BEING GOOD

BEING GOOD

Christian Virtues for Everyday Life

Edited by

Michael W. Austin

R. Douglas Geivett

William B. Eerdmans Publishing Company

Grand Rapids, Michigan / Cambridge, U.K.

Published 2012 by
Wm. B. Eerdmans Publishing Co.
2140 Oak Industrial Drive N.E., Grand Rapids, Michigan 49505 /
P.O. Box 163, Cambridge CB3 9PU U.K.

Printed in the United States of America

18 17 16 15 14 13 12 7 6 5 4 3 2 1

Library of Congress Cataloging-in-Publication Data

Being good: Christian virtues for everyday life /
edited by Michael W. Austin, R. Douglas Geivett.
p. cm.
ISBN 978-0-8028-6565-6 (paper: alk. paper)
1. Theological virtues.
I. Austin, Michael W. II. Geivett, R. Douglas.

BV4635.B45 2012
241'.4 — dc23

2011027505

www.eerdmans.com

To my father-in-law, Jon Sederquist,
for his consistent display of Christlike goodness.

Mike

In memory of my father-in-law, Gerald Weitz.

Doug

Contents

Introduction: Virtues and the Good Life

Michael W. Austin and R. Douglas Geivett

Why Christian Virtues?

In some segments of the church it is now routinely suggested that Christianity is not about ethics; rather it is about a relationship with Christ. While we applaud any resistance to reducing Christianity to an ethical system, we are concerned that Christian antipathy toward ethical theory is itself unchristian. Christianity is not *merely* about ethics, but it does *essentially include* ethics. The Christian, as a follower of Jesus, should seek to embody the moral and intellectual virtues of Jesus Christ, our Lord. This book seeks to assist in this task as, together, we follow Jesus Christ. He is our moral and intellectual exemplar.

We live in a period of moral confusion and decay. The world threatens to press followers of Christ into its mold (Rom. 12:1-2). There is an abundance of Christian leaders, charismatic figures who create an impressive wake with their gifts and scholarship. There are Christian celebrities aplenty. But living models of unequivocal virtue are in short supply. Christians collectively are frequently charged with hypocrisy, perhaps especially because of inconsistencies in the lives of prominent Christians. Sadly, what is not true of everyone is true of far too many, which leaves even ordinary Christians confused. Cynicism replaces respect for genuinely virtuous persons because of suspicion born of disappointment by the examples of self-appointed leaders of the church. We are diminished by wave upon wave of moral failure. No time has been more ripe for a Christian treatment of specific virtues that are largely ignored or misunderstood.

We and the other contributors to this book believe there is something distinctive about a Christian approach to the virtues. First, Christians order the virtues in ways that non-Christians do not. For example, love is a fundamental Christian virtue (see 1 Cor. 13); for Stoics, love is subordinate to the virtue of equanimity. Second, Christians understand certain individual virtues in ways that non-Christians do not. Hope means something different to the Christian than it does to someone who believes her life is delimited by the period of her earthly existence. Third, Christians acknowledge the existence of virtues (for example, humility) that are not considered virtues at all within some non-Christian approaches, such as those espoused by philosophers like Friedrich Nietzsche and David Hume. For this reason, historical figures whom Christians regard as models of virtue have often been subject to scorn by others who conceive of virtue in different ways (see Heb. 11). Fourth, 2 Peter 1:2-9 lists many qualities that we must possess if we are to avoid being unfruitful and unproductive in our knowledge of Jesus Christ, including moral excellence, godliness, and love. In fact, if we have these qualities, Peter tells us, we are participating in the divine nature. In these and other ways, Christianity charts a peculiar course.

In addition, being virtuous is essential to the abundant life Christ came to offer and it is an important component of our witness in the world. Christianity has the resources, as a worldview and way of life, to explain why the intellectual and moral virtues are conducive to our flourishing, and why they are excellences of character. Virtues are conducive to flourishing and the abundant life because God designed us to function best when possessing and exemplifying the virtues. As James Spiegel puts it, "To be virtuous is to live up to the divine standard for human life. Or better, it is to embody that standard, to display it in one's conduct."[1] Virtues are excellences of character because they reflect the perfect character of God, and they are good for individuals and communities because we were designed to function at our best as virtuous creatures.

To grasp the relevance of particular virtues, we must grasp the fact that human persons are proper objects of moral evaluation. Character counts. As his followers, we know that Jesus Christ, the perfect embodiment of virtue, was and is good. He is the morally perfect specimen of hu-

1. James Spiegel, *How to Be Good in a World Gone Bad* (Grand Rapids: Kregel, 2004), p. 15.

manity. He was, you might say, a virtuoso when it comes to being a person. His moral excellence was so great that he was literally sinless. And he is our example. Jesus exemplified moral virtue in all that he did. We follow his example, not in doing the precise acts that he did, but in cultivating the same virtues he had and in acting from those virtues in whatever we do.

As followers of Jesus Christ who aspire to act from virtue as he did, it is wise for us to understand key Christian virtues more fully. This book speaks to that need. There is a broad consensus among Christians about the meaning and implications of some of the virtues. Much of what contributors to this book write clarifies and reinforces what has been said elsewhere. On some points, however, common assumptions and intuitions are challenged. Whether in agreement with common notions about the virtues, or in disagreement with how they are sometimes understood, our goal is to achieve a genuinely Christian conception of several virtues, informed by Scripture and nourished by philosophical and theological reflection. Here you will find an accessible exploration of key virtues that discusses their significance, explains how they can be nurtured individually and corporately, and seeks to inspire a zeal for personal growth in virtue — all from a distinctively Christian point of view.

Each chapter includes (i) a description of a single virtue, (ii) a philosophical exploration of the virtue, (iii) a Christian perspective on the virtue, (iv) some practical advice with respect to Christian spiritual formation and exemplification of the virtue in everyday life, and (v) several reflection questions suitable for individual or group study. We ourselves desire to deepen our understanding of the virtues, and to grow more fully in virtue. You probably do, too, or you wouldn't be reading this book. We hope that by study, reflection, discussion, and application, you will be better equipped to grow in your imitation of Christ, to be more like him — to be good — in the depths of your being and in your everyday life.

Overview of the Book

1 Corinthians 13 is known as the great "love chapter" of the Bible. But this chapter describes love in terms of numerous other inter-related virtues, suggesting that there is a unity to the virtues and that love brings a multitude of virtues into proper relation to each other. The Apostle Paul con-

cludes his love chapter with these words: "So now faith, hope, and love abide, these three; but the greatest of these is love" (1 Cor. 13:13, ESV).

With this reference to the three great and abiding virtues in mind, we have organized this book into three parts, under the headings of Faith, Hope, and Love. Part 1 begins with the virtue of Faith (chapter 1). This foundational chapter is followed by chapters on three closely related virtues: Open-mindedness (chapter 2), Wisdom (chapter 3), and Zeal (chapter 4). This part of the book elucidates virtues that govern our knowledge practices and the types of actions that are grounded by these practices. Part 2 begins with the virtue of Hope (chapter 5). Standing in intimate relation to hope are the virtues of Contentment (chapter 6) and Courage (chapter 7). The cluster of virtues treated in this part of the book pertain to personal expectations and aspirations. Part 3 begins with Love, the greatest virtue of all (chapter 8). The virtues of Compassion (chapter 9), Forgiveness (chapter 10), and Humility (chapter 11) complement love in the concreteness of actual relationships between persons. In this part of the book we explore virtues that bear most directly on our relations with one another.

Of course, all of the virtues treated in these chapters have overlapping claims on our lives. We hope that you will consider how any one of the virtues relates to all of the others. The exposition of each virtue should enable you to see important connections. We suggest that you first reflect on the ways that virtues in the Faith section of the book are related, then how those in the Hope section overlap, and then the close communion of the virtues treated in the Love section. Having done that, it would be wise to explore connections across parts of the book.

Here are a few questions to assist in this comparative study:

- Part 1. How are faith, open-mindedness, wisdom, and zeal related to each other? Does faith include open-mindedness? Does wisdom provide goals and boundaries for the operation of zeal?
- Part 2. How are hope, contentment, and courage connected? How is courage an aid to contentment? Does having the virtue of hope make contentment easier?
- Part 3. How do love, compassion, forgiveness, and humility work in concert with each other? Can love exist without compassion, or forgiveness, or humility? Do the virtues of humility and compassion provide guidance in the practice of forgiveness?

- What connections exist between the faith-grounded virtues, the hope-directed virtues, and the love-conditioned virtues? Consider the image of a three-sided pyramid, one side representing each cluster of virtues. Imagine the sides rising up through habits corresponding to the virtues of each cluster, so that the sides are built up and converge through practice. How do the individual components of each side contribute to the support and integrity of the whole pyramid of virtuous living? What must be said of this pyramid if it is deficient in any one virtue? How might the other virtues enable cultivation of what is deficient?

Faith

A crucial virtue for the Christian life, fundamental in many ways, is the virtue of faith. Paul Moser examines faith — its value and its relation to knowledge. He considers how faith is connected to good works. He reasons that when we have faith in God, we entrust our very selves to God. Faith in God, then, is not merely faith that God exists; it includes a rational entrustment of oneself to God which is a means to friendship with God and results in loving obedience to his will. Faith in God is not cognitively defective. It resembles trusting one's best friend. As we trust God, God transforms our hearts, so that we become more like Christ. Moser encourages us to engage in *kardiatheology* — theology of the heart — which is aimed at changing the motivations of the heart and is oriented towards action. One of the moral virtues of the heart, then, is faith. This faith is the means by which we have new life in God, and the potential to love our enemies and to be freed from the tyranny of selfishness.

Open-mindedness is not often included in the catalogue of Christian virtues. Jason Baehr recognizes that many Christians are actually a bit wary of open-mindedness, perhaps because it suggests to them a kind of relativism or an uncritical acceptance of other beliefs. However, open-mindedness, understood the right way, should be seen as an excellence of Christian character. Baehr argues that an open-minded person is one who is able and willing to transcend some default cognitive standpoint in order to take up or consider a different cognitive standpoint. This means, in part, that in their quest for truth, open-minded people can set aside their beliefs about some issue in order to consider an opposing viewpoint.

Doing this is not wishy-washy, or cowardly, or foolish, as some Christians might think. Rather, the virtue of open-mindedness is grounded in a love of the truth and a desire to know it. And given the intellectual impact of sin, Christians have a reason to avoid taking any belief to be beyond error. Open-mindedness, however, is also consistent with a firm and realistic adherence to the central tenets of the Christian faith. If we understand these tenets and possess a deep spiritual life, open-mindedness functions as a virtue.

Wisdom, according to James Spiegel, is a countercultural virtue. Popular culture focuses on fame, fortune, beauty, pleasure, and a host of other pursuits, but rarely does it elevate wisdom. Unfortunately, wisdom does not enjoy its proper place even in the world of higher education, where many focus primarily or even solely on education as preparation for a job, and not also as a means of forming the mind and heart. Spiegel poses and answers the most fundamental questions concerning wisdom. What is wisdom, and what is its connection to other virtues? Why is wisdom valuable? How do we become wise? In answering these questions, Spiegel explores the insights of Scripture, and turns to philosophers and theologians past and present. The wise person, it turns out, understands the deleterious effects of vice as well as the benefits of virtue on the mind. The goodness of our minds and the goodness of our character are intricately related to one another.

Zeal, especially religious zeal, is considered by many to be a vice rather than a virtue, since it does, in some cases, motivate people to do vicious things. Zeal today is often associated with Islamic terrorists or the Christian Crusaders. However, as David Horner and David Turner point out, a truly Christian conception of zeal shows that it is essential to life in Christ and is in fact an excellence of character. Zeal, on their account, avoids the vices of both sloth and fanaticism. The zealous person diligently (eschewing sloth) pursues the good (eschewing fanaticism). Zeal is a trait of God himself, who is zealous for his people. Zeal for the house of the Lord consumed Jesus when he overturned the tables of the moneychangers in the temple. As followers of Christ, we also are to be zealous for what is good (1 Pet. 3:13). The problem for contemporary Christians in general is not excessive zeal, rightly understood, but rather sloth, or lack of zeal. In their chapter, Horner and Turner offer a penetrating and thorough analysis of the most relevant passages of Scripture, coupled with a philosophical exploration of zeal as a virtue.

Considerable space has been devoted to an exposition of this much neglected and misunderstood virtue.

Hope

God himself is both the source and goal of Christian hope. William C. Mattison explains both what hope is and what sorts of actions it produces. Hope is not merely a feeling, nor is it merely wishing that something be true. Rather, Christian hope is an excellence of character directed towards God, made possible by grace, and fulfilled in our complete happiness in union with God. Since our union with God is only partial in this life, hope is fixed upon the next life as well. But given the "intrinsic" continuity between "abundant life" and "eternal life," hope clearly is relevant to the way we live our lives now, in a variety of ways. Mattison explores many of these — showing how Christian hope contravenes despair, idolatry, and presumption; how it kindles a desire for justice; and how it induces fortitude in the lives of believers.

Contentment, as Steve Porter points out, is an elusive thing. Whether on the freeway or in line at the store, or when faced with more difficult trials, discontent threatens to take over. Christian contentment goes beyond being satisfied in or with our circumstances. It is, in fact, a virtue. As such, it is not reducible to passive acceptance of circumstances, whatever they may be. On the contrary, we may be content while also working passionately to rectify some injustice. Contentment is also connected in a variety of ways to other desirable traits, such as patience, gratitude, generosity, compassion, and kindness. Porter investigates the formation of contentment in its relation to other virtues. Confidence in the consistent and loving presence of God in our lives is a central component in Porter's analysis.

Courage is also essential for following Christ, though only if it is understood in a properly Christian manner. Rebecca Konyndyk DeYoung explains that a Christian conception of courage differs in some ways with the dominant cultural understandings of this virtue, especially those associated with action-adventure heroes. Courage is not, from a Christian perspective, primarily concerned with the battlefield or with any form of aggressive action; nor is it the domain of rugged individualists. It turns out that love, rather than mere human power, is central to acting with courage. In her analysis of courage, Konyndyk DeYoung draws on the perspective of Thomas Aquinas. She also turns to the fictional character of Harry Potter, particularly in *The Deathly Hallows*, to shed light on this virtue. She admonishes Christians to seek and practice a form of courage that imitates the courage of Christ, where love is central and powerful enough to move us to sacrifice everything for what is good, even our very lives.

Love

We come to new life in Jesus Christ by faith, and we persevere in this life of faith with hope. In this we are sustained by love. But we are also expected to exhibit love. "Whoever does not love does not know God": just as love is foundational to all that Christ does, it is to be an essential characteristic of any disciple of Jesus. In his chapter, Charles Taliaferro notes that loving another person involves an affirmation of her value, but also simply taking pleasure in her very existence. Many Christians today stress that love is not a feeling. Taliaferro points out that, though love is not mere emotion, it does include a disposition to take pleasure in the well-being of the beloved. Taliaferro asks and answers several questions: Are there different kinds of love? What does it mean to say that "God is love"? Would it make any sense to say that "love is God"? What might be dangerous about loving love? Does Christianity have any distinctive resources for assisting us in the practice of love? The Triune God, Taliaferro argues, exemplifies love in its fullness as the mutual co-inherence of Father, Son, and Holy Spirit, portraying an ideal convergence of the highest forms of love. When we exhibit the virtue of love, we are imaging what God is like for all to see.

A natural offspring of love is compassion. Jesus was noted for his compassion. And this compassion has been exemplified in diverse ways throughout Christian history, as Jesus' disciples have endeavored to follow his example. Michael Austin argues that seeking to be like Christ means seeking to acquire the virtue of compassion. This virtue is to be nurtured in our hearts and minds, and demonstrated in our actions. Austin first discusses the cognitive, emotional, and active aspects of this trait, then argues that the scope of compassion is broader than we often think. It is not merely a virtue called for in our treatment of the poor, sick, and suffering. It is also important for us as we seek to be good neighbors, friends, and spouses. Compassion is connected to justice, mercy, and faithfulness. As such, it is essential for life in Christ.

Christians are a community of people whose sins have been forgiven by a loving and compassionate God. We are to emulate the forgiveness of God in our dealings with one another. R. Douglas Geivett offers a close analysis of key passages in Scripture that should inform our understanding of forgiveness. He argues that forgiveness is a virtue and discusses the implications of regarding it as such. In the course of his discussion, he considers whether repentance is needed before there can be forgiveness, briefly assesses the "therapeutic" conception of forgiveness, and challenges us to think about what it means to have the virtue of forgiveness when we or others have been wronged. The centrality of forgiveness in Christian belief and our neglect of the specific teachings of Jesus concerning it merits the extended treatment we have given this virtue.

Our final chapter addresses humility, a virtue that is given a more prominent place within Christianity than in many other moral and religious traditions. Andrew Pinsent describes how we ought to think about humility, and what it is to be truly humble in the best and truest sense of the word. In his chapter, humility is contrasted with its opposing vice, pride, and is understood as incorporating two essential dispositions. First, it involves having a sense of God's majesty and of the gift of participating in the divine nature. Second, it disposes us to receive friendship with God as a gift given out of love. Many thinkers, both classic and contemporary, have neglected or criticized the claim that humility is a virtue. However, Christian humility is essential for both the attainment and the enjoyment of heaven. As with the other virtues considered in this book, humility was an essential trait of Jesus Christ himself. Like Christ, we ought to make the presence and practice of humility a priority in our lives.

Other Resources Past and Present

We hope that this book will encourage and facilitate deep reflection on the virtues. We hope, also, that you will be stimulated to greater growth in the particular virtues that we have examined. Growth in the virtues, with the help of the Holy Spirit, is a lifelong project. With this in mind, we suggest that you continue to study and pursue a life of virtue, following in the steps of Jesus Christ. In recent years there has been an explosion of interest in spiritual formation, and many new resources have been developed to help in this process. Much of the literature focuses on specific practices, such as meditation, fasting, service, and solitude. We believe that sustained attention to Christian virtue is a crucial aspect of this process. And so we refer you to several resources that may help you on your journey.

A few contemporary works are both conceptually insightful and practically beneficial for spiritual and moral formation. In his book *Spiritual Emotions: A Psychology of Christian Virtues* (Eerdmans, 2007), Robert C. Roberts examines several of the traits treated in this book — compassion, humility, and hope. In addition, he considers several other "emotion-virtues," including contrition, joy, and peace. James Spiegel's book *How to Be Good in a World Gone Bad* (Kregel, 2004) is essentially a handbook for the virtues. Spiegel discusses eighteen different virtues and seeks to inspire readers to live a good life. Finally, Rebecca Konyndyk DeYoung's *Glittering Vices: A New Look at the Seven Deadly Sins* (Brazos, 2009) makes a unique contribution. In the introduction, she quotes Horace: "To flee vice is the beginning of virtue." Knowledge of the seven deadly sins, which today are minimized, psychologized, and even celebrated, enables us to see where we are going wrong. Konyndyk DeYoung discusses remedies for these vices, and offers practical counsel for counteracting their influence and presence in our lives as we seek to fight the good fight.

Any short list of classic treatments of the virtues must include the magisterial *Summa Theologica* by Thomas Aquinas (1225-1274). Saint Thomas presents a rich analysis of virtuous character. Much of his moral theology is informed by his study of Aristotle (384 BC–322 BC), whose *Nichomachean Ethics* continues to be influential. D. D. Raphael's two-volume collection on *British Moralists: 1650-1800* contains valuable selections by a few Christian thinkers from the late seventeenth and eighteenth centuries, including Francis Hutcheson, Joseph Butler, William Paley, and Thomas Reid. Reading, reflecting upon, and, where appropriate, applying insights from these works will, we believe, be helpful in your journey with Christ.

FAITH

Faith

Paul K. Moser

According to Jewish and Christian theism, God authoritatively invites and highly values human *faith in God.* What exactly is such faith? What, in addition, is its primary value? Is it a virtue of some sort? How, furthermore, is it related to human knowledge and evidence, and how does it contrast with human "works"? This chapter addresses these questions, and puts the idea of faith in God in an illuminating theological, cognitive, and moral context. It thereby sheds light on the idea that "without faith it is impossible to please God" (Heb. 11:6, NIV).

Faith in God

God's valuing of human faith became apparent, according to the Hebrew Bible, even before the origin of national Israel and of Judaism. Thus Genesis 15:5-6, NRSV: "He [God] brought him [Abram] outside and said, 'Look toward heaven and count the stars, if you are able to count them.' Then he said to him, 'So shall your descendants be.' And he believed the LORD; and the LORD reckoned it to him as righteousness." The Hebrew word translated "believed" derives from the same root as our word "Amen." So, we might offer this paraphrase: "Abram 'amen-ed' the Lord, and the Lord counted it for him as a right relationship with the Lord." The word "trust" is among the best in the English language for the relationship in question. The NEB, REB, NAB, and NJB translations use language consistent with the title of this essay: "Abram put his faith in the

LORD." We can treat "faith in God," "trust in God," and "belief in God" as interchangeable phrases in this context.

The kind of faith ascribed to Abraham in Genesis 15 is not merely intellectual or psychological. It involves the central purpose and direction of Abraham's life relative to God's redemptive promise and call to him. Such faith may best be understood as "entrusting oneself." Thus, we should consider this paraphrase: "Abraham entrusted himself to the Lord, and the Lord counted this entrusting as a right relationship with himself." The entrusting required Abraham's *living* into an ongoing relationship with God as the authoritative promise-giver and promise-keeper, and thus his faith was itself ongoing (or, diachronic) rather than static (or, synchronic). This entrusting exceeded intellectual assent, given that it was life-involving, and not just mind-involving. In particular, Abraham was entrusting *himself* to God relative to God's unique promise to bless all the families of the earth through him, even though it was unclear to him exactly how this promise would be realized (see Gen. 12:2-3; 13:16).

According to Genesis 15, God calls Abraham into an entrusting relationship, and then responds to Abraham's entrusting himself to God by crediting this entrusting commitment as righteousness, that is, as a right relationship with God. In other words, God thereby offers a means to exercise mercy rather than condemnation toward wayward humans, without condoning the rebellion, the supposed self-righteousness, or any other wrongdoing of humans toward God. God thus seeks the redemption of humans via the human response of faith, or entrustment, toward God. We will return to this important lesson later in the chapter.

The temporal order in the divine process of crediting righteousness to humans via faith, or entrusting oneself, is crucial. Mercifully, God moves first, with a redemptive promise, for the needed good of humans, and with a corresponding authoritative invitation to humans to entrust themselves wholeheartedly to God. Specifically, God calls Abraham into a needed relationship *before* Abraham calls God (Gen. 12:1-3). We might thus say that "in this is love, not that we loved God, but that he loved us. . . . We love, because he first loved us" (1 John 4:10, 19, NASB). God's promise and corresponding invitation to humans manifest divine love, as various biblical writers have noted (see, for example, Hosea 11:1-9; Rom. 5:1-11; 9:25-33). We are, accordingly, called by God to put our faith in, or entrust ourselves to, the God who first loved us. This distinctive theme of divine grace, appropriated through faith as entrustment, emerges in both the Old and New Testaments. We will return to this theme in due course.

Philosophy and Faith

The topic of faith in God has attracted considerable discussion throughout the history of philosophy, at least from Socrates to the present. One important theme of this discussion is that the notion of faith "in God" is not reducible to the idea of faith "that God exists." Faith that God exists, if it amounts simply to a belief that God exists, is merely a psychological attitude toward a judgment, or a proposition. That is, it is simply *de dicto,* related to a propositional dictum, the dictum that God exists. In contrast, faith *in God* is best understood as having a *de re* component that is irreducible to a judgment, or a proposition. In particular, faith in God relates one *to God,* and not just to a judgment, or a proposition, *about God.* Some writers, under the influence of Søren Kierkegaard, would say that human faith in God involves a distinctive "I-Thou" relationship between a human and God that goes well beyond belief that God exists. What exactly such an I-Thou relationship consists in has been a topic of controversy in the philosophy of religion. Clearly, given its *de re* component, it involves more than just historical information.[1]

Writing as Johannes Climacus in *Concluding Unscientific Postscript,* Kierkegaard has emphasized the importance of the "inwardness of faith." He proposes that such inwardness "cannot be expressed more definitely than this: it is the absurd, adhered to firmly with the passion of the infinite."[2] He adds that the relevant inwardness includes ". . . placing [a person] decisively, more decisively than any judge can place the accused, between time [viz., human finitude] and eternity [viz., God], between heaven and hell in the time of salvation."[3] Faith in God, according to Kierkegaard, involves a commitment to mystery, the presence of God in

1. For relevant discussion, see Herbert H. Farmer, *The Servant of the Word* (New York: Scribner, 1942), chap. 2; also Paul K. Moser, *The Elusive God: Reorienting Religious Epistemology* (Cambridge: Cambridge University Press, 2008), chap. 3.

2. Søren Kierkegaard, *Concluding Unscientific Postscript to Philosophical Fragments* [1846], trans. H. V. Hong and E. H. Hong (Princeton: Princeton University Press, 1992), vol. 1, p. 214. Subsequent references to Kierkegaard are to this edition.

3. Kierkegaard, *Postscript,* p. 215.

human inwardness, that does not go away or yield to explanation, nonparadoxical description, or philosophical resolution.

Human philosophical speculation about God and God's purposes, according to Kierkegaard, "is a temptation, the most precarious of all" temptations.[4] The speculative philosopher, he claims, is *not* the prodigal son who comes home to his waiting Father, but is rather "the naughty child who refuses to stay where existing humans belong, in the children's nursery and the education room of existence where one becomes adult only through inwardness, but who instead wants to enter God's council, continually screaming that, from the point of view of the eternal, . . . there is no paradox."[5] Kierkegaard makes his anti-speculative point in connection with divine forgiveness of human sins. He proposes that "the simple wise person," even after reflection on God's forgiveness of human sins, would say: "I still cannot comprehend the divine mercy that can forgive sins; the more intensely I believe it, the less I am able to understand it."[6] On this basis, Kierkegaard concludes: "Thus probability does not seem to increase as the inwardness of faith is augmented, rather the opposite."[7] This seems to accord with his suggestion that Christian faith "is not a matter of knowing."[8]

Faith in God, according to Kierkegaard, does not require comprehending God or God's ways. If "comprehending" means "fully understanding," this position is compelling, or at least worthy of serious consideration. We should not expect cognitively limited humans to be able to comprehend God or God's purposes in the sense of "being able fully to explain God or God's purposes." Still, we should be careful about the implications of this position for reasonable faith in God, particularly in connection with such a remark as this: "Faith has . . . two tasks: to watch for and at every moment to make the discovery of improbability, the paradox, in order then to hold it fast with the passion of inwardness."[9] Kierkegaard's rhetoric yields a dubious message in this connection; it suggests that the inwardness of faith is antithetical, or at least inversely proportional, to reasonable belief as probably true belief.

4. Kierkegaard, *Postscript,* p. 214.
5. Kierkegaard, *Postscript,* p. 214.
6. Kierkegaard, *Postscript,* p. 228.
7. Kierkegaard, *Postscript,* p. 228.
8. Kierkegaard, *Postscript,* p. 215.
9. Kierkegaard, *Postscript,* p. 233.

At times Kierkegaard suggests that his talk of the "absurd" and the "paradox," with regard to the inwardness of faith, is just talk of an eternal, infinite God entering temporal, finite human history, particularly in the divine incarnation in Jesus as a human with historical existence.[10] *If* this is all Kierkegaard means, his talk of "absurdity" and "contradiction" is potentially very misleading, because it suggests much more than this when taken at face value. The proclaimed divine incarnation in Jesus is shocking and mysterious indeed, but it is not, strictly speaking, absurd or contradictory. Any suggestion to the contrary should deliver a careful demonstration of the alleged contradiction. In addition, we should avoid blocking people who existed before the assumed incarnation in Jesus from the "inwardness of faith" as the human means of receiving divine grace. Abraham, for instance, should be a candidate for faith in God, in keeping with Genesis 15 and Romans 4, even if (quite naturally, given his historical location) he did not believe in the divine incarnation in Jesus.

Faith in God, as suggested, is most plausibly regarded as a human response of entrustment of oneself to God and God's promises. In addition, as illustrated by the case of Abraham in Genesis 15, such faith can enjoy a cognitive basis in the human experience of God's intervening in human lives with redemptive actions and thereby calling people to trust and to obey God. Indeed, human faith in God should be grounded in supporting evidence of that distinctive kind in order to avoid being mere wishful thinking or being otherwise cognitively arbitrary. Ideally, such faith is cognitively grounded in experienced evidence of its divine personal object: the God who authoritatively calls humans before they call God.[11] Faith in God should thus not be characterized as an inward embracing of absurdity or contradiction, at least in any ordinary sense of those terms. That approach to faith would undermine the important need for supporting evidence. Kierkegaard's language about faith, then, is misleading and harmful if taken at face value. Even so, Kierkegaard is correct about the independence of human faith in God from philosophical speculation. If such faith is a human response of entrustment to an experienced divine call, it does not depend for its existence on philosophical speculation.

Kierkegaard suggests that Socrates manifested and recommended a

10. Kierkegaard, *Postscript,* pp. 209-10, 213, 217.

11. On the relevant cognitive basis as purposively available authoritative evidence, see Moser, *Elusive God.*

kind of "existential inwardness" akin to faith.[12] Even if he did, we should hesitate to compare Socrates favorably to Jesus on the matter of faith in God. The difference between them is, in the end, vast and irreducible. Jesus, as the self-avowed authoritative Son of his divine Father (see Mark 12:1-12; Matt. 11:25-27; Luke 10:21-22), commands people to have faith as obedient and loving entrustment of themselves to his Father (see Mark 11:22), on the basis of God's purportedly redemptive intervention in human lives. Such entrustment of oneself moves outward obediently in love, by divine command, toward God and thereby toward others. It transcends mere discussion in order to represent the primacy of a life of faithful obedience under divine authority. Accordingly, the apostle Paul speaks of "faith [or trust, in God and Jesus] working through love *(agapē)*" (Gal. 5:6). Such faith in God is a consistent focus of Jesus as divinely appointed Lord, and it is absent from Socrates as represented by Plato. In this respect, the difference between Jesus and Socrates is more substantial than any similarity.

Kierkegaard captures an important dimension of faith in God in his emphasis on human *decision* regarding God's call. He remarks that "the speculative thinker . . . believes only to a certain degree — he puts his hand to the plow and looks around in order to find something to know."[13] The entrustment central to faith in God requires a definite commitment to God, and this commitment demands a human decision to yield oneself to God, relative to God's authoritative will and promises. In this respect, faith in God is a kind of obedience, even morally virtuous obedience because morally excellent (at least in one respect), as we shall see below. It is thus a mistake to oppose faith in God to human obedience. Even so, the required decision and commitment need not be cognitively arbitrary or otherwise unreasonable. They can rest on evidence supplied by divine intervention in human experience.

We have characterized human faith in God as human *entrustment* to God in response to human experience of God's redemptive intervention in human lives. Such faith as entrustment of oneself to God is a needed motivational anchor for human *faithful actions* toward God, in obedience to God. It includes one's general *receptive volitional commitment* to receive manifested and offered divine power of redemptive love as a gra-

12. Kierkegaard, *Postscript,* pp. 204-7.

13. Kierkegaard, *Postscript,* p. 230.

cious gift and thereby to obey God in what God commands and promises. This commitment can be firmly in place even if one occasionally disobeys God and thus violates one's general commitment. Such a volitional commitment, when actually carried out by a person in action, includes that person's submitting his or her will to God's authoritative will in a particular case of action, just as Jesus did in Gethsemane and Abraham did in the context of Genesis 15. This kind of commitment is morally virtuous owing to its reception of divine moral excellence. Mere belief that God exists can be altogether selfish, and thus need not be virtuous at all in that respect (see James 2:19).

Faith in God, at its heart, includes one's *obediently receiving, and volitionally committing oneself to,* God and what God graciously offers for the sake of reconciled fellowship with God. A life of faith in God is inherently a life that obediently receives, and volitionally entrusts oneself to, God and God's authoritative call to reconciled divine-human fellowship. The obedient receptivity of faith in God toward God's call leads to the kind of human transformation that enables a human to become suited to divine-human fellowship. It would be a mistake, then, to draw a contrast between faith in God and obedience to God's call to reconciled divine-human fellowship. Such faith is an obedient response of volitional commitment to receive and to follow agreeably an authoritative divine call that offers lasting forgiveness and reconciled fellowship. Faith in God is, accordingly, a means to reconciled fellowship with God. Abraham, the biblical exemplar of faith in God, is thus called a "friend" of God, given the role of fellowship with God in his faith in God (see 2 Chron. 20:7; Isa. 41:8; James 2:23). The receptive feature of this kind of faith, toward an experienced divine call, excludes a characterization in terms of pure imagination or wishful thinking, and points to a kind of experiential cognitive support. We will explore this important lesson in connection with a distinctively Christian understanding of faith in God.

Christian Faith

The apostle Paul offers a distinctively Christian approach to faith in God, and this approach is unmatched in its profundity. He uses talk of *obedience* and talk of *belief/faith* interchangeably in some important contexts that can illuminate our notion of faith in God (see, for instance, Rom.

10:16-17; cf. Rom. 1:5; 6:16; 16:26; Gal. 5:5-7). Jesus, setting the authoritative model for Paul, likewise acknowledged a necessary role for human obedience to God's will in entering God's kingdom family (see Matt. 7:21; 16:24-26; 19:16-22; 21:28-32; cf. Matt. 6:24-29). In addition, Jesus commanded that his followers have faith in God, in himself, and in the Good News of divine redemption in himself (see, e.g., Mark 1:15; 5:36; 11:22; John 14:1). The "obedience of faith" in question is *attitudinal obedience* that includes obediently receiving, and volitionally committing and thus yielding oneself to, God as perfectly authoritative, for the sake of living into God's redemptive offer of volitional fellowship with God. We may call such faith in God *obedience of the heart.*

We should acknowledge that heart-based obedience of faith can be, for various reasons, imperfectly represented in corresponding actions. In other words, we can entrust ourselves to God in faith but still make moral mistakes, including serious moral mistakes. Even so, the God of Abraham, Isaac, Jacob, and Jesus, seeks to attract and to transform the very center of human motivation, that is, the motivational "heart" of a person (*kardia* in ancient Greek). This consideration suggests a distinctive kind of theology: *kardiatheology,* as theology aimed at one's motivational heart, including one's will, rather than just at one's mind or one's emotions.

Christian faith, in keeping with the teaching of Jesus and Paul, should be understood in terms of kardiatheology, as an entrustment of oneself to God that involves one's motivational heart and is therefore inherently action-oriented. In addition, if we regard a moral virtue as a motivating moral excellence of a person, we may understand kardiatheology as promoting moral virtues of the heart, anchored in fellowship with God, the ultimate source and sustainer of human moral virtues. Faith in God is among those moral virtues, and, in the perspective offered here, it can also be cognitively virtuous owing to its enabling a person to receive some otherwise unavailable evidence of divine activity. The latter point accords with (one reading of) the Augustinian thesis that "I have faith [in God] in order to understand."

Many theologians have disregarded the important idea of faith as including a general volitional commitment to receive and to follow God and God's authoritative call to fellowship and thus as being a distinctive kind of obedience of the heart to God's call and will. Some fear that, if this idea were accepted, faith could be confused with human "works" that are not only unnecessary for but also incompatible with any gracious divine redemption of humans. The heart-based "obedience of faith," however, is not what Paul calls "works" in contrast with faith. Instead, Paul thinks of "works," at least in Romans 4:4 (and in Rom. 9:30-33), as what one does to *obligate* God or to *earn* (or, to merit) something from God. In contrast with an ordinary use of the term "works," the word is a technical theological term in Paul's remarks in Romans 4 and 9.

In keeping with faith in God as obedient entrustment of one's heart to God, Paul says the following regarding identity markers for God's redeemed people: "For neither circumcision counts for anything nor uncircumcision, but *keeping the commandments* of God" (1 Cor. 7:19, RSV, italics added). In Paul's understanding, God's commandments include not only the divine love commands issued by Jesus (Mark 12:28-31; cf. Gal. 5:14), but primarily the gospel of Jesus Christ itself, in virtue of its authoritatively calling people to "the obedience of faith" in God and Jesus (see Rom. 16:26; cf. Matt. 28:18-20). Thus, after presenting the Good News of divine grace as gift-righteousness through Jesus (Rom. 3:21-26), Paul speaks of "obedience which leads to righteousness" (Rom. 6:16, RSV). He characterizes this obedience as one's being "obedient from the heart," and suggests that it underlies one's "having been set free from sin" (Rom. 6:17-18, RSV). These remarks cohere with Paul's talk of the "obedience of faith" (Rom. 1:5; 16:26), which is best understood as one's general volitional entrustment of oneself, at the level of one's heart, to God and God's call to fellowship as one obediently receives the transformative gift of reconciled fellowship with God.

Paul acknowledges an indispensable *human role* in the divine redemption of humans. This role includes *obedient reception of,* and *volitional commitment to,* the Good News gift of divine righteousness in Jesus. Avoiding extreme divine sovereignty that forecloses a crucial role for human volitional response,[14] Paul states *why* Abraham and many other humans are reckoned with divine righteousness. Specifically, *their faith,* as their response of entrustment of themselves to God, is reckoned to them as divine righteousness (see Rom. 4:16-25). In contrast, the rejection of such faith will exclude some humans from fellowship with God (see Rom. 11:20). The divine redemptive gift on offer without coercion in the Good News of Jesus Christ falls short of its salvific goal in the absence

14. See Edward Meadors, *Idolatry and the Hardening of the Heart* (London: T&T Clark, 2006).

of being voluntarily received in faith, or entrustment, by humans. When, however, this gift is received by human faith, and divine righteousness is credited to a human, an actual divine gift of righteous reconciliation of humans is present.

We might think of faith in God as itself a divine gift, following a common reading of Ephesians 2:8, but in that case there would still be a crucial role for human volitional response in *willingly receiving* this gift. In any case, Paul, following Jesus, speaks of human faith as the means of receiving the gift of divine redemptive grace (Rom. 4:16) and as something that humans can willingly reject by adopting resolute distrust in God (*apistia,* Rom. 4:20). Abraham, according to Paul, did not fail in that way relative to God and God's redemptive promise (despite his occasional acts of disobedience). In Paul's theology, "*that* is why his faith was 'reckoned to him as righteousness'" (Rom. 4:22, RSV, italics added; cf. Gal. 3:6-9). Such faith resists any motive for human boasting, earning, or self-credit before God, because it is just the human means, for Jews as well as Gentiles, to receive the gracious gift of redemption promised by God, including the gift of divine-human fellowship via God's Spirit (see Rom. 3:29-30; 4:16; 5:2; Gal. 3:14).

Paul links human faith in God to reception of God's Spirit, the Spirit of Jesus according to Romans 8:9. In particular, he thinks of human faith in God, in terms of obedience of the heart, as the means of receiving God's empowering Spirit whereby divine love commands can actually be obeyed in virtue of the power of divine love in one's receptive heart (see Rom. 5:5; Gal. 3:2-5, 14; 5:5-7, 22). This empowering Spirit leads one to love as God loves, by "killing the deeds" that are antithetical to divine love (Rom. 8:13). Of course, we should not confuse killing evil *deeds* and killing *people* who perform evil deeds. Commenting on the familiar kind of theology found in Psalms 5:5 and 11:5, Jesus calls his followers to hate evil deeds but to follow his divine Father in loving people who do evil deeds, even evil enemies (see Matt. 5:43-48).

Paul thinks of divine love, received via trust in God, as what empowers the human *fulfillment* of (the purpose of) God's law when such love is lived out toward God and others (see Rom. 13:8-10; Gal. 5:15; cf. 2 Cor. 3:5-8; Gal. 6:2; Matt. 5:17, 20-22). God's offering as a gift what the love commands require underwrites Paul's Good News of God's grace in Jesus for all humans. This Good News, according to Paul, is nothing less than "the power of God for salvation to everyone who has faith [in God]"

(Rom. 1:16, RSV; cf. 1 Cor. 4:20). Such faith, then, is a crucial means to receiving crucial power, and that power, being divine, transcends all merely human sources. It is the saving power of God's Spirit, the Spirit received only as a gift by the human entrustment of faith, and not by human earning. Let's briefly explore how humans can live into this desperately needed faith and power.

Living Faith

Human faith in God, as characterized above, includes an affirmative response of entrustment to God's redemptive call. This fits with Paul's remark that "faith comes from what is heard" (Rom. 10:17, RSV). This is faith as a receptive response of volitional commitment to God's call heard by a person, and it includes the person's *willing reliance,* grounded in experienced evidence of the call, on the God whom humans need to overcome death with lastingly good life. This is thus *not* faith as guesswork or a leap without evidence, as if faith in God were automatically defective from a cognitive point of view. Faith in God can be at least as cognitively sound as trusting in one's best friend, and thus need not, and should not, be a cognitive embarrassment at all. We will return to this important point below.

Our entrusting ourselves to God includes our willingly counting on God as our authoritative Lord, in response to God's redemptive intervention in our lives. Christian faith offers the life, death, and resurrection of Jesus as the central divine intervention and the focus of the preached Good News. As Paul expresses this: "God was in Christ reconciling the world to himself" (2 Cor. 5:19). Faith in God, accordingly, is for the sake of reconciliation in fellowship with God through Jesus. In counting on God as authoritative Lord, I manifest my having committed myself to God volitionally as *my* God and *my* Lord. I thus commit, obediently, to putting God's will over my own will in my life, even with regard to my impending death. This is consistent with the way Jesus prayed to God in Gethsemane upon his impending redemptive death by crucifixion: "Not what I will, but what *you* will."

In entrusting myself to God, I commit to dying to my own selfish ways to live to God's unselfish loving ways, in fellowship with God. In short, I resolve to die to my selfishness to live to God and God's ways of perfect love. Paul understands the human reception of divine grace via such a commitment of faith in terms of "dying and rising with Christ" (see Rom. 6:1-14; Phil. 3:9-11; for the same general lesson offered by Jesus himself, see Mark 8:34-36). This entails a commitment to reject selfishness, in particular any selfishness that involves exalting my will above God's will of perfect love. The relevant trust, or faith, thus includes my obediently *entrusting myself* to God as God, in response to God's authoritative call that makes a claim on me and my whole life. This call is thus a call to wholehearted entrustment of oneself to God. Nothing in one's life is to be excluded from God's authoritative call to faith as entrustment.

In selfishness (the antithesis of loving others), I fail to honor God *as authoritative Lord,* because I put myself and my own ways above the superior ways of a perfectly loving God. I would, however, not necessarily be selfish in putting God's ways first in order to bring good *to myself.* My doing something good for myself is not automatically selfish on my part. *Self-interestedness* and *selfishness* are not one and the same thing, and, of the two, only selfishness inevitably conflicts with the will of a perfectly loving God. Selfishness threatens if I seek to fulfill my desires in ways that knowingly bring harm to others. The divine call to faith in God is, in contrast, a call to die to selfishness in order to live to the God who seeks to empower unselfish love in us and to overcome death for us.

The suggestion that I must die to my selfish ways to live to God may seem to rest on an unduly harsh understanding of what faith in God requires. Still, the suggestion merits acceptance, given an empirically verifiable feature of the human condition: namely, deep-seated selfishness, the antithesis to the unselfish love, including the love of enemies, characteristic of a morally perfect God. Selfishness is the immoral toxin inside us that leads us to hoard the wealth and other resources that are desperately needed by others. We need a powerful remedy, or antitoxin, and we gain nothing of significance by ignoring this urgent problem. Our facing the problem of human selfishness honestly will enable us to apprehend our genuine need of the divine power of perfect love, and thereby will encourage us to become sincerely open to available evidence of divine reality and of the reconciliation on offer from God through Jesus.

If we could free ourselves of selfishness on our own, we would doubtless find much less of it around us and even within us. In any case, we cannot plausibly be encouraged about our taking care of the problem of human selfishness on our own, particularly because we typically protect our own selfishness. Obviously, our persistent selfishness makes us morally defective (and arguably worthy of judgment) by the divine standard of unselfish perfect love, and it thus disqualifies us as morally equivalent to God and even as deserving of, or owed, redemption by God. Still, we humans have a lingering tendency to "play God" in assuming supreme authority in some areas of our lives. This tendency has harmful cognitive consequences, in that it obstructs our receiving available evidence of divine reality that is intended to challenge our moral deficiencies. In particular, we become inclined to ignore or to suppress needed evidence of God's authoritative call in human conscience that challenges us in our selfish tendencies antithetical to God. As Paul suggests, in our immorality we "suppress" what God offers to us by way of corrective challenges (Rom. 1:18). We have the God-given freedom to suppress challenges in conscience, and we often exercise that freedom, even to our own cognitive and moral detriment.

We tend to consider ourselves to be authoritative lords over our lives, particularly in areas we find crucial to our well-being. A particularly revealing area concerns the way we treat our enemies who clearly threaten our (perceived) well-being. In some cases, we ignore them, but in other cases, we seek to destroy them, perhaps with heavy artillery and toxic chemicals or perhaps with slander that undermines their reputation. We very rarely, if ever, offer our enemies unselfish forgiving love, the kind of merciful enemy love found in the perfectly loving God of Jesus' Sermon on the Mount (see Matt. 5:43-48; cf. Luke 6:27-36). Such enemy love is, however, a crucial feature of what enables the Jewish-Christian God to be inherently morally perfect and worthy of worship, and thereby to satisfy the maximally honorific title "God." Not just any maximally powerful being, of course, will qualify as titleholder of the morally demanding title "God." Once we acknowledge this, we can readily exclude as imposters a long list of proposed candidates for titleholder, and carefully focus on the very small list of candidates worthy of the wholehearted entrustment appropriate to faith in God. The perfectly loving God represented by Jesus is, in the end, the only remaining serious candidate, once we acknowledge the crucial role of enemy love.

We are inclined to suppose that the risk of unselfish love is too great for us, because it is too threatening to *our* (perceived) well-being. We thereby often choose contrary to the ways of a perfectly loving God, given our presumption to know better and our selfish fear (on fear as an impediment to faith, see Mark 4:40-41; 5:36). Accordingly, we play God in the area of ethical conduct, and we proceed with destructive actions against our enemies who seem to threaten our own well-being. In contrast to such selfish fear and destructiveness, faith in God is inherently the volitional commitment to *let God be God* in our lives. Such faith includes the heart-based commitment to refuse to play God by going against God's ways of perfect love, including enemy love. If we would have such faith in God, we would decisively renounce selfishness as ultimately counterproductive and destructive.

Let's briefly consider a serious cognitive obstacle to a lived faith in God. We humans sometimes play God in connection with what is to count as needed adequate evidence of God's existence. Boldly, we presume to be in a position to say, on our own authority, what kind of evidence God *must* supply regarding God's existence. We reason in a dubious manner familiar from Bertrand Russell,[15] N. R. Hanson,[16] and many other philosophers who have overlooked that we should expect evidence of God's existence to be purposively available to us, that is, available in a manner that suits the authoritative purposes of a morally perfect God. The dubious reasoning runs, in outline, as follows. If God actually exists, God would certainly be revealed in a way readily noticed by all concerned. For instance, God would be revealed with considerable fanfare readily noticed by all observers. God, however, is definitely not revealed in that way. Therefore, according to many casual observers, God does not actually exist. Russell, accordingly, anticipated as follows his preferred response if he were to meet God after death: "God, you gave us insufficient evidence." Using this line of reasoning, we intentionally exalt ourselves as cognitive judge, jury, and executioner over God. Our preferred cognitive standard thus consigns God to the impotent category of the non-existent.

The uncritical presumption here is that God must be revealed on *our* preferred cognitive terms, as if our own terms were cognitively above reproach. This amounts to a kind of cognitive idolatry whereby we replace God's cognitive authority with our own. In particular, we set up our cognitive standards in ways that undermine "reasonable" acknowledgment

15. Bertrand Russell, "The Talk of the Town," *The New Yorker,* February 21, 1970, p. 29.

16. N. R. Hanson, *What I Do Not Believe and Other Essays* (Dordrecht: Reidel, 1971).

of God's reality, but we ignore that the relevant evidence would be purposively available to humans in keeping with *God's* perfectly loving (and thus sometimes subtle) character and purposes. Cognitive idolatry typically stems from cognitive pride wherein we play God in the cognitive domain, to our own demise. One's epistemology matters, then, because it can have life-or-death consequences.

Obviously, we are imposters in playing God, in any domain, because we fail undeniably to be worthy of worship. In particular, we lack the kind of powerful divine moral perfection that delivers not only an opportunity for lasting life in the face of our impending death, but also an offer of unselfish love in the presence of our destructive selfishness. God's power contrasts sharply, then, with familiar human power, especially in supplying what humans desperately need in their dire predicament. We should allow, accordingly, for *cognitive grace* whereby God freely gives us purposively available evidence of divine reality on God's perfectly loving terms, without either our trivializing God's morally profound character or our earning knowledge of God.

A perfectly loving God would call us to die to our playing God in order to live lastingly in fellowship with God. Our playing God wreaks havoc, wherever it is played, because we are at most a weak and pathetic counterfeit in place of the morally perfect and powerful true article. In the presence of our impending physical death, a perfectly loving God calls us to the realization that our playing God, including in the cognitive domain, will lead ultimately to the grave, with no happy ending. This God also calls us to yield our selfish wills to God's unselfish ways rather than to have our selfish wills extinguished altogether, given their destructive tendencies. On the basis of purposively available evidence of divine reality, we are called by God to fold now (i.e., repent) and to welcome (i.e., to trust) divine redeeming power in a new Spirit-led mode of living and dying. The life, death, and resurrection of Jesus perfectly model this new mode, receptively and obediently under divine authority that, in perfect redemptive love, is for our good. Faith in God is the human means of receiving this new mode of life under God, in fellowship with God.

In our selfishness antithetical to divine love, we fear not getting something (perhaps an opportunity or a relationship) we want to get, even at the expense of harming others (perhaps by blocking them from things they need). One motive at work is self-indulgent fear, which typically underwrites greed, covetousness, bias, and various other evils. Such fear haunts our natural behavioral tendencies, and looms large over much of human history, including national wars, racial and ethnic battles, and religious violence. Such fear can capture and bind us at the expense of flourishing and loving human relationships, and, in any case, it is always contrary to the life-giving ways of a perfectly loving God. Faith in God is a needed antidote, because such faith, as human entrustment to God, is the avenue of receiving the perfect divine love that casts out selfish fear and offers reconciled fellowship instead (see 1 John 4:18).

Ordinary knowledge in the form of information will not free us from our selfishness or our impending death, because we need volitional, purpose-directed *power* to move beyond selfishness and death. We can, of course, know what is good but fail to conform to it in our intentions and actions. Selfishness is inherently a matter of the will, and therefore cognitive enlightenment by itself will not solve our problem of selfishness. Although many philosophers and religious thinkers have overlooked this important lesson, we should embrace it and acknowledge our need for power beyond intellectual illumination.

Faith in God points to a place of rescue and safe refuge from our selfishness where we are set free of selfish fear even in the face of death. This is a place of divine-human *interpersonal fellowship* where humans are volitionally related and reconciled, via entrusting themselves, to a personal agent who first calls them into reconciled fellowship. This call comes with distinctive *power* of morally perfect love. Such divine love can bring good to us, even in suffering and dying, in ways that make selfishness undesirable and even repulsive. In suffering and dying, we often have a clear opportunity to see that the lasting power of redemption we humans need does not come from us but must come from God. God's authoritative power of unselfish lasting love, particularly in the life, death, and resurrection of Jesus, *shows* us (perhaps even without fully explaining) that we do not need selfishness to receive what is vitally good for us, and that even physical death can be overcome in resurrection by God. This is a central part of the Good News of powerful divine redemption by grace through faith in God and Jesus.

We should ask, finally, whether we are morally and cognitively *fit* to recognize on our own a personal power of perfect love that can liberate us from our selfishness if we are willing. We may be too far into the darkness of destructive selfishness to see on our own what we truly need to see and to do. This suggests cognitive pessimism about *our own resources* relative to a perfectly loving God, but it is *not* unqualified pessimism about all available resources. Perhaps the needed divine resources are purposively available to us if we are suitably willing, in a manner that fits with divine redemptive purposes for us as people desperately in need of volitional transformation, in reconciled fellowship with God.[17] At least we now face this urgent question: Are we *willing* to hear, and then to obey in the entrustment of faith, a call to ever-deepening fellowship with a God who manifests and commands love of others, even of enemies? This is the life-or-death question now before us. It takes us well beyond philosophy, into a self-defining decision we have to make before God.

Questions for Further Reflection

1. What is the relation between faith in God and belief that God exists? See James 2:19.

2. Can faith in God be supported by evidence? If so, how? Specifically, what should we expect the relevant evidence to look like? Might it be subtle and elusive? If so, how and why?

3. How is faith related to obedience, love, and "works"? Can faith be commanded? If so, are we morally responsible for having faith in God? Might we be disobedient in not having it? Can we selfishly have faith in God? If so, is it genuine faith?

4. Is human faith in God a means to a divine end? If so, what is that end, and how exactly does faith contribute to it? Might one satisfy that end more or less perfectly?

5. How does selfish fear bear on faith in God? How might such fear be a motive for intellectual doubt that God exists?

17. This is argued in Moser, *Elusive God.*

Open-mindedness

Jason Baehr

Many Christians are wary of open-mindedness. It suggests to them a kind of wishy-washy relativism or uncritical acceptance of others' beliefs. Indeed, the prevailing attitude toward open-mindedness, at least within large segments of the Christian community, is captured by the cynical but familiar adage: "Don't be so open-minded that your brains fall out."

This chapter is an exploration and partial defense of open-mindedness undertaken from a Christian standpoint. The defense is partial in that I am interested in defending a fairly specific conception of this trait. This leaves open the possibility that there are other personal qualities that can reasonably be described as "open-mindedness" but that I will make no attempt to defend.

I shall begin with a very brief sketch of open-mindedness together with an attempt to identify the source of Christian unease with it. Next I shall develop and illustrate a particular account of the basic character of open-mindedness. Armed with this account, I shall turn to the question of whether Christians should regard open-mindedness as a genuine virtue, that is, as a genuine *excellence* of personal character. I shall defend an affirmative answer to this question. This in turn will lead to an important and challenging objection to my proposal, my response to which will shed some additional light on the critical features of open-mindedness.

Thanks to Doug Geivett for comments on an earlier draft of this chapter. Thanks also to Michael Pace and Dan Speak for helpful conversations about the topics discussed herein.

In the final part of the chapter, I shall offer some remarks about the process of becoming open-minded.

Some Misgivings about Open-mindedness

Whatever its more detailed features, open-mindedness has *something* to do with how we respond to others' beliefs, and typically at least, to beliefs or ideas that conflict with our own. An open-minded person does not cling blindly to her beliefs in the face of challenges or counter-evidence to them. She is not dismissive of beliefs or positions with which she disagrees. Nor does she shy away from rational dialogue or engagement with people who believe differently from her. In these ways, open-mindedness is the *opposite* of traits like narrow-mindedness, closed-mindedness, dogmatism, intellectual dismissiveness, provincialism, and the like. These are (arguably, at any rate) the *vices* or character defects associated with the virtue of open-mindedness.

But even under this rather positive description, many Christians are likely to be suspicious of open-mindedness. This suspicion is rooted, I think, in at least three different negative perceptions of open-mindedness:

1. Open-mindedness as *wishy-washy.* Open-mindedness is often equated with relativistic ways of thinking. It is thought to connote a kind of intellectual flaccidity or flabbiness, a lack of intellectual seriousness and rigor. In a recent discussion of open-mindedness, Robert Roberts and Jay Wood imagine a young college student taking a survey course in philosophy whose intellectual life is marked by this way of thinking. The student "treats the survey as a smorgasbord at which she partakes with an appetite. With a course of sixteen weeks she may have been a Platonist, an empiricist, a skeptic, a Cartesian, a Kantian, a utilitarian, a social contractor, a mind-body dualist, a Berkeleyan idealist, a reductive materialist, a theist, an atheist, and an agnostic. Having scratched the surface of a debate, having followed for a few steps the flow of a dialectical exchange, she commits quickly to each theory, easily relinquishing its contrary, then passing on to the next. She is bright, but under the pressure of successive presentations of ideas, her intellectual character is too soft to hold

onto a position."[1] Understood in this way, it is not difficult to see why Christians (or any thinking person) might object to open-mindedness.

2. Open-mindedness as *cowardly.* Some Christians are suspicious of open-mindedness on the grounds that it represents a failure of intellectual *nerve.* Particularly for Christians of a more conservative stripe, the question of whether to be open-minded typically arises in the context of intellectual "combat" or "assault." They often feel "under attack" within the culture at large. They sense that the broader, secular community is hostile and antagonistic to what they believe. To be open-minded in this context, they think, is to betray a kind of intellectual weakness or cowardice: it represents a failure to stand up to one's intellectual accusers or enemies.
3. Open-mindedness as *foolish.* A third misgiving about open-mindedness comes from a place of relative intellectual *confidence* (rather than weakness or defensiveness). Some Christians, convinced that their beliefs about God, morality, and the like, are correct, see no reason to be open-minded. "My Christian beliefs are true," they think, "so what's the point of taking seriously the beliefs of people who disagree with me?" Indeed, to these folks, open-mindedness threatens to do considerable intellectual *damage.* It threatens to lead them away from truth and down the path of deception. In this way, open-mindedness can be regarded as downright intellectually foolish, as a guaranteed *squandering* of cognitive goods.[2]

1. *Intellectual Virtues: An Essay in Regulative Epistemology* (Oxford: Oxford University Press, 2007), p. 188. Roberts and Wood do not endorse this way of thinking about open-mindedness. Their immediate concern is the virtue of intellectual firmness, a virtue that I would argue complements genuine open-mindedness.

2. While related to the first misgiving, the present worry about open-mindedness is distinct. For one thing, it presupposes that the person in question thinks of himself as already possessing the truth. The first misgiving makes no such assumption, since one could be opposed to wishy-washy thinking about a given subject matter (or in general) even if one did not think of oneself as already possessing the truth about this subject matter (or in general). Furthermore, the present misgiving focuses on the (alleged) negative *consequences* of open-mindedness. But a disapproval of wishy-washy thinking need not be consequentialist in nature: one might object to such thinking on the grounds that it is *irrational* and that irrationality is an *intrinsically* bad intellectual state.

We shall return to these objections to open-mindedness below. Before we do so, however, it will be helpful to have a more precise and intuitively plausible conception of open-mindedness before us. I turn now to develop such a conception.

The Nature of Open-mindedness

My aim here is to sketch an account of open-mindedness whereby it is at least initially plausible to think of open-mindedness as a genuine excellence of personal character. In the section that follows, I shall take up the question of whether open-mindedness thus conceived really *is* a virtue — or rather, whether it really is a virtue when examined from a distinctively Christian standpoint.

How, then, should we think about open-mindedness? What are its essential or defining features? In attempting to answer this question, I shall begin with an account of open-mindedness which, while initially very plausible, has some significant limitations. Once the relevant cases and criticisms are on the table, I shall proceed to articulate a more plausible account.

On one initially attractive model, open-mindedness is essentially *a willingness to "set aside" or loosen one's grip on a particular belief in order to give a fair or impartial hearing to arguments or evidence against this belief.* A great deal could be said in explanation and support of this definition. What I wish to focus on here, however, is the fact that if this definition is correct, an exercise of open-mindedness necessarily (a) presupposes a *conflict* between an open-minded person's beliefs and the beliefs toward which she is open-minded and (b) involves a certain amount of rational *assessment* or *adjudication* (for instance, an assessment of the plausibility or force of the relevant counterargument). I shall argue that, in fact, neither (a) nor (b) is necessary.

First, an exercise of open-mindedness does not presuppose a conflict between the open-minded person's beliefs and the beliefs toward which she is open-minded. To see why, consider the case of a judge preparing to hear opening arguments in a particular case. The judge might have no prior opinions or biases about any part of the case. And she might have no stake in its outcome. There might, then, be no conflict between the beliefs of the judge and the beliefs or arguments she is preparing to assess. Nonetheless, it seems clear that the judge might give an open-minded hearing to or make an open-minded assessment of these arguments. Open-mindedness might lead her, say, to *follow the arguments where they lead and to refrain from drawing any hasty or premature conclusions.* If so, then contrary to (a), open-mindedness need not involve a conflict between the open-minded person's beliefs and the beliefs or arguments at which her open-mindedness is directed.

This case is consistent, however, with the idea that open-mindedness necessarily involves *some* kind of intellectual disagreement or dispute, for clearly there is a conflict between the arguments toward which the judge is being open-minded. Accordingly, it might be thought that open-mindedness is something like *a willingness to adjudicate two or more conflicting viewpoints in a certain impartial, detached, or "open" way.* But even this represents an overly restrictive way of thinking about open-mindedness. To see why, consider a group of high school physics students who have just been led by their teacher through a rigorous unit on Einstein's Special Theory of Relativity. The unit has been a considerable challenge for the students, but they are, by and large, on board; they understand the core concepts, principles, and claims of the Special Theory. In the next unit of the course, however, the teacher plans to introduce his students to Einstein's General Theory of Relativity. This unit is bound to prove extremely challenging for them. The material will require an even greater and more radical departure from their usual concepts of space, time, laws of nature, velocity, frames of reference, and the like. It will require them to think even further "outside the box." Here there is no relevant intellectual conflict or disagreement whatsoever. The students are preparing to study the General Theory, and this theory is a natural (if complex and mind-bending) *extension* of the Special Theory; it does not *conflict* with the Special Theory. And yet it is reasonable to think that the students' efforts to understand the General Theory might be facilitated by a kind of open-mindedness. Open-mindedness might help them "detach" or depart from some of their usual ways of thinking and to "wrap their minds around" the core elements of this challenging theory.[3] This

3. Other intellectual virtues might be relevant here as well — for instance, curiosity or perseverance. However, the point is that there may be students who are curious (perseverant, etc.) but who, in order to grasp the subject matter, still need to "stretch their minds" or "think outside the box" in a manner characteristic of open-

shows that an exercise of open-mindedness does not, in fact, presuppose a conflict between any of the beliefs or standpoints at which it is directed.

Cases of this sort also make clear, contrary to (b) above, that open-mindedness need not manifest in the activity of rational *assessment* or *adjudication*. For the physics students are not attempting to *assess* the General Theory; they are not attempting to judge whether it is true or false, or to identify its logical strengths or weaknesses. Rather, at this point, they are simply trying to *understand* or *comprehend* the theory.[4]

For a similar kind of example, imagine a detective attempting to solve an especially confounding case. His investigation is complete: he has examined the crime scene in painstaking detail, studied the forensics reports, interviewed all the witnesses, followed up on possible suspects, and so forth. He is in possession of all of the relevant evidence. Yet the evidence is perplexing and contradictory — so much so that he is unable to conceive of a single coherent explanation of it. Like the previous case, this case is void of any intellectual dispute or disagreement.[5] And the person in question is not attempting to assess or evaluate any particular belief. Again, he is merely attempting to identify *some* possible explanation of a certain perplexing set of data. He is not yet at the stage of attempting to assess or evaluate this explanation. And yet, here again it seems that open-mindedness might be relevant. Specifically, open-mindedness might permit the detective to imagine or conceive of an explanation of the relevant data that would otherwise be beyond his reach. We might imagine him muttering to himself, "Now, keep your thinking open. Consider all the relevant possibilities. Just keep an open mind." What this suggests is that open-mindedness, in addition to facilitating rational assessment and attempts to grasp a certain subject matter, can also facilitate attempts to *identify* or *conceive* of a certain (otherwise unthinkable) possibility or explanation.[6]

---

mindedness. Anything less than open-mindedness may be insufficient for cognitive success in this case.

4. Of course, upon grasping the theory, the students might immediately proceed to attempt to evaluate it, and open-mindedness might be relevant here as well. But the former application of open-mindedness would be distinct from the latter.

5. There is a kind of "disagreement" or (apparent) lack of rational coherence among the data, but this is not the sort of disagreement we are concerned with; nor is open-mindedness needed to "move between" or adjudicate these data.

6. While closely related to understanding or comprehension, the kind of "conceiv-

We have seen that neither (a) nor (b) above are essential features of open-mindedness and thus that our initial definition of open-mindedness, while perhaps a good start, is too narrow. What, then, might a broader, more plausible account of open-mindedness look like? I propose the following multi-part definition, the key terms of which I will then go on to clarify (in reverse order):

> An open-minded person is one who is (a) able and willing (b) to transcend a certain default cognitive standpoint (c) in order to take up or take seriously a distinct cognitive standpoint.[7]

Part (c) of the definition addresses the immediate aim or motivation of open-mindedness. A person who sets aside her belief about some issue in order to consider a competing standpoint, but who fails to give an honest, fair, or impartial consideration to this standpoint, fails to manifest genuine open-mindedness. While she may *appear* open-minded, inasmuch as she ignores, distorts, or misrepresents the view she is considering, her cognitive activity is not truly open-minded. Thus, in cases in which open-mindedness involves a kind of rational assessment or adjudication, it necessarily involves "taking seriously" the view or standpoint at which it is directed. This underscores the fact that open-mindedness is a "facilitating" trait or virtue, that is, that it can facilitate or support an exercise of other putative virtues like intellectual fairness, honesty, and impartiality. That said, we have seen that open-mindedness does not necessarily involve the activity of rational assessment. And where it does not, the question of "taking seriously" an alternative standpoint does not arise.[8] Again, the open-minded physics students, for instance, need not

---

ing" I have in mind here is prior and distinct. The detective, for instance, might seek to *understand* or *comprehend* the details of a particular theory *after* he conceives of it — the latter being his immediate focus. Indeed, his attempt to comprehend the theory *presupposes* his already having conceived of or identified it in the relevant sense.

7. These are not intended as jointly *sufficient* conditions for open-mindedness, at least not if open-mindedness is to be considered a genuine *virtue.* To be a virtue, the relevant disposition must, on my view, be rooted in a certain good or admirable motivation. More on this momentarily.

8. Of course, it might arise immediately thereafter, since, again, one might move from an open-minded "taking up" of a particular perspective to an evaluation or assessment of this perspective.

be attempting to "take seriously" or to give a fair or impartial hearing to Einstein's General Theory. Instead, their open-mindedness is aimed immediately at *understanding* or *conceiving* — that is, at "taking up" — the standpoint in question.[9]

Part (b) of the definition gets at the conceptual core of open-mindedness. It says that open-mindedness is principally a kind of cognitive "transcending" of an initial or "default" cognitive standpoint. This characterization fits well with standard cases of open-mindedness, where the open-minded person sets aside her belief about some issue in order to consider an opposing position, argument, or the like. Here the "default" cognitive standpoint is the one that the open-minded person sets aside or moves beyond. This characterization also fits well with the other cases discussed above. For instance, the open-minded detective is attempting to "transcend" or move beyond his limited grasp of what might explain the relevant evidence. Similarly, the physics students are attempting to "transcend" their present understanding of space, time, and the like.

The case of the open-minded judge is a bit trickier in this regard. While the judge might be attempting to adjudicate or "take seriously" the merits of the competing arguments, in what sense is she "transcending" a "default" cognitive perspective? For again, she is presently *neutral* with regard to the matter at hand (that is, the guilt or innocence of the defendant). This case illustrates the point that while open-mindedness is typically a matter of *doing* something — of a kind of positive or forward cognitive movement — it sometimes consists in *refraining* from engaging in cognitive activity. The judge, for instance, refrains from drawing any hasty or premature conclusions about the case she is hearing. This shows that open-mindedness sometimes consists, not in a positive opening of one's mind, but rather in an *unwillingness to close it.* In cases of this sort, the "default" standpoint is one that the open-minded person might otherwise be tempted or likely to take up (for example, the standpoint of a

9. A similar point holds for the detective case. Open-mindedness is relevant to the detective's attempt to *imagine* or *conceive* of a particular explanation; the detective is not (at present) trying to assess any explanation. Of course, recognizing that an explanation *could* account for a certain data set amounts to an evaluation of some sort (for presumably not every proposed explanation would have this quality). I am thinking of "assessment" or "evaluation" in somewhat narrower terms, however — terms that presuppose the *possibility* or *possible truth* of the explanation or other item being assessed.

hasty conclusion); the open-minded person "transcends" this standpoint by remaining apart or detached from it.

Finally, as indicated by (a), open-mindedness on my view involves both a willingness and an ability. Clearly, if a person is capable of taking seriously objections or counterevidence to her beliefs, say, but is consistently *unwilling* to do so, then she is not genuinely open-minded. Indeed, it is tempting to think that open-mindedness is nothing more than a willingness to engage in the relevant sort of cognitive "transcending." But this is not quite right. For suppose that a person is genuinely *willing* to consider alternative viewpoints regarding some matter but has been so indoctrinated regarding this matter, or holds so tightly to her beliefs about it, that she is psychologically *incapable* of doing so. Such an agent would not be genuinely open-minded. An open-minded person, then, is necessarily willing *and* able to "transcend" a default cognitive standpoint for the sake of "taking up" or "taking seriously" some alternative or distinct standpoint.[10]

Before turning to consider how open-mindedness conceived along these lines should be assessed from a Christian standpoint, I want to supplement the account just sketched with two additional claims. First, as I am thinking of it, open-mindedness necessarily ranges, not merely over the relevant cognitive detaching or transcending, but also over the open-minded agent's *cognitive response* to certain judgments that arise from this activity. Suppose, for instance, that I set aside or transcend a particular belief of mine in order to consider the merits of the "opposing side," that I come to judge that the preponderance of evidence actually supports this opposing standpoint, but that I fail to give up or even to loosen my grip on my original belief; instead I go on believing precisely as I did prior to encountering the relevant counterevidence. Presumably it would be a mistake to consider me genuinely open-minded.[11] Were I

10. However, the required ability in question has its limits. For if a person were able and willing, in the ways just described, to engage in the activity characteristic of open-mindedness, but were prevented from doing so by some *external* source, then it might still make sense to think of this person as open-minded. Here, the inability is a matter of bad luck; it is beyond the control of the agent.

11. I qualify this claim in a limited way below. See the section "Open-mindedness and Christian Faith." It is worth noting that in the sort of case just described, I would indeed have a *semblance* of open-mindedness or be open-minded to a *degree.* But again, my concern here is with a version or kind of open-mindedness that at least

truly open-minded, then, in addition to giving a serious hearing to the merits of the "opposing side," I would also adjust my beliefs in light of what I learned from this hearing — which in this case would likely mean abandoning my original belief. This, then, points to a further general feature of open-mindedness: namely, that where an exercise of open-mindedness involves rational assessment, it also involves adjusting one's beliefs or confidence levels in a way that reflects the outcome of this assessment.[12] This is not, however, an essential or required feature of open-mindedness, for we have seen that open-mindedness does not always involve rational assessment.

Second, as I am thinking of it here, open-mindedness is characteristically motivated by or "flows" from a "love" of intellectual goods like truth, knowledge, and understanding.[13] This is to say that an open-minded person is typically motivated to consider counterevidence to her beliefs, to think "outside the box," and so on, *because* she desires to know or understand; and, more specifically, because she desires knowledge or understanding and is convinced that the activity characteristic of open-mindedness is an effective way of achieving this goal. Therefore, on the present account, open-mindedness is characteristically accompanied by a certain intellectual *motivation.*[14] I take it that G. K. Chesterton had something like this point in mind when he famously quipped: "Merely having an open mind is nothing. The object of opening the mind, as of opening the mouth, is to shut it again on something solid."[15]

---

stands a chance of counting as a genuine *excellence;* and it is doubtful that whatever kind of open-mindedness I might exhibit in the example just noted fits this description.

12. This requirement is discussed in more depth in the sections that follow.

13. I say "characteristically" rather than "necessarily" mainly because I want to leave open the possibility that the sort of open-mindedness I am interested in might be motivated by other valuable ends. In the section that follows, I explain, for instance, that it might be motivated by a kind of neighbor- or enemy-love.

14. Clearly this — or any similar — motivation is not necessary for open-mindedness *per se,* which is why the present point is not included in the foregoing *definition* of open-mindedness. A person could be open-minded, even in a reasonably "deep" or habitual sense, for the sake of other, far less noble ends — for example, because she wants to be well-liked or because she sees being open-minded as necessary for winning a certain prize. I exclude such cases from my present characterization since, again, my aim is to identify a kind or variety of open-mindedness that at least stands a chance of qualifying as a Christian *virtue.*

15. *Collected Works,* vol. 16 (San Francisco: Ignatius, 1988), p. 212.

We now have before us a fairly robust and, I hope, familiar and plausible conception of open-mindedness. I turn now to consider whether open-mindedness conceived in this way should be regarded as a Christian virtue.[16]

Open-mindedness as a Christian Virtue

Should someone attempting to be faithful to the Christian scriptures and theological tradition regard the foregoing account of open-mindedness as picking out a genuine virtue, that is, as identifying a genuine *excellence* of personal character?

At some level, the answer is undoubtedly "yes." New and Old Testament scriptures alike place a premium on a concern for truth (see, for instance, Ps. 51:6; Ps. 15:2; James 1:5, Acts 17:10-11; and 1 Thess. 5:21). And again, according to the account just sketched, open-mindedness is characteristically rooted in or flows from precisely such a concern. Moreover, as illustrated by several of the cases discussed above, open-mindedness has clear intellectual "benefits" that should be welcomed by anyone. No reasonable Christian would deny, for instance, that open-mindedness might be valuable in contexts like those of the physics students or the detective discussed above. Again, in situations like these, open-mindedness can facilitate its possessor's attempt to *understand* a foreign or challenging subject matter or to *conceive* of a coherent explanation of a perplexing set of data. Likewise, no Christian should have a hard time recognizing the value of open-mindedness relative to certain *intramural* disputes, for example, in the context of good faith theological disagreements or discussions with other believers.

The more difficult question is whether Christians can plausibly regard open-mindedness as a virtue when it is directed at beliefs that conflict with their own distinctively *Christian* beliefs. Let us refer to the former beliefs as *unchristian* beliefs. These, again, are beliefs that are incompatible with the acceptance of a distinctively Christian view of the world. While I will not venture to specify all of the elements of a "distinctively Christian" worldview, I shall assume that they include beliefs such

16. Special thanks to Michael Pace for several helpful discussions about the content of this section.

as that there exists an omniscient, omnipotent, and omnibenevolent deity, that human beings have an eternal existence, that Jesus is the son of God, that he was resurrected from the dead, and so on. Accordingly, unchristian beliefs would include beliefs to the effect that such claims are false (for example, that Jesus was not raised from the dead) or beliefs that are otherwise incompatible with these claims (for example, that only material things exist). The pressing question, then, is whether Christians can reasonably regard open-mindedness directed at unchristian beliefs as a genuine virtue. We will have occasion to engage this question later in the discussion. For now let us return to the three misgivings about open-mindedness identified at the outset of this chapter.

According to the first objection, open-mindedness is essentially wishy-washy or relativistic: it involves intellectually flaccid or flabby ways of thinking or believing. It should be clear that when conceived in the way I have suggested, to be open-minded is *not* essentially or inherently to be wishy-washy, relativistic, or flaccid. For one thing, to be open-minded in this sense is not necessarily to adopt or embrace the views toward which one manifests open-mindedness. Nor does open-mindedness require giving serious consideration to just *any* view with which one disagrees. For, insofar as open-mindedness is constrained by something like a love of truth, it will involve an appropriate kind of selectivity or discrimination. A person who cares deeply about "getting things right," about developing an *accurate* view of the world, is unlikely to give an open-minded consideration to a belief or argument which she has little or no reason to think might actually be true.[17] For these and related reasons, there should be little concern that open-mindedness, when understood in the suggested way, involves wishy-washy or relativist thinking.

The second misgiving about open-mindedness identified earlier stems from the idea that for many Christians, the question of whether to be open-minded often arises in an intellectually combative context — that is, in a context in which the Christian or her worldview is being "attacked"

17. A possible exception here, which will be developed in more detail momentarily, is open-mindedness motivated by a kind of Christian love. Here open-mindedness may not be directed strictly at beliefs that the open-minded person has reason to think might be true. However, in this manifestation, open-mindedness is hardly wishy-washy, especially when considered from a Christian standpoint. I say considerably more about when exactly it is appropriate to manifest open-mindedness in my as yet unpublished essay,"The Structure of Open-Mindedness."

by another person or by the culture at large. And again, the suggestion is that to be open-minded vis-à-vis one's intellectual enemies or opponents amounts to a kind of intellectual weakness or cowardice. This prescription embodies a rather striking "enemy ethic." It suggests that the stance Christians should have toward their enemies is one of defensiveness and force — perhaps even of retaliation. But this prescription is, in fact, diametrically opposed to the New Testament's teaching about how Christians should be oriented toward their enemies. Jesus of Nazareth taught, not only that we should "love our *neighbors* as ourselves," but also, and much more radically, that we must love our *enemies* (Matt. 5:43-44). What does such "enemy love" require of us? While I cannot pursue this question in depth, surely it involves respecting and giving serious consideration to our enemies' *beliefs* — and particularly to those beliefs that really "matter" to them. If I feed and clothe my neighbor or enemy, but ignore, distort, or otherwise fail to "take seriously" his deeply held beliefs, then surely I fail to embody the kind of love that Jesus commands.[18] This suggests, contra the objection, that Christians have a *special* obligation, that there are in fact distinctively *Christian* reasons, to be open-minded.[19]

Two additional points are worth making in connection with this objection. First, it bears repeating that "taking seriously" a particular belief need not involve accepting this belief. As already noted, open-mindedness is principally a matter of "transcending" an initial or default cognitive standpoint. While it *can* — for reasons sketched above — require giving up or loosening one's grip on one's beliefs, there is no immediate reason to think that this is likely to be required especially often. Second, it is important to regard the kind of open-mindedness that is part and parcel to Christlike enemy-love as being rooted in a place of deep *confidence and power.* When Jesus calls his followers to love their ene-

18. This is at least partly because our deeply held beliefs are central to our identities or self-conceptions, such that to have them disrespected or disregarded is to be disrespected ourselves.

19. I do not want to deny that contexts of the sort in question might also call for a kind of intellectual *courage.* Indeed, it might take courage to be open-minded in such contexts. What I do wish to deny is that a genuine Christian courage might license closed-minded or dogmatic ways of engaging with our intellectual enemies. Also, the "Christian reasons" in question are not necessarily overriding, for among the beliefs that we ought to be open-minded about is the belief that we might be mistaken about our Christian beliefs.

mies, he is not asking them simply or irrationally or against the full force of their wills to *cast* themselves at the feet of their enemies; he is not calling his followers to a kind of blind or arbitrary self-sacrifice. Rather, Christlike enemy-love is, at least in its purest form, rooted in a deep knowledge, trust, and acquaintance with God himself.[20] The same goes for the kind of open-mindedness entailed by such love. We shall return to this point below.

According to the third misgiving, open-mindedness is a foolish intellectual gamble. Again, the idea here can be put thus: "We as Christians already *have* the truth. So why should we bother being open-minded toward people that disagree with us? Indeed, doing so seems bound to lead us down a path of cognitive error. Therefore, open-mindedness is no virtue." We have already identified part of the problem with this objection, namely, that even if we do possess the truth, Christian love may require us to give serious attention to the beliefs of those that disagree with us.[21] An equally serious problem is that the objection bespeaks an extremely unchristian intellectual *arrogance.* It is remarkable that Christians in particular (and especially Christians of a more conservative or traditional stripe) are known for touting humanity's "fallen" (even "depraved") nature while at the same time displaying an apparently unshakable confidence in their own beliefs. Such a mindset is remarkable because surely our fallenness extends, not just to the "moral" dimension of our nature, but also to its *cognitive* or *epistemic* dimension.[22] This suggests an additional distinctively Christian reason for being open-minded. Again, if we

20. For a recent treatment of this theme, see Dallas Willard, *Knowing Christ Today* (New York: HarperCollins, 2009).

21. This kind of case illustrates a potential tension, noted above, between a desire for truth and Christian love. This tension is not a problem, however, unless one thinks (implausibly) that a desire for truth should always trump the demands of Christian love.

22. For more on this topic, see Alvin Plantinga, *Warranted Christian Belief* (New York: Oxford University Press, 2000); Abraham Kuyper, *The Principles of Sacred Theology* (Grand Rapids: Eerdmans, 1954); and Merold Westphal, "Taking St. Paul Seriously: Sin as an Epistemological Category," in *Christian Philosophy,* ed. Thomas Flint (Notre Dame: University of Notre Dame Press, 1988), pp. 200-226. See Jonathan Adler, "Reconciling Open-Mindedness and Belief," *Theory and Research in Education* 2 (2004): 127-42, for a more general, non-theological account of how an acceptance of cognitive fallibility is relevant to open-mindedness.

believe (as we should) that original sin extends even to our cognitive or epistemic nature, we ought to be especially willing to listen and give serious consideration to those with whom we disagree. An appropriate Christian humility demands nothing less.

Open-mindedness and Christian Faith

At this point the following objection is likely to arise: "On the present account, when open-mindedness leads to a favorable assessment of some belief that one presently rejects, it requires that one adjust or change one's beliefs in response to this assessment. Do you really mean to suggest that Christians should be open-minded in this way relative to their *Christian* beliefs — that we ought, say, to repudiate one of these beliefs if our assessment of a corresponding nonchristian belief seems to call for it? Wouldn't this involve holding loosely to our Christian beliefs in a way that is incompatible with genuine Christian *faith?*"

My answer, in short, is that I think we *should* be open-minded in connection with our Christian beliefs — even to the point of repudiating these beliefs if the result of an open-minded inquiry calls for it.[23] I do not, at any rate, believe that there are any *Christian* (or other good) reasons for thinking otherwise. Indeed, given the point above about the cognitive or noetic dimensions of sin, I think Christians have a special reason *not* to regard any of their beliefs as beyond error or doubt. It is also important to bear in mind that, as I have described it, the relevant willingness to give up or revise a particular belief is characteristically motivated by something like a "love of truth," that is, by a desire to see or understand things as they really are. And this again is something on which the Jewish and

23. Important questions can be raised pertaining to when exactly an open-minded inquiry might "call for" or "demand" the repudiation of a particular belief. One such question concerns the epistemic threshold a belief must meet if one is to be justified in *holding onto* (not repudiating) it. For instance, must a belief have positive evidential support? Or might it be "properly basic"? The position I am defending here is intended to be neutral with respect to this question (and with respect to the philosophical views that lie behind it). For present purposes, it will suffice to say that, on the view I am defending, an open-minded inquiry calls for the repudiation of a belief just in case it yields a *defeater* relative to this belief. This is something that evidentialists and Reformed epistemologists should be able to agree upon.

Christian scriptures place a premium. Finally, to refuse to be open-minded about one's Christian beliefs is to open the door to a kind of intellectual *dishonesty.* For, if one makes such a refusal, and is confronted with compelling evidence against one's Christian beliefs, then one is likely to ignore, distort, or suppress this evidence: one is likely, as it were, to "hide" from what one has reason to think is actually *true.* But surely the God of the Bible does not welcome (let alone *require*) this kind of dishonesty.[24]

It is important, however, to clarify or qualify my position here in several ways. First, I am open to the possibility that *if* one's Christian worldview is on the whole adequately supported, then one is justified in holding somewhat more firmly to (and thus being somewhat *less* open-minded about) those beliefs that are especially central or integral to a Christian worldview (for example, the "essentials" or "majors" of the Christian faith).[25] This is not to suggest that the beliefs in question are immune to counterevidence or that they are beyond reflective questioning or revision. Rather, the suggestion is merely that they can reasonably be given an initially privileged position relative to the other elements of one's Christian worldview (and again, this only if one's Christian worldview is adequately supported on the whole). While I cannot explore this proposal in any detail here, I think it has considerable plausibility.[26] And

24. In fact, it might even be said that (to the extent that God disapproves of dishonesty) the Christian has a special obligation to give up her Christian beliefs if she finds that the evidence is stacked against them. But there is, of course, a paradox here, since as soon as she gives up her Christian beliefs, she (presumably) is no longer a Christian, and therefore no longer has the reasons in question! I will not stop to pursue this point here, except to say that the paradox is not unique to Christian or any other kind of religious belief. A similar problem arises in connection with philosophical skepticism, for example, when one is led to doubt the reliability of sense perception based on beliefs that arise from sense perception or when reason itself leads one to be skeptical about the reliability of reason.

25. Again, I will not attempt to say what exactly counts as "adequate support"; however, in this case, I do think it involves having some *positive* evidential support (that is, it is not enough that the belief in question be "properly basic" and that one lack any defeaters for this belief).

26. Something like this principle is at work in some fairly standard philosophical ways of thinking about knowledge and rationality. For instance, it is often held (roughly) that if a scientific theory T is on the whole well-confirmed, it takes more in the way of empirical counterevidence to "dislodge" or refute the more central or integral elements of T than it does those elements that are less central or that are, as it

if it is correct, it suggests a subtle but important qualification to the claim that we should be open-minded even about our Christian beliefs.

Second, when I say that open-mindedness requires adjusting one's beliefs or confidence levels in light of one's open-minded rational assessments, I take the cognitive or evidential perspective in question to be a *settled, all-things-considered* one. Suppose, for instance, that I have a well-supported belief that P, but that my open-mindedness leads me to make an honest and impartial assessment of a certain argument for not-P, and that I come to find this argument compelling. It does not follow from this that I shall have to give up my belief that P. For it might remain that, while I now have some evidence against P, the *totality* of my evidence still supports P, that is, that *all things considered* I have good reasons in support of P.[27] Relatedly, it is important to do justice to the fact that our assessment of our own reasons or evidence for our beliefs can fluctuate from one moment to the next, even when these reasons remain more or less the same. This is at least partly a function of the fact that the evidence we have relative to a given belief can be vast and complicated, such that it can be very difficult, at any given moment, to keep the totality of this evidence "before our minds," so to speak. For instance, suppose again that while having good reasons for my belief that P, I come to find a particular argument for not-P compelling. As the force of this argument sinks in, I might (momentarily) lose sight of the *support* I have for P, and thus be led to think (mistakenly) that the totality of my evidence now supports not-P. Surely, given the fact that the totality of my evidence actually supports P, I need not repudiate my belief that P. Accordingly, the position I wish to defend is that open-mindedness requires adjusting one's beliefs or confidence levels only when, from a *set-*

---

were, on the "periphery" of T. The corresponding point about rational or justified belief is that it takes more (by way of counterevidence) to defeat the justification of a belief in the integral elements of T than it does the more peripheral elements. While W. V. O. Quine famously argued in "Two Dogmas of Empiricism" (*From a Logical Point of View* [Cambridge, MA: Harvard University Press, 1980], pp. 20-47) that *no* belief (not even the most central or integral) is immune to empirical refutation, he presumably accepted the much weaker principle just noted. See also Imre Lakatos, "Falsification and the Methodology of Scientific Research Programmes," *Criticism and the Growth of Knowledge,* ed. Imre Lakatos and Alan Musgrave (Cambridge: Cambridge University Press, 1970), pp. 91-96. Thanks to Tim Shanahan for the latter reference.

27. I may, however, need to reduce my confidence level regarding P.

tled (and all-things-considered) perspective, one's open-minded inquiries call for such an adjustment.[28]

Third, I see little reason to think that being open-minded about one's Christian beliefs in the suggested way is incompatible with the very notion of *faith* understood in a Christian way. As indicated above, Christian faith is not a matter of accepting what, on the whole or from a settled perspective, one has little if any reason to think is actually *true* — or worse, what one has reason to think is *false.*[29] This again would amount to a kind of intellectual *dishonesty.* Furthermore, while open-mindedness applied to Christian belief does bring with it a certain intellectual tentativeness, this tentativeness need not be a matter of "holding loosely" to the relevant beliefs, or at least not of "holding loosely" in a way that conflicts with a genuine and robust faith. On the contrary, it is consistent with a very firm and realistic acceptance of the tenets of the Christian faith.

These qualifications notwithstanding, I do not wish to deny that being an open-minded Christian is likely to prove challenging in various ways. It is likely, for instance, to demand a considerable amount of intellectual effort and to involve periods of doubt and uncertainty. The *easier* and more *comfortable* route is to be closed-minded and dogmatic about one's Christian beliefs. But again, we have seen that such comfort comes only at the expense of a kind of intellectual integrity and honesty. And, especially *as* a Christian, I regard this as a price that is decidedly *not* worth paying.

We have seen that, when understood in a certain way, there are a va-

28. This talk of "adjusting" confidence levels or "repudiating" beliefs raises the question of whether the present view presupposes an implausible doxastic voluntarism. I believe it does not: first, because I think it is clear that for the most part we have *enough* (at least *indirect*) control over our beliefs and confidence levels to satisfy the requirements I am defending; and second, because, where a person happens to lack such control, I think the relevant normative judgments may still be warranted. Concerning the latter point, if a person is *so* dogmatic or clings *so* tightly to *every one* of his Christian beliefs that he simply *cannot* bring himself to revise these beliefs in the light of counterevidence that comes his way, I think we are right to view his clinging to the relevant beliefs as unjustified or irrational — despite the fact that he has no real control over them.

29. Here again I am sidestepping the question of exactly what epistemic standard a belief must satisfy before it qualifies as intellectually dishonest or before open-mindedness might require giving it up. See note 23 above.

riety of reasons for thinking that open-mindedness is indeed a Christian virtue: not only is it useful for acquiring knowledge that Christians do and should value, but there are also some distinctively Christian reasons for being open-minded. A call to open-mindedness is embedded, I have suggested, in the biblical injunctions to care about truth and to love our neighbors and enemies, as well as in any plausible theology of original sin. Finally, we have seen that open-mindedness, when properly conceived, is neither wishy-washy, cowardly, nor foolish in the ways suggested at the outset of this chapter.

Becoming Open-minded

In this final section, I shall attempt to say something concerning the "how to" of open-mindedness. This is not a task that I feel especially qualified to perform as a *philosopher* (rather than, say, as a psychologist or spiritual advisor). Nonetheless, I am convinced that the process of becoming open-minded is to a significant extent a matter of reflective commonsense. This is, in any case, the spirit in which the following remarks are offered.

First, a word about how *not* to pursue open-mindedness. Like any character trait, open-mindedness is not achievable by immediate or direct choice. I cannot successfully *will* to be open-minded any more than I can will to be patient or compassionate or generous. This is because, in its purest form at least, open-mindedness is a deep inner trait or "heart attitude." It makes significant demands on one's desires, emotions, thoughts, and actions. And one's habits or dispositions in this regard are not the sort of thing that can be changed or modified on demand. The result is that any strategy or practical steps relevant to becoming open-minded are bound to be at least somewhat *indirect.*[30]

Second, it is a truism that to a very significant extent we get our "values" and other normative standards from the company we keep. The same can be said for our *comfort level* with these values. Suppose I harbor considerable animosity toward my colleague Jones. If the majority of my other colleagues feel the same way about Jones, then I am likely to feel at

30. One can, of course, will to *try* to become more open-minded, patient, or courageous. But, alas, this is hardly sufficient for actually *becoming* virtuous in these ways.

ease with and be unlikely to address my own attitude toward him. If, on the other hand, my colleagues tend to think very well of Jones, then my dislike of him is likely to be a source of discomfort for me, and I am considerably more likely to question it and try to repudiate it. Accordingly, if we desire to become more open-minded, intellectually fair, honest, or the like, then we must choose to surround ourselves with people who embody (or at least *value*) these qualities; and we must seek to avoid the company of those who are narrow, dogmatic, intellectually uncharitable, dishonest, and so on. Our selection of social environment is critical to our prospects of becoming more open-minded.

Third, if we wish to cultivate open-mindedness, it is also critical that we make specific intentional *efforts* to this end. I think here of the apostle Paul's remark that he "buffets" or "disciplines" his body "lest after preaching to others I myself should be disqualified" (1 Cor. 9:27). Implicit in this remark, I take it, is the idea that if we wish to achieve certain inner qualities, we must undertake specific actions or "exercises" that will help bring these qualities about.[31] In a similar vein, Aristotle says that to cultivate a particular virtue, one must repeatedly practice (even if imperfectly) the activity specific to or characteristic of this virtue. What might this look like in connection with open-mindedness? In general, the idea is that we must make repeated efforts to practice the kind of cognitive "detaching" or "transcending" described above. This is likely to be no small challenge, since we are often deeply attached to those beliefs which, on reflection, we recognize as presenting an opportunity for greater open-mindedness.

But what, more specifically, might such efforts amount to? The following is but one of a wide range of potential examples. Suppose I have some rather strong beliefs regarding a certain political issue X, but that I recognize that my grounds for my beliefs about X are not conclusive, and indeed, that my possession of these beliefs is probably attributable more to the community in which I was raised than to any careful or thorough examination of the relevant evidence. Out of an interest in becoming more open-minded, I might choose to expose myself to one or more of the better, more in depth defenses of the perspective on X that I reject. This might involve committing to read an entire book by one of the better respected proponents of the relevant view, regularly visiting a website at

31. For a comprehensive and masterful treatment of this issue, see Dallas Willard, *The Spirit of the Disciplines* (San Francisco: HarperCollins, 1988).

which this view is discussed and defended by other intelligent, well-motivated inquirers, or some such activity.[32] As I engage in this activity, I might also pose the following sorts of questions to myself: What temptations am I experiencing to ignore, distort, or otherwise exhibit a "closed" mind toward the perspective I am considering? How do I *feel* when I am reading the relevant material? Am I irritated? Do I rush to get to the end of the chapter or article? Can I see how an intelligent, well-meaning person might be led to disagree with me about X? Am I able to accept this fact? Or does it make me feel uncomfortable? My answers to these questions are, at a minimum, likely to give me a sense of *how far I have to go* before I am as open-minded as I would like to be. Nonetheless, if pursued and practiced repeatedly, and especially if done so out of a firm and sincere desire to become more open-minded (or to become a more virtuous "inquirer" or a better lover of my friends or enemies), exercises of this sort are likely to have a significant and favorable impact on my character.

Fourth, and perhaps most importantly, I think that if we are to be open-minded in the truest, deepest, or most Christian sense, we must possess a well-grounded understanding and acceptance of the central tenets of the Christian faith together with a rich and meaningful spiritual life. As noted above, the sort of open-mindedness that flows from Christian love is not blind; it does not amount to an arbitrary or irrational casting of ourselves or our beliefs at the feet of our intellectual adversaries. Rather, it comes from a place of deep intellectual confidence and nearness to God. A person whose Christian beliefs, say, are not well-grounded or who in her "heart of hearts" harbors significant (unwelcome) doubts about them, is likely to have a difficult time being at all open-minded about these beliefs — let alone being open-minded in the deeper or truly Christian sense. Instead, she is likely to be anxious, irritable, defensive, and arrogant in the face of challenges to her beliefs. Likewise, a person whose grasp of his Christian beliefs is firm and well-informed may, while perhaps possessing the confidence and courage to be open-minded, nonetheless be *uninclined* to do so, for he might lack the kind of concern or love for his neighbor that would lead him to give a respectful, open-

32. Such a commitment will have its intended effect, however, only if I am properly equipped to assess the relevant views in a competent and rational way. This underscores the importance of training in formal and informal logic, particularly within the Christian community.

minded hearing to his neighbor's beliefs. On one plausible account, the richest source of such love is an intimate, experiential relationship with the One who *is* love. Philosopher and theologian Richard Mouw makes a similar point in connection with Christian "civility," which he says entails a kind of curiosity and empathy regarding others' beliefs: "We keep coming back to this point: we live in the presence of God. We cannot consistently develop empathy and curiosity and teachability in our relationships without the reinforcing experiences of divine grace. We can sustain open hearts toward others only because of the love that flows from the heart of God."[33] What this suggests, then, is that the Christian's pursuit of greater open-mindedness should include attempts to better understand and know the foundations of her faith and to cultivate a rich and active spiritual life. In this regard, the process of becoming open-minded, when pursued with Christian aims and motivation, has deeply theological and spiritual dimensions.

Questions for Further Reflection

1. Do you think it is possible to be open-minded (in the sense developed in this chapter) about your Christian beliefs while also maintaining a genuine and robust Christian faith? How exactly is this possible? What might this look like "from the inside," so to speak?

2. What are some qualities that are importantly related to open-mindedness? How exactly are they related? Which qualities do you think are *opposed* to open-mindedness? Are these traits common in the Christian community? If so, why do you think this is the case?

3. Identify someone you regard as an exemplar of open-mindedness. How have you seen this person's open-mindedness "in action"? How did it make you feel? What do you think motivates this person's open-mindedness? How do you think this person came to be open-minded? What do your answers to these questions suggest about what *you* might do to become more open-minded?

33. *Uncommon Decency: Christian Civility in an Uncivil World* (Downers Grove: InterVarsity, 1992), p. 69. Thanks to Bob Covolo for directing me to Mouw's book, which, while about Christian "civility," contains a great deal of insight about the importance of open-mindedness from a Christian standpoint.

4. What other biblical principles or passages do you think bear upon the question of whether or how a Christian should be open-minded? Do these principles or passages fit with what has been said in this chapter? Do they conflict with it? Finally, how do characters from the Old and New Testaments stack up in relation to the conception of open-mindedness developed here? What lesson should we take from this?

Wisdom

James S. Spiegel

If there is a singular aim where the fields of philosophy and theology converge it is the attainment of wisdom. In ancient Greece, that great moral reformer Socrates established this as the original agenda of Western philosophy. In fact, the discipline takes its name from his call to fellow Athenians to love *(phileō)* wisdom *(sophia)* above all things. In Scripture we find the same priority placed on this virtue: "Wisdom is supreme; therefore get wisdom. Though it cost all you have, get understanding" (Prov. 4:7, NIV).[1]

Today in American society, such a perspective could not be more countercultural. From Hollywood to Wall Street, it seems the last thing on people's minds is wisdom. Even higher education is often seen as a mere means to the attainment of wealth and social status. And in many professional quarters, prioritizing wisdom over money or fame can be rather costly. If Socrates' commitment to wisdom led to his persecution, the same commitment in our culture today might not be much less demanding in terms of self-sacrifice.

Still, today, as in Socrates' Athens, wisdom is generally acknowledged as a noble aim, even if genuine devotees of this virtue are rare. But what, exactly, *is* wisdom and how is it related to other moral virtues? What is it about this trait that makes it so valuable — more valuable, in fact, than anything else one can pursue in this life? What practical steps, if any, can one take in order to become wise? Is it a matter of simple ded-

1. All subsequent biblical references, unless otherwise noted, are to this translation.

ication in study, or are there other things involved in the attainment of wisdom? As we address these questions, we will see why the biblical writers laud this virtue as "more precious than rubies" (Prov. 8:11) and why Socrates' willingness to be martyred in its pursuit was perhaps the surest sign of his genius.

Wisdom and Understanding

Let us begin with the Aristotelian concept of practical wisdom or *phronesis.* Generally speaking, this refers to a certain kind of insight which pertains to right conduct, enabling a person to discern what courses of action are best. Aristotle defines *phronesis* as "a reasoned and true state of capacity to act with regard to human goods."[2] While Aristotle regarded this as an intellectual virtue, he also recognized it as a prerequisite for moral excellence. Without the virtue of *phronesis,* he claimed, a person cannot be morally virtuous. Aquinas took essentially the same view of the matter with his concept of *prudentia,* which he defined as "good counsel about matters regarding man's entire life and the end of human life."[3] Like Aristotle, Aquinas maintained, "There can be no moral virtue without prudence."[4]

Practical wisdom *(phronesis)* is distinguished from speculative wisdom *(sophia),* the virtue from which philosophy takes its name. To possess *sophia* is to have a theoretical understanding of things, a certain insight into the nature of reality, including matters of logic, metaphysics, and science. However, *sophia* has nothing essentially to do with conduct, how to live a good life. So, in contrast to *phronesis,* it is a purely intellectual virtue.

Phronesis and *sophia* are closely related to another intellectual virtue: understanding. Linda Zagzebski and others have bemoaned the neglect of understanding in contemporary epistemology, a lacuna attributable to the widespread but dubious notion that individual propositions are the

2. Aristotle, *Nicomachean Ethics,* trans. W. D. Ross, in *The Basic Works of Aristotle,* ed. Richard McKeon (New York: Random House, 1941), p. 1027.

3. Thomas Aquinas, *Summa Theologica,* vol. 1, trans. English Dominican Fathers (New York: Benziger Brothers, 1947), p. 831.

4. Aquinas, ST, p. 836.

unique objects of knowledge. On the contrary, Zagzebski observes, "Understanding is not a state directed toward a single propositional object at all. This is not to deny that there is a sense in which one can be said to understand a proposition *p*. But the understanding of *p* is not directed primarily at *p* itself. One understands *p* as part of and because of one's understanding of a system or network of truths, or . . . we could say that one understands *p* as part of one's understanding of the pattern of a whole chunk of reality."[5] To understand something is to possess a certain kind of insight into how things work or fit together. Thus, to have understanding is to be able to explain it or communicate its meaning. When I say I understand an event, such as the Democrats gaining majority control of the House of Representatives, I mean that I have insight into the principal causal factors involved in this state of affairs. When I say I understand how an internal combustion engine works, I mean that I can describe the basic physical and chemical processes involved in its operation.

Understanding is also applicable to personal knowledge. When I say that I understand my wife I do not simply mean that I possess exceptional propositional knowledge about her. In fact, no matter how formidable my knowledge of discrete facts about her might be, this in itself does not constitute my genuinely understanding her. When I say I understand her (or that I "get her" or "know what makes her tick") I mean that I grasp something of her character or nature. In a sense, to understand someone is to be able to see *past* many of the incidental facts about the person and to glimpse her essential qualities, what makes her who she is as an individual.

What understanding, *phronesis,* and *sophia* seem to have in common is insight. What distinguishes them is that *phronesis* pertains particularly to practical moral matters, *sophia* regards theoretical matters, and understanding is more general than either one. Each of these traits is a bona fide intellectual virtue, a mental disposition enabling the knower to succeed in the acquisition of truth.

Zagzebski adds an important wrinkle to the concept of *phronesis,* noting that it is a higher-order virtue governing the whole range of moral and intellectual virtues.[6] This way of conceiving *phronesis* has explana-

5. Linda Zagzebski, *Virtues of the Mind: An Inquiry into the Nature of Virtue and the Ethical Foundations of Knowledge* (Cambridge: Cambridge University Press, 1996), p. 49.

6. Zagzebski, *Virtues,* p. 229.

tory power in several key respects. First, it helps to explain Aristotle's and Aquinas's insistence that this trait is a prerequisite for any moral virtue. Second, the notion that *phronesis* is a higher-order virtue explains how the moral virtues can function together toward a unified end. Since there are multiple moral virtues, and sometimes conflicts emerge when, say, justice and compassion appear to lead a person in opposite directions regarding a particular issue, some particular trait or skill is necessary to mediate and enable the person to arrive at a single considered judgment. Conceiving *phronesis* as a higher-order virtue explains how this is possible. Third, in parallel fashion, the intellectual virtues, if they are to function in a unified way, demand mediation as well, since such traits as open-mindedness and intellectual discretion might incline a person in opposite directions regarding some inquiry. Thus, a higher-order virtue is necessary to provide this mediation, and *phronesis* seems to be that virtue. Finally, intellectual and moral virtues must sometimes be balanced against one another, such as when intellectual rigor conflicts with the moral virtue of kindness or courtesy. A higher-order judgment call is necessary to assess which of these virtues should trump the other. Again, *phronesis* explains how this is possible.

If Zagzebski's analysis is correct, then *phronesis* is one of the most important virtues of all, since its operation governs all of the virtues, both moral and intellectual. But even if practical wisdom does not also serve this higher-order function, its place in the moral life remains significant, for practical moral insight is essential in all moral conduct and decision-making. Given this premium on practical wisdom, then, let us next consider the factors that influence the development of this virtue.

Belief and Behavior

The nineteenth-century German poet Heinrich Heine wrote that "the thought precedes the deed as the lightning the thunder."[7] This line reveals a particularly modern dogma about the relationship between belief and behavior, namely that our cognitions come first and our volitions flow from them. This idea is supported by ordinary experience. When I make a

7. Heinrich Heine, *Religion and Philosophy in Germany: A Fragment* (Albany: SUNY Press, 1986), p. 159.

choice and perform a particular action, such as hug my child or log on to my computer, I do so on the basis of various beliefs. But is this the whole story when it comes to the dynamics of human belief and behavior?

Biblical and Psychological Themes

In Scripture we find a theme that runs counter to this usual way of looking at the matter. In the Old Testament wisdom literature we are told that God makes wise the simple and grants understanding to those who humble themselves (see Ps. 19:7; Ps. 25:9; Prov. 1:4; and Prov. 11:2). And some New Testament passages underscore the critical role of behavior when it comes to belief formation. For example, in the book of Ephesians Paul refers to Gentiles who "are darkened in their understanding . . . due to the hardening of their hearts," which in turn he explains by the fact that "they have given themselves over to sensuality so as to indulge in every kind of impurity" (Eph. 4:18-19). Such passages suggest that the causal relation between cognition and conduct is actually a two-way street.

It is a truism in psychology today that behavior affects attitudes. As we interact with other people and things, are exposed to mass media, and are subject to conditioning through the social activities in which we engage, our beliefs are impacted in a variety of ways. For example, someone might develop a strong dislike for factory farms through an up-close, personal encounter with a confined animal feeding operation. After being overwhelmed by the stench of the place and the sounds of the tortured animals inside, she might form a negative attitude toward such operations. Or one might run in social circles in which factory farming is strongly opposed. Even a person who has never thought much about the practice might form a negative attitude toward it by witnessing her friends' strong opposition. Formal membership within a group, such as a political party, business, or sports team may further reinforce certain attitudes.[8]

But how does my *own* behavior affect my *own* attitudes and beliefs? One way is derivatively, through my conduct, which exposes me to some of the influences just noted. I may or may not choose to expose myself to

8. For a good summary of the basic ways in which behavior affects attitudes, see Dennis Coon, *Psychology: A Journey* (Belmont, CA: Thomson/Wadsworth, 2003), pp. 558-59.

a factory farm. If I never bother to observe what goes on at these operations, then my attitude toward them is not likely to change one way or another. But if I take the time to make direct contact, then my attitudes and beliefs about them will almost surely be significantly impacted. Similarly, I may or may not choose to expose myself to people outside my usual social circles. If I do so, then their opinions which differ markedly from those of my friends are likely to have some impact upon me, either reinforcing my attitudes or challenging these, perhaps even changing them. Also, all of us choose, to a large degree, how much to expose ourselves — and perhaps our family members — to mass media. How much television will I watch and which programs? How much internet will I browse and which websites? How much radio will I listen to and which stations? And to how many of these things, if any, will I expose my children? Most of us recognize that these are not petty questions, because we are aware of the impact that our behavior regarding mass media has on our attitudes and beliefs.

Plantinga's Reformed Moral Psychology

Alvin Plantinga's *Warrant* trilogy, a landmark study in Christian epistemology, also contains a surprisingly rich Christian moral psychology. Plantinga's purpose in the series is to present a distinctively Christian — and, more specifically, theologically Reformed — account of what it means to have knowledge. Like most epistemologists, Plantinga recognizes that true belief must be the basis of any theory of knowledge. But what, in addition to these two conditions (belief and the truth of what is believed) must obtain for one genuinely to know something? Plantinga's answer lies in the concept of "warrant." A belief has warrant, says Plantinga, if it is produced by cognitive faculties which: (1) are functioning properly, (2) are operating in a favorable environment, and (3) are successfully aimed at the production of true beliefs. Now each of these conditions for warrant requires some explanation. To say that a thing functions properly is just to say that it operates according to its design plan. There is no corruption or dysfunction in the system interfering with its operation. And a *design plan* is simply the way a thing is made to work. For example, a thermos is designed to hold liquid and maintain its temperature. Now, of course, to apply this idea to human cognitive faculties entails the concept of intelligent creation, which Plantinga specifies as follows: "Human beings and their organs are so constructed that there is a way that they should work, a way they are supposed to work, a way they work when they work right."[9]

Plantinga's second condition for warrant stipulates that properly functioning cognitive faculties *operate in a favorable environment.* With any organ system some environments are congenial to proper operation and others are not. Human eyes cannot function properly in smoky air, nor can our lungs work well at the top of Mount Everest. If the atmosphere is not congenial to a particular system, then its operation cannot be counted on to achieve the end for which it was designed. The same is true of cognitive systems. Some environments are more congenial than others, and proper cognitive function will be contingent upon there being a sufficiently favorable environment for thinking and forming beliefs.

The third condition for warrant regards the ultimate aim of cognitive faculties, namely to produce true beliefs. A cognitive system could be aimed at any number of things, from wish fulfillment to simple survival value of the beliefs it tends to produce. But in order for beliefs to have warrant, says Plantinga, truth must be the target. And it is not even enough that the cognitive processes be aimed at truth. Their design plan must be a good one, "one that is successfully aimed at truth, one such that there is a high (objective) probability that a belief produced according to that plan will be true (or nearly true)."[10]

Combining these conditions for warrant, then, a belief has warrant for a person only if it was produced by properly functioning cognitive processes successfully aimed at truth and operating in a congenial environment. If one's cognitive faculties operate according to their design plan in this way, then they will be more or less reliable and the consequent beliefs warranted. Crucial to our cognitive design plan is what John Calvin dubbed the *sensus divinitatis.* Plantinga describes this as "a kind of faculty or cognitive mechanism . . . which in a wide variety of circumstances produces in us beliefs about God."[11] Its operation is triggered by diverse stimuli, from perceptions of nature's beauty to feelings of shame.

9. Alvin Plantinga, *Warranted Christian Belief* (Oxford: Oxford University Press, 2000), p. 154.

10. Plantinga, *Warranted Belief,* p. 156.

11. Plantinga, *Warranted Belief,* p. 172.

Originally, the *sensus divinitatis* guaranteed an intimate natural knowledge of God. And our affections were naturally geared to love and hate the right things.

However, sin has tarnished both our cognitions and affections. Our natural knowledge of God is impeded by sin and its consequences so that we form false beliefs about God or even disbelieve in him altogether. We suffer a sort of blindness, which Plantinga characterizes as an "imperceptiveness, dullness, stupidity" with regard to the knowledge of God's beauty, glory, and love.[12] Accordingly, the *sensus divinitatis* has been badly damaged, such that it is only partly operational. We also suffer a skewing of affections, so that we love and hate the wrong things, even hating and resenting God because we are not in his position. We display selfishness and abject pride, whereby we overestimate our own importance and put ourselves before others. Consequently, our ability to make judgments about moral-spiritual matters is particularly hampered.

Plantinga adds that the *sensus divinitatis* can be further impeded through disobedience, bad nurturing, the false testimony of others, and perverse philosophizing. Our knowledge of God, even at its most basic level, can be disturbed, even altogether squelched by these influences, which make for an unfavorable environment for our cognitive faculties and cause them to malfunction. And, of course, dysfunction in turn gives rise to further false beliefs which may in turn further impede the *sensus divinitatis.* Plantinga has very little to say about how disobedience corrupts cognition. My purpose in what follows is to explore this notion in some depth, along with the corresponding positive idea that obedience enhances our capacity for right thinking, whether we are thinking about God or other things. All of this has important implications for the development and preservation of the virtue of wisdom.

The Epistemic Effects of Behavior

If Plantinga's Reformed moral psychology is approximately correct, then our behaviors constantly impact our attitudes, and this impact is often not neutral. These influences may have a positive influence on our cognitive faculties, reinforcing their proper function and making for a more

12. Plantinga, *Warranted Belief,* p. 207.

congenial environment for the formation of true beliefs. Or they may disrupt proper function and make for a less congenial environment for true belief formation. I want to look at a variety of ways in which our *moral* conduct impacts our cognitive abilities and, more specifically, our proper function when it comes to the exercise of *phronesis.*

The Epistemic Costs of Vice

In the first chapter of the book of Romans the apostle Paul makes some remarks which are particularly apposite, given our topic. He writes, "The wrath of God is being revealed from heaven against all the godlessness and wickedness of men who suppress the truth by their wickedness, since what may be known about God is plain to them, because God has made it plain to them" (Rom. 1:18-19). Here Paul explicitly recognizes the negative impact that bad behavior has on belief. A few verses later he says that "although they knew God, they neither glorified him as God nor gave thanks to him, but their thinking became futile and their foolish hearts were darkened" (v. 21). Notice Paul's acknowledgment that they originally *knew* God, but this epistemic condition was corrupted. Thus, a little later he says, "since they did not think it worthwhile to retain the knowledge of God, he gave them over to a depraved mind, to do what ought not to be done" (v. 28). So their wickedness not only drove out the knowledge of God but led to a "depraved mind," which in turn culminated in more bad behavior. So we have here a literally vicious cycle, from initial wickedness to the suppression of truth about God to the loss of knowledge of God to profound epistemic corruption to yet more wickedness.

One obvious lesson to draw from this passage is that a person's bad behavior corrupts her own mind. My present concern is to draw attention to some ways in which this corruption occurs. One of these ways pertains to the natural tendency to justify existing practice. Psychological studies have shown that, when faced with a conflict between their personal beliefs and behavior, people will often reconcile this conflict by changing the way they *think* about their behavior. Rather than alter their conduct, they will take the less demanding route and search for some way to justify it rationally. This response is almost always unconscious, which of course makes for a morally insidious dynamic in contexts involving vicious behavior.

A Christian minister in a community near mine might serve as an illustration of this pattern. During one of his talks to a men's group he addressed the issue of pornography and glibly dismissed the practice of viewing porn as morally insignificant. His message was essentially "If you're into porn and feeling shame about it, get over it. It's perfectly natural and harmless. After all, looking is different from touching. It's not like viewers are actually having sex with the women in those pictures." Given such a distortion of the biblical ethic of purity, it is natural to raise questions about this minister's motives. Could it be that he simply found it too difficult to overcome his own struggle with pornography so his eventual response was to rationalize it?[13]

Whether or not my suspicions in this case are correct, the changing of one's convictions to accommodate one's immoral behavior is a common phenomenon. Even scholars, for whom intellectual fairness is an essential quality, are not immune to this.[14] Twentieth-century novelist Aldous Huxley confessed that his own sexual conduct and that of his peers had a decisive influence on their worldview: "For myself as, no doubt, for most of my contemporaries, the philosophy of meaninglessness was essentially an instrument of liberation. The liberation we desired was simultaneously liberation from a certain political and economic system and liberation from a certain system of morality. We objected to the morality because it interfered with our sexual freedom."[15]

The psychological mechanism described by Huxley, and perhaps exemplified by the aforementioned minister, is an example of a certain kind

13. Sidney Callahan has observed how the same tendency to justify existing behavior occurs on a societal level as well, specifically in the context of the abortion debate. Because of the widespread practice of abortion, the American public is naturally more inclined to rationalize it. If our national behavior will not change, and concluding that we are guilty of an on-going horrendous evil is too psychologically stressful, then the search for a justification of our current practice is a natural response. See Callahan's "Abortion and the Sexual Agenda," in *Commonweal* 112 (April 25, 1986): 232-38.

14. Two books which powerfully document this fact among many leading modern scholars are Paul Johnson's *Intellectuals* (New York: Harper & Row, 1988) and E. Michael Jones's *Degenerate Moderns: Modernity as Rationalized Sexual Misbehavior* (San Francisco: Ignatius, 1993).

15. Aldous Huxley, *Ends and Means: An Inquiry into the Nature of Ideals and into the Methods Employed for Their Realization* (New York: Harper & Brothers, 1937), p. 316.

of self-deception, what Alfred Mele has analyzed as "motivationally biased beliefs." It is a psychological dynamic in which one's desires inordinately impact one's beliefs. Mele notes that this happens in a variety of ways, including what he calls *negative interpretation,* a process in which a person's desire in favor of some belief causes him to underestimate the force of the evidence against it. Another psychological process involved in this category of self-deception, says Mele, is *selective evidence-gathering,* which occurs when a person's preference for a belief inclines him or her to overlook obvious evidence against it and search for less accessible evidence in its favor.[16]

In the case of the minister, whom I'll call "Jack," something like the following analysis might apply. After struggling at length with internal conflict over his use of porn, Jack began to despair over his moral failure. Eventually, through his repeated exposure to people who "have no problem" with porn, Jack began to consider the possibility that his feelings of shame were misplaced and that the practice is actually not wrong after all. Considering this possibility, and the prospect of being released from his feelings of shame while being able to continue indulging his porn habit, there kindled in him a *desire* to believe that there was nothing wrong with it. This prompted the negative interpretation phase of Jack's self-deception, as he began to downplay the evidence against the moral legitimacy of porn use. Consequently, he began to give undue evidential weight to the fact that viewing porn involves no physical contact with the pictured women. Jack was further motivated to do selective evidence-gathering. Ignoring the facts that the porn industry exploits women and entices viewers to lust and to view women as mere objects and means, Jack began a dogged search for evidence favoring his belief, apparently locating it in the notion that porn use "relieves sexual tension" and that so many guys use porn that it seems perfectly "natural."

The psychology of self-deception is complex and difficult to analyze,[17] and my purpose here is simply to draw attention to the phenome-

16. Alfred Mele, "Real Self-Deception," *Behavioral and Brain Sciences* 20 (1997): 94.

17. There are other instructive models of self-deception besides the one I've discussed here, such as the "existential" approach. This focuses on disavowal, a common strategy for dealing with psychic moral conflict where one refuses to acknowledge one's immoral behavior as one's own. See, for example, Herbert Fingarette, *Self-Deception* (London: Routledge and Kegan Paul, 1969). For a fuller discussion of the

non as one significant way in which our behavior may corrupt us epistemically, even culminating in a change of important ethical beliefs and commitments. Another way of conceiving how sinful actions may corrupt beliefs is less complex and more direct, involving emotions. Historically, philosophers have tended to regard belief and emotion as fundamentally distinct categories of mental activity, even putting them in opposition and recommending that great care be taken not to allow emotions to contaminate rational inquiry and the process of belief formation. In recent years, however, some philosophers have noted the close connection between belief and emotion, and some have even suggested that emotion is a significant avenue to certain kinds of truths.[18]

A pioneer of this latter approach was William James, who argued not just that beliefs and emotions are closely connected but that beliefs essentially *are* states of emotion. Consider a paradigm case of conviction regarding some truth, such as the answer to the question "What two English words contain all five vowels in alphabetical order?" When we learn the answer[19] to this question and subject our new belief to phenomenological analysis, we discover that the sense of its reasonableness is, at bottom, a feeling. In James's words, "The transition from a state of puzzle and perplexity to rational comprehension is full of lively relief and pleasure."[20] When we reflect upon many other beliefs that we hold, we will come to the same conclusion. Whether our convictions are the result of deductive inference, inductive or probabilistic reasoning, inference to the best explanation, hypothesis testing, or any other method, the fundamental phenomenological feature of these convictions is emotional: our belief *feels* right. This, says James, is the "sentiment of rationality."

Now this analysis of the emotional nature of belief suggests another way in which bad conduct may corrupt cognition. Consider a sinful action, such as intentionally spreading a false rumor about a colleague. When one

---

major models of self-deception, see my *Hypocrisy: Moral Fraud and Other Vices* (Grand Rapids: Baker, 1999), chap. 3. By my analysis, Mele's motivated bias model and Fingarette's existential approach typify the two major forms of self-deception: cognitive (or belief-formation phase) and volitional (or reflection phase) self-deception.

18. See Robert C. Roberts, "Emotions as Access to Religious Truths," *Faith and Philosophy* 9 (1992): 83-94.

19. The two words are "abstemious" and "facetious."

20. William James, "The Sentiment of Rationality," in *The Will to Believe and Other Essays* (New York: Dover, 1956), p. 63.

performs this act and finds pleasure in it, what typically follows are various emotional pleasures associated with it, such as a feeling of emotional release in the venting of hostility or a certain satisfaction based on a perverse sense of justice. The experience of these pleasures contradicts and thus tends to displace negative emotional associations with slanderous behavior. Keep in mind that such negative feelings are, on the Jamesian analysis, an actual *component* of the belief about the act's moral wrongness. Consequently, the overall reduction of negative feelings about the act of slander weakens the strength of one's conviction that it is morally wrong, at least in the present context.[21] This, in turn, increases the likelihood that the person will indulge in similarly immoral behavior in the future. So we have here a vicious cycle of vice, and it is easy to see how with enough turns of the cycle the person's original belief that slander is wrong can eventually disappear. A similar cycle yielding negative epistemic fallout might occur for just about any other vice. (See Figure 1 on p. 66.)

Returning to Plantinga's Reformed model of moral psychology, we may see both self-deception and perverse emotional pleasures as corruptions of our original cognitive design plan. A properly functioning belief-forming mechanism would not be motivationally biased, nor would pleasurable emotions associated with vice tilt one's doxastic tendencies away from ethical truth and proper moral commitments. Over the long term, self-deception and perverse emotional pleasures create a hostile environment for the formation of true beliefs. Such disruption directly impacts a person's capacity to exercise the virtues of understanding and *phronesis.* And with corruption of the latter, she would lose the capacity to comprehend her own foolishness or be rationally sensitive to even the most insightful rebukes of friends. The biblical comparison of the fool to a dog returning to its vomit comes to mind as a particularly apt image in this connection (cf. Prov. 26:11).

The Epistemic Benefits of Virtue

The above are just some of the ways in which sinful behavior corrupts one's cognitive design plan, causing one's belief-forming mechanisms to

21. Note that this analysis helps to explain why both beliefs and emotions come in degrees.

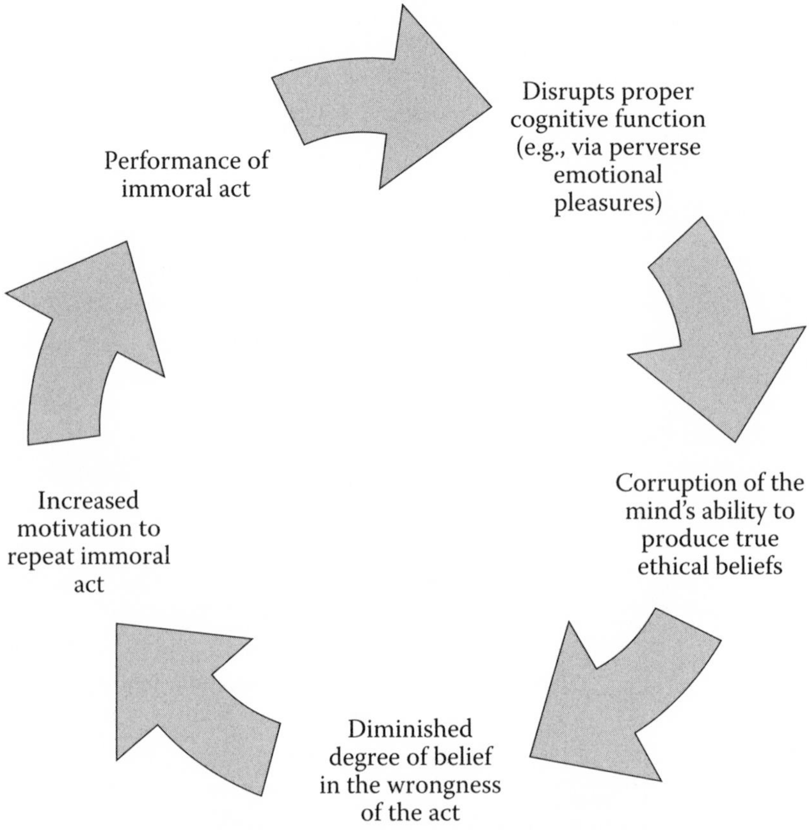

Figure 1. The Vicious Cycle of Vice

yield false beliefs, and causing the diminution of *phronesis* within the person. But just as vice has negative epistemic fallout, virtue yields epistemic benefits. The first thing to note is that moral virtue is epistemically advantageous if only because by behaving morally we avoid the negative ramifications of vice on our cognitive processes. This by itself constitutes a significant advantage for the virtuous person. Her *sensus divinitatis* is less impeded, her belief-forming apparatus is able to function according to design, and her capacity to successfully display *phronesis* is preserved.

There are also more substantive ways in which a person's virtuous conduct provides her with a favorable epistemic environment. One of these concerns the unity of the virtues. Many virtue ethicists maintain that the virtues are unified in the sense that growth in one virtue naturally begets growth in other virtues as well. So, for example, to become more kind or patient will naturally dispose one to be more generous or courageous. The same might also be said of intellectual virtues, such that to grow in curiosity or epistemic circumspection will naturally make a person more intellectually magnanimous or courageous. Now if there is unity within each of these domains, then might not there be a higher order unity of the virtues, in the sense that moral virtues beget intellectual virtues and vice versa? After all, both kinds of virtues regard character traits. And if there is a natural wholeness to a person's character, then such a higher-order unity of the virtues is likely. If this is right, then here we have a further way in which good conduct has salutary epistemic effects.

Another epistemic benefit from moral virtue can be understood in light of Plantinga's moral psychology. The apostle Paul encouraged believers to dwell on "anything excellent or praiseworthy" (Phil. 4:8). Among other things, this should direct us to the contemplation of anything beautiful, since beauty is aesthetic excellence. Now aesthetic involvement may enhance or attune our cognitive design plan both directly and indirectly. Plantinga asserts that experiences of beauty "trigger" the *sensus divinitatis,* making us more aware of God. Exactly how this happens Plantinga does not attempt to explain. A possible explanation might lie in the fact that God is most beautiful and is himself the source of all beauty. Aquinas notes that God "gives beauty to all created beings, according to the properties of each."[22] God is the ontological spring of all beauty, says Aquinas, because God is himself "super-beautiful." Jonathan Edwards echoes the same theme when he declares God to be "infinitely the most beautiful and excellent: and all beauty to be found throughout the whole creation is but the reflection of the diffused beams of that being, who hath an infinite fullness of brightness and glory."[23] Now if God is most beautiful and in fact the wellspring of all other beauty, then any beautiful objects we apprehend in nature or among the arts are just so many reminders of God. In this way, then, aesthetic experiences of all kinds will improve one's knowledge of God and thus are a direct boon to one's epistemic well-being.

22. Quoted in Michael A. G. Haykin, "Beauty as a Divine Attribute: Sources and Issues," *Churchman* 116 (2002): 131.

23. Jonathan Edwards, "The Nature of True Virtue," in *The Works of Jonathan Edwards,* vol. 1 (Edinburgh: Banner of Truth Trust, 1974), p. 125.

Obeying Paul's maxim might have epistemic benefits in some less direct ways. First, exposure to aesthetic excellence and beauty of all kinds builds the moral imagination, which in turn is crucial for careful application of the Golden Rule. When applying this basic moral principle, we all must strive to consider in many cases what it is like to be in another person's place. A strong imagination is, of course, essential for doing this well. So by improving the imagination, aesthetic experience has potentially significant moral benefits. And these moral benefits, in turn, improve a person epistemically in the ways already noted.

Second, some philosophers, most notably Jonathan Edwards,[24] have argued that moral goodness is itself a sub-category of beauty. That is, to be virtuous is to be beautiful in a specifically moral way. If this is correct, then to attune one's aesthetic sensibility is *ipso facto* to attune one's moral sensibility. Otherwise put, to improve one's ability to make aesthetic judgments is to improve one's ability to make moral judgments. In this way, then, following Paul's counsel through involvement in the arts and contemplation of the beautiful will, other things being equal, make a person wiser.

The upshot of all of the above is that we must behave well in order to maximize our cognitive functionality and to minimize cognitive impairment due to sin. This will give us our best chance at operating at our epistemic potential and, in particular, gaining wisdom and understanding. Among other things, I have tried to identify some of the moral-psychological mechanisms at work behind the biblical theme that God grants wisdom and understanding to the humble. Humility preserves proper function of one's cognitive design plan by serving as an antidote to selfishness and abject pride, which are arch-vices, catalysts for self-deception, and fundamental impedances to the *sensus divinitatis.*[25] So the humble person is morally inoculated against some of the more powerful antagonists of *phronesis.*

This analysis also casts light upon Paul's cryptic exhortation to "work out your salvation with fear and trembling" (Phil. 2:12). Since behavior impacts belief, and the things we believe are crucial to our faith commit-

24. Edwards, "True Virtue," p. 122.

25. Some have questioned whether humility is a genuine moral virtue. I have argued that it is in "The Moral Irony of Humility," *Logos: A Journal of Catholic Thought and Culture* 6.1 (2003): 131-50. See also Andrew Pinsent's chapter on humility, below.

ment, the preservation of our faith very much hinges upon how we conduct ourselves. Our good works do not secure our salvation, as some have mistakenly interpreted Paul as suggesting. Rather, by acting virtuously we strengthen our own faith, as we preserve proper epistemic function and avoid the negative influences which corrupt cognitive processes. Consequently, we continue believing the right things about God and how to live before him. This in turn improves our ability to live virtuously, which again in turn improves us cognitively. Indeed, this whole process of sanctification can be construed as a "virtuous cycle" in which moral and epistemic virtues beget one another. (See Figure 2 below.)

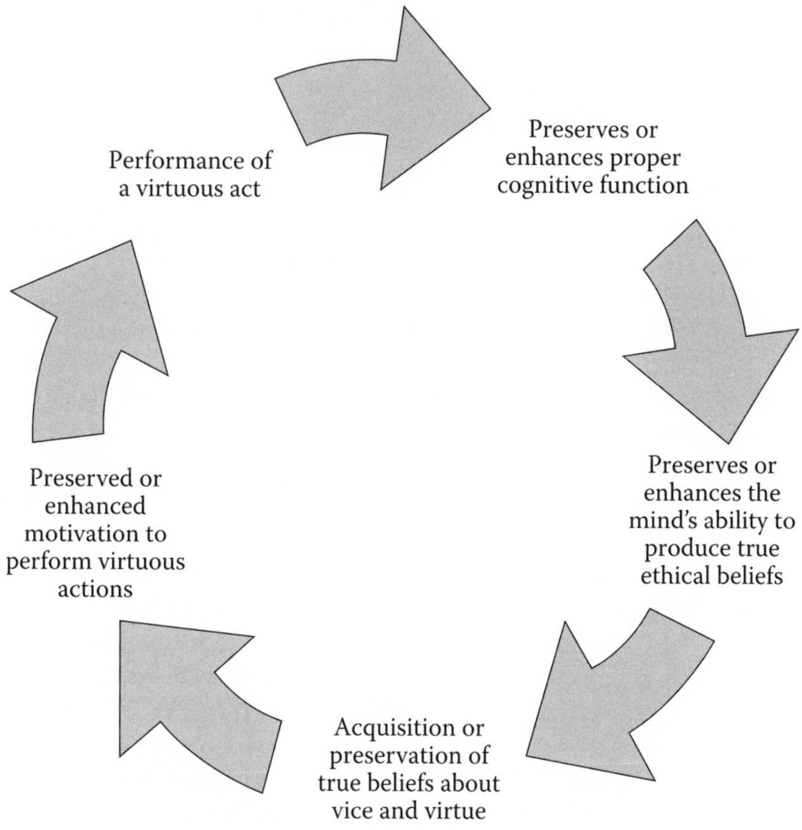

Figure 2. The Virtuous Cycle of Virtue

Final Thoughts on *Phronesis*

Phronesis is a virtue of sound judgment regarding conduct and, as a higher-order mediating virtue, governs both moral and intellectual virtues. What I've said above about the deleterious effects of vice can be seen essentially as an analysis of sin's corruption of the virtue of *phronesis.* All sin opposes *phronesis,* and since this virtue governs both moral and intellectual virtues, there is necessarily negative epistemic fallout from sin as well. The role of *phronesis* as a higher-order virtue also helps to shed light on why good behavior benefits us epistemically. As a mediating virtue among intellectual virtues as well as moral virtues, *phronesis* is crucial to good judgment of any kind, as it is the virtue enabling the knower to apply such discrete intellectual virtues as curiosity, open-mindedness, intellectual courage, and so on. To behave in such a way as to build *phronesis* and avoid its corruption, then, will put the knower in the best position for exercising the intellectual virtues and thus being, overall, a good knower.

So how does one acquire *phronesis?* Our discussion has explored one crucial *necessary* condition for acquiring this virtue, namely good conduct. (I will not attempt here the much more challenging task of identifying *sufficient* conditions for the acquisition of *phronesis.*) Since good conduct is, in large part, a matter of living virtuously, development of all of the other virtues discussed in this book is essential to gaining wisdom. And, of course, one should also strive to develop other virtues which are not discussed here, such as gratitude, kindness, justice, patience, discretion, and modesty.

Another important means of acquiring wisdom is prayer. As James says, "If any of you lacks wisdom, he should ask God, who gives generously to all without finding fault, and it will be given to him" (James 1:5). The truth of this promise is illustrated in the case of King Solomon, who begged God to give him wisdom above all else, a prayer which God granted and supplemented with many tangible blessings as well (see 2 Chron. 1:7-12). Note, however, James's caveat: When one asks God for wisdom, "he must believe and not doubt, because he who doubts is like a wave of the sea, blown and tossed by the wind. That man should not think he will receive anything from the Lord; he is a double-minded man, unstable in all he does" (James 1:6-8). These are sobering words, which underscore just how fundamental the virtue of faith is in every aspect of the

Christian moral life. The act of trusting in the Lord is a sign of wisdom; it is also crucial in the process of becoming wise.

Questions for Further Reflection

1. What practical steps can I take to become wiser? Besides prayer, what spiritual disciplines might be especially useful in gaining practical moral insight?

2. How can I encourage others in the quest for wisdom? Are there things I can do to assist my friends, family, and others in my community in this process?

3. Every person has moral "blind spots" — faults of which we are unaware or particularly insensitive. Are there ways in which we can become more aware of our own blind spots or at least diminish their practical fallout in our lives? What, if anything, can we do to avoid self-deception or falling victim to the tendency to have motivationally biased beliefs?

4. Do I strive to build my moral imagination and thus improve my ability to apply the Golden Rule? What further steps can I take toward this end?

Zeal

David A. Horner and David R. Turner

A significant obstacle to personal growth in virtue is sloth, or moral lethargy — a characteristic that, in our view, is particularly prevalent in Christian discipleship these days.[1] At the same time, enthusiasm, passion, and initiative — when they are found — often take the form of thoughtless, and even destructive, fanaticism. As a result, fervency, particularly in religious matters, is typically viewed with great suspicion — more so, indeed, than is sloth. Both sloth and fanaticism, however, are vices — vicious extremes in relation to a proper passion in pursuit of the good. In fact, both extremes are condemned in Scripture. What is commended there is the virtue of *zeal:* an orientation toward the good that is consistently expressed in wise, fervent, and diligent pursuit. In the Bible, zeal characterizes God and his purposes, the ministry of Jesus, and the moral and spiritual life of the Christian. "Never be lacking in zeal," says Paul, "but keep your spiritual fervor, serving the Lord" (Rom. 12:11, NIV).

We think that it is necessary in our time to recover a proper understanding of this important but underrated and misunderstood trait.[2] Be-

1. The problem is more general, of course, but we draw particular attention here to Christian spiritual and moral formation.

2. We are not entirely alone here. Law professor Anita Bernstein laments the loss of zeal as a central value in legal ethics, tracing the gradual disappearance of zeal language in the American Bar Association Code of Lawyers, where once it was prominent in the legal profession's ideals. See Anita Bernstein, "The Zeal Shortage," *Hofstra Law Review* 34 (2006): 1165-1205. Rosa Chun also identifies zeal as a dimension of virtuous ethical character in business, along with integrity, empathy, courage, warmth, and conscientiousness, in Rosa Chun, "Ethical Character and Virtue of Organizations:

cause zeal is relatively unknown as a virtue, and because of the confusion and controversy surrounding it, we will devote more space to clarification and defense than may be needed in other chapters. Since our chief aim is to provide an account of zeal as it is reflected in Scripture, we begin with a specific examination of the biblical materials, particularly several important New Testament ethical texts, and develop an initial understanding of biblical zeal. We then clarify and defend our understanding through analysis of opposing vices — competitors, confusions, contrasts — and we conclude with specific suggestions for encouraging and developing zeal in practical discipleship and spiritual formation.

Zeal: An Initial Account

Although the Bible is replete with considerations of character, it does not provide taxonomies, catalogues, or theoretical accounts of virtue or virtues. Indeed, virtues are seldom denominated as such in the biblical text. For example, Paul describes the traits of love, joy, peace, patience, kindness, goodness, faithfulness, gentleness, and self-control as "fruit of the Spirit" (Gal. 5:22-23).[3] However, most or all of these correspond to a standard understanding of "virtues" as *character traits:* developed dispositions to feel, act, respond, perceive, or be motivated in certain ways, in relation to certain kinds of ethical consideration.[4] In any case, while biblical authors commend such traits, it is left to others (like the authors of these

---

An Empirical Assessment and Strategic Implications," *Journal of Business Ethics* 57 (2005): 269-84.

3. Henceforth, unless noted, biblical citations are from the English Standard Version (ESV), emendations appearing in brackets. Other translations indicated are the New International Version (NIV) and the New American Standard Bible (NASB). Biblical citations throughout are representative, not exhaustive.

4. A representative contemporary definition of a virtue is: "a disposition to act, desire, and feel that involves the exercise of judgment and leads to a recognizable human excellence, an instance of flourishing": Lee H. Yearley, "Recent Work on Virtue," *Religious Studies Review* 16 (1990): 2. This understanding of virtue is consistent with the developed Christian virtue ethics of Thomas Aquinas, perhaps the chief theorist in the Christian virtue-ethical tradition. In the case of the "fruit of the Spirit," however, Aquinas understands them to be virtuous actions, rather than virtues themselves (*Summa Theologica* [hereafter, ST], 1a2ae.70).

chapters, happily) to develop theoretical accounts of them as virtues. In the case of zeal, however, there is yet a further challenge: not only is zeal not explicitly identified in Scripture as a virtue, it also does not appear in the standard virtue taxonomies of classical authors such as Aristotle — as does, for example, self-control.[5] Still, on the general understanding of virtue described above, zeal can be seen to function importantly in Scripture as a virtue.

Zēlos

Two primary Greek terms (and their cognates) are translated as zeal terms in the New Testament. The chief is *zēlos,* which directly and obviously underlies the English term. In its classical usage, *zēlos* refers to a capacity or state of passionate commitment,[6] an emotional going out to a person, idea, or cause.[7] It is used, broadly, in two ways. On the one hand, it may express an eager striving or enthusiasm in relation to an object;[8] on the other, it may express jealousy, ill-will, or envy in relation to an object.[9] *Zēlos* is used in the Septuagint, the ancient Greek translation of the Old Testament, to translate *qinah* (and its cognates) — a Hebrew term which also bears this two-fold connotation. Thus, *zēlos* and *qinah* are frequently rendered in English Old Testament translations as envy (Gen. 26:14) and jealousy (Gen. 30:1) as well as zeal. Although in contemporary usage jealousy is typically thought of solely in negative moral terms, this is not the case in biblical usage. Both zeal and jealousy (positively) are attributed to God, who is described as a "jealous God" (Exod. 20:5) — that is, jealous for his honor and for the covenant loyalty and worship of his people (Deut. 32:21) — and as zealous for the accomplishment of his purposes, particularly as expressed in judgment. God is said to have zeal for

5. We shall qualify this point below. See note 17.

6. Gerhard Kittel and Gerhard Friedrich, eds., *Theological Dictionary of the New Testament: Abridged in One Volume by Geoffrey W. Bromiley* (Grand Rapids: Eerdmans, 1985), s.v. *zēlos,* pp. 297-98. (Hereafter, TDNT)

7. Colin Brown, ed., *The New International Dictionary of New Testament Theology* (Grand Rapids: Zondervan, 1971), s.v. zeal, vol. 3, p. 1166. (Hereafter, NIDNTT)

8. Using "object" here in the philosophical sense of intentional object, not in the sense, for example, of a physical object.

9. Brown, NIDNTT, 3:1166.

his people (Isa. 26:11), to wrap himself with zeal as with a mantle (Isa. 59:17), and to judge the earth by the fire of his zeal (Zeph. 3:8). Indeed, zeal appears in the capstone of the messianic vision of Isaiah 9:7:

> Of the increase of his government and of peace
> there will be no end,
> on the throne of David and over his kingdom,
> to establish it and to uphold it
> with justice and with righteousness
> from this time forth and forevermore.
> The zeal of the LORD of hosts will do this.

Humans are also described as zealous in the Old Testament. The context may be negative, as when Saul broke a covenant with the Gibeonites and sought to kill them "in his zeal for the people of Israel" (2 Sam. 21:2). But zeal is typically treated as positive, as when David describes his passionate concern for God's honor in Psalm 69:9: "For zeal for your house has consumed me, and the reproaches of those who reproach you have fallen on me." Human jealousy is generally viewed negatively in the Old Testament, but it is seen as positive where it corresponds to God's jealousy, as in the case of Phinehas, who is described as rightly jealous of God's honor (Num. 25:11).

Zēlos in the New Testament follows a similar pattern. Its sole occurrence in the gospels is in John 2:17, where John notes that, when they observed Jesus' passionate "cleansing" of the Temple, "his disciples remembered that it was written, 'Zeal for your house will consume me,'" referring to Psalm 69:9 (cited above). *Zēlos* is common in the rest of the NT, however, especially in Paul. In 2 Corinthians, for example, it is used to refer to the passionate interest the Corinthian believers have in Paul's welfare (7:7) and in their own spiritual formation (7:11), as well as to their eagerness to meet the needs of others (9:2). Besides referring to "zeal," *zēlos* is sometimes translated in the New Testament as jealousy or envy in a negative sense (Acts 5:17; Gal. 5:20), as jealousy in the positive sense of godly jealousy (2 Cor. 11:2), as earnest desire or eager seeking, both good and bad (1 Cor. 14:1, 39; Gal. 4:17-18), and as fury (Heb. 10:27). The Jesus of the Apocalypse warns the spiritually lukewarm church in Laodicea: "Those whom I love, I reprove and discipline, so be zealous and repent" (Rev. 3:19).

Paul acknowledges that zeal may be ignorant, as in the case of Israel's "zeal for God, but not according to knowledge" (Rom. 10:2), or misdirected, as in the case of his own earlier fervency in persecuting the nascent Christian church (Phil. 3:6). Yet zeal is clearly, and chiefly, commended. In an important passage that explicitly connects redemption and ethics, evoking a familiar Old Testament description of the nature and mission of God's people,[10] Paul identifies zeal as a chief ethical distinctive of the church:

> For the grace of God has appeared, bringing salvation for all people, training us to renounce ungodliness and worldly passions, and to live self-controlled, upright, and godly lives in the present age, waiting for our blessed hope, the appearing of the glory of our great God and Savior Jesus Christ, who gave himself for us to redeem us from all lawlessness and to purify for himself a people for his own possession who are *zealous for good works.* (Titus 2:11-14, emphasis added)

Peter likewise affirms that it is characteristic of God's people that they are "zealous for what is good" (1 Pet. 3:13).

What is clear in all of these usages of *zēlos* and *qinah* are notions of fervency, passion, and single-mindedness in the pursuit of some end, whether good or bad. Following a recent study of biblical jealousy by K. Erik Thoennes, we may understand the biblical notion of "zeal" as a general concept denoting fervency in pursuit of some object, with "jealousy" (both good and bad) as denoting a specific form of zeal in relation to an object or a relation between a person and an object (for example, where there is a "perceived infidelity to covenant exclusivity").[11] Our concern here is with the general notion of zeal, rather than the more specific forms that comprise jealousy.[12]

10. Exodus 19:5-6: "Now therefore, if you will indeed obey my voice and keep my covenant, you shall be my treasured possession among all peoples, for all the earth is mine; and you shall be to me a kingdom of priests and a holy nation."

11. K. Erik Theonnes, *Godly Jealousy: A Theology of Intolerant Love* (Fearn, Scotland: Christian Focus Publications, 2005), p. 12.

12. For our purposes, good jealousy may be considered simply as zeal (as the NIV translates *qinah* in Numbers 25:11, the case of Phinehas referred to in text, above), and bad jealousy as envy, one of the traditional seven capital vices (Aquinas, ST 1a2ae.28.4.c, ad 2).

Spoudē

A second Greek zeal term, *spoudē,* is featured in two New Testament passages of particular ethical importance. In classical Greek, *spoudē* (and its cognates) referred, first, to haste, speed in carrying out a matter, or quick movements in relation to some interest, and then to being zealous, active, earnest, industrious, and serious (such as taking persons or things seriously, as opposed to joking or playing).[13] In later classical use, *spoudē* took on a more distinctively moral sense, of being good, excellent, weighty, or worthy of serious attention.[14] In the *Nicomachean Ethics,* for example, Aristotle describes a life according to virtue as including relaxation, not for its own sake, but for the sake of action — "a life involving serious *(spoudē)* actions [or purposes], not consisting in amusement" (1177a1-2).[15] In fact, Aristotle uses the adjective, *spoudaios,* as equivalent to "virtuous" and "good," and indeed to refer to the person of highest ethical achievement, the one who is sober, serious, and excellent, who applies himself to human matters and attains moral virtue.[16] "For the excellent person *(spoudaios)* is far superior, because he sees what is true in each case, being himself a sort of standard and measure" (1113a30-32).[17]

Old Testament (Septuagint) use of *spoudē* is restricted to the more basic sense of urgency and haste.[18] Besides "zeal," it is rendered in the New Testament in various ways, such as haste (Mark 6:25), eagerness (Gal. 2:10; Phil. 2:28), striving (Heb. 4:11), and making an effort or doing one's best (2 Tim. 4:9, 21). The two most common English renderings of *spoudē* in

13. Brown, NIDNTT, 3:1168-69.

14. Alexandrine Schniewind, "Remarks on the spoudaios in Plotinus I 4 [46]," *The Paideia Archive* (1998), http://www.bu.edu/wcp/Papers/Anci/AnciSchn.htm.

15. Citations from Irwin translation, in Aristotle, *Nicomachean Ethics* (Indianapolis: Hackett, 1999). Cf. Aristotle's description of the magnanimous person, who takes things seriously (1125a11). On magnanimity and Christian virtue, see David A. Horner, "What it Takes to be Great: Aristotle and Aquinas on Magnanimity," *Faith and Philosophy* 15 (1998): 415-44.

16. Irwin, *Nicomachean Ethics,* glossary, s.v. *spoudaios,* p. 328; Schniewind, "Remarks."

17. Although we shall not pursue the point, it is worth noting that we do see here some common ground — albeit obscured in standard English renderings — between the classical virtue picture and biblical zeal. This qualifies our earlier point about this (see note 5).

18. Brown, NIDNTT, 3:1169.

Paul, however, are earnestness and diligence. In 2 Corinthians alone, *spoudē* is rendered in the ESV as earnestness in seeking vindication against wrongdoing (7:11), in seeking to please Paul (7:12), in excelling in faith, knowledge, and love (8:7), in caring for the welfare of others (8:16), and as reflected in a general passion and initiative toward Christian faith and obedience (8:22). *Spoudē* is also commonly rendered as diligence.[19]

Romans 12 *Spoudē* appears in two New Testament passages that are of particular interest to us, as they are situated in important, explicitly ethical contexts. First, at the beginning of Romans 12, Paul transitions from his eleven-chapter theological discourse on God's mercy to identify the Christian's proper response to this mercy: a lifestyle of worship, involving every aspect of life (v. 1). Paul spells out this lifestyle in specifically moral terms, as characteristics and behaviors that reflect the transformation of the believer's character (v. 2). Verses 3-8 describe the character transformation as it is expressed in the "body life" of the Christian community, where all members use their own gifts for the good of the church. In verses 9-13, Paul lists specific areas in which the character transformation is expressed in moral virtues and actions. He begins with a summary command to let love be genuine or authentic (v. 9),[20] and unpacks this in a chiastic series of terse phrases, generally of the form: "in C, be or do[21] X," where C specifies a context of concern (for example, brotherly love, honor, hope, affliction, prayer) and X specifies a state or activity (for example, loving, preferring, rejoicing, constancy). Within this list appears verse 11: "Do not be slothful in zeal, be fervent in spirit, serve the Lord" ("Never be lacking in zeal, but keep your spiritual fervor, serving the Lord," NIV). Literally, the verse reads: "in zeal *(spoudē)* not [being] slothful, [but] in spirit being fervent, serving the Lord." In this verse we find a commendation of zeal, an identification of sloth as its contrast, and a further characterization of zeal in terms of spiritual fervency and Christian service. We shall look at these components more closely later.

19. The preceding references reflect a mixture of NIV, NASB, and ESV translations.

20. Literally, this statement functions more as a label or title than a command: "authentic love" (there is no verb — the imperative is supplied in the translation).

21. Literally, "being" or "doing." Although these are characteristically translated as imperatives, the Greek text typically uses participles.

It is relevant here, however, to note that several features of the overall context of this passage (continuing through v. 21) not only provide general insight into the biblical picture of the moral life, but also give specific shape to our understanding of biblical zeal. First, the passage comprises neither an abstract list of moral principles or impersonal duties nor requirements for acquiring God's mercy. Instead, it is framed as the Christian's appropriate *response,* in moral terms, to God's love and mercy. The motivation for moral action here is wholly one of love and gratitude. Second, this response to God's love is itself expressed in practical *love* for others, even persecutors, and especially the lowly and needy. Third, Paul portrays this moral vision as an essentially *rational* one. It is an expression of rational *(logikos)* worship (v. 1), both in its constituting a believer's reasonable response to the magnitude of God's mercy and in its expressing the form of worship appropriate to a rational being — that is, involving the mind rather than merely bodily or mindless practices.[22] Further, the character transformation in which such worship is expressed is itself produced by the renewing of the believer's mind *(noūs),* resulting in her increasing ability to discern what is truly valuable in relation to God's will (v. 2). Indeed, Paul portrays the various moral traits and actions as being grounded in a transformed understanding that includes correct thinking about oneself (v. 3), about other believers (v. 16), and about what is truly good (*kalos,* v. 17).[23] The biblical zeal that is commended in this context is thus not only motivated by and oriented toward love, but also rationally guided by an accurate, transformed vision of reality.[24]

Fourth, the ethical picture here is *teleological,* in the classical sense, rather than deontological. That is, it is structured as an orientation toward the pursuit of *good* (what is supremely valuable and excellent) as an end *(telos),* rather than toward the performance of right actions or the preservation of certain principles, and duties, however important they

22. See Douglas J. Moo, *The Epistle to the Romans* (Grand Rapids: Eerdmans, 1996), pp. 752-54.

23. *Kalos* is an important term in classical virtue ethics. Aristotle, for example, repeatedly emphasizes that the virtuous person aims specifically at the "fine" or the "noble" *(to kalon)* in his actions (see *Nicomachean Ethics,* 1115b12). For a biblical passage loaded with classical virtue language, including *kalos,* see Heb. 5:14.

24. The centrality of thinking in these verses is somewhat obscured in English translations. In verses 3, 16, and 17 there appear eight terms related to mind and thinking.

may be in the pursuit of the good. Verse 2 strikingly casts God's will in classically teleological terms, as being in fact that which is the good, the pleasing, and the perfect or complete *(teleion)* — the right, and rightly attractive, object of ultimate pursuit. One's understanding of God's will in these terms, according to Paul, results from one's mind being renewed (v. 2). Moreover, Paul frames an extensive set of specific moral admonitions in verses 10-20 in teleological terms, sandwiching them between two general statements about pursuing good and rejecting evil. He starts by initially unpacking the overall aim of "authentic love" as abhorring or hating the evil and holding fast or uniting oneself to the good (v. 9). His language is strong; as one commentator notes, "'abhor' could also be translated 'hate exceedingly,' and 'cling' can be used to refer to the intimate union that is to characterize the marriage relationship."[25] Paul's subsequent moral admonitions constitute exhortations to do good and not evil, within various areas of life, concluding with the summary principle, "Do not be overcome by evil, but overcome evil with good" (v. 21). The command to be zealous is thus framed within a teleological context, as an aspect of pursuing what is good.

Finally, Paul characterizes this teleological pursuit as requiring a *passionate* response, in light of its strenuous difficulty. The ethical shape and texture of the passage is active, aggressive, and aspirational, rather than passive, automatic, and minimalistic.[26] Even beyond the explicit mention of zeal in verse 11, Paul describes the moral life here as one of deeply passionate action — loving, holding fast, abhorring, outdoing one another, contributing, blessing, weeping, meeting needs. In verse 13, he speaks literally of "pursuing" hospitality — using another zeal-related word *(diōkō)*.[27] This is a far cry from understanding morality as simply a matter of not violating moral prohibitions, staying within prescribed moral boundaries, trying not to offend, coasting in safe

25. Moo, *Romans*, p. 776.

26. For an excellent treatment of moral minimalism as characteristic of modern ethics, see David L. Norton, "Moral Minimalism and the Development of Moral Character," *Midwest Studies in Philosophy*, vol. 13: *Ethical Character and Virtue*, ed. P. A. French, T. E. Uehling, and H. K. Wettstein (Notre Dame: University of Notre Dame Press, 1988), pp. 180-95.

27. Another vivid picture of the Christian life as passionate pursuit, which uses this term, is Phil. 3:12. See also 1 Cor. 14:1; 1 Thess. 5:15; 1 Tim. 6:4; 2 Tim. 2:22; Heb. 12:14; 1 Pet. 3:11.

moral waters as one awaits heaven — being "nice." There is nothing comfortable — much less, boring — about this vision of life. Neither is it easy, immediate, or automatic. The assumed life context of Romans 12 is one of affliction, persecution, tears, and need, and this requires constancy in prayer and perseverance in action. The moral life, on this understanding, is one of intentional, consistent, diligent action. That is to say, it requires *zeal* — characterized here in terms of a passionate, intentional, rational, diligent pursuit of what is good, motivated by and expressed in love.

2 Peter 1 Finally, and much more briefly, we turn to the appearance of *spoudē* in 2 Peter 1:3-11, a passage which, although this is somewhat obscured in some English translations, explicitly appeals to moral virtue as central to spiritual formation. The picture is aspirational and virtue-oriented to the limit, as Peter identifies the aim of Christian formation to be nothing less than to partake of God's nature, that is, for the Christian to reflect God's moral character or virtue (verse 3). It is a pursuit, chiefly, of love, and it is one that is constant and diligent, rather than immediate or automatic. The natural or dominant human tendency, the context assumes, is, by contrast, to *fail* to attain, to drop out. What is needed, therefore, is zeal.

> His divine power has granted to us all things that pertain to life and godliness, through the knowledge of him who called us to his own glory and excellence [virtue — *aretē*], by which he has granted to us his precious and very great promises, so that through them you may become partakers of the divine nature, having escaped from the corruption that is in the world because of sinful desire. For this very reason, make every effort [exerting all zeal — *spoudē*] to supplement your faith with virtue, and virtue with knowledge, and knowledge with self-control, and self-control with steadfastness, and steadfastness with godliness, and godliness with brotherly affection, and brotherly affection with love. For if these qualities are yours and are increasing, they will keep you from being ineffective or unfruitful in the knowledge of our Lord Jesus Christ. For whoever lacks these qualities is so nearsighted that he is blind, having forgotten that he was cleansed from his former sins. Therefore, brothers, be all the more diligent [zealous — the verb, *spoudazō*] to make your calling and election sure, for if you

> practice these qualities you will never fall. For in this way there will be richly provided for you an entrance into the eternal kingdom of our Lord and Savior Jesus Christ.[28]

In sum, a biblical understanding of the intended character and behavior of God's people (Titus 2), the teleological, aspirational, and arduous shape of the Christian moral life (Romans 12), and the awesome aim of spiritual formation as coming to share in God's moral character (2 Peter 1), points to the role and importance of zeal as a virtue, and indicates some essential aspects of its nature. The biblical picture of zeal is of a disposition to rational, fervent, and diligent pursuit of what is good, motivated by and expressed in love.

Fanaticism: Bad Zeal

In order to refine our initial understanding of zeal, let us consider its alternatives. On the Aristotelian picture, a virtue expresses the proper balance, in a particular matter, between two opposing vices: one of deficiency, one of excess. It is helpful to understand zeal and its alternatives in these terms. Paul, as we have seen, explicitly contrasts zeal to sloth, one of the classic seven cardinal vices; in Aristotelian terms, the vice of sloth would represent a deficiency of zeal. In our time, however, sloth has lost its sting as a vice, while zeal has lost its luster as a virtue. Indeed, surrounded by examples of fanatics who pursue their visions of the good with deadly passion, we are today more likely to consider zeal — especially religious zeal — as the vice. However, the common understanding of zeal that this assumes actually corresponds to the vice that is opposed to zeal by excess: *fanaticism.* Or so we shall argue.

Clearly there *is* bad zeal, including bad religious zeal, or at least bad

28. Peter continues to emphasize zeal in what follows (v. 15): "And I will make every effort [*spoudazō*] so that after my departure you may be able at any time to recall these things." Note that while both *spoudē* and virtue are emphasized here, zeal is not listed *as* a virtue. It functions here, rather, as a condition for the development of the virtues that are listed. This suggests that zeal may be best considered as what has been called an "executive virtue," like practical wisdom, whose function is to direct the other virtues. In this case, zeal's function is to energize, motivate, and sustain the development and practice of the other virtues.

cases of such.[29] Critics of religion like Sam Harris see religious zeal as particularly problematic, as it is based upon religious faith, which is in Harris's view essentially irrational, immoderate, and intolerant.[30] Many Christian believers are also concerned about religious zeal, however — not only that of Islamic terrorists, but also the "Crusader zeal" expressed in the holy wars of medieval Christendom.[31] Indeed, some believers worry, along with many outside the faith community, that the sort of "certitude" that is central to orthodox religious faith, particularly with respect to the authority of religious texts, leads naturally and perhaps ineluctably to this sort of violence.[32]

There are legitimate concerns here, but also much confusion. More issues are involved than we can address in this chapter, including broader questions about the relationships between faith and reason, the nature of tolerance, and the nature and role of authority, especially religious authority.[33] We limit ourselves here to what is specific to zeal itself.

Several questions need to be untangled. To begin, we distinguish, in decreasing degrees of strength, three positions concerning the scope of bad zeal, both with respect to zeal as such and to religious zeal more specifically. First, zeal as such may be considered suspect — *all zeal is bad zeal* — including, by implication, all religious zeal. Second, it may be thought that, while zeal may be good in general, specifically religious zeal is inherently problematic — *all religious zeal is bad zeal.* Or, third, zeal, including religious zeal as such, may be thought in general to be good, but particular instances of zeal (religious or not) may be bad, when zeal is misdirected or excessive. On the third view the presence of zeal is not by itself morally determinative; that is a function, rather, of zeal's direction and force. Problematic instances, on this view, constitute not so much cases of *bad zeal* as they do *bad cases* or *mis*applications of zeal. The sec-

29. "Good" and "bad" here refer to broadly moral evaluations.

30. See Sam Harris, *The End of Faith: Religion, Terror, and the Future of Reason* (New York: Norton, 2005).

31. See Timothy M. Renick, "Crusader Zeal: Holy Wars, Then and Now," *Christian Century* 122 (2005): 26-29.

32. See John J. Collins, "The Zeal of Phinehas: The Bible and the Legitimation of Violence," *Journal of Biblical Literature* 122 (2003): 3-21.

33. For an excellent introduction and response to contemporary concerns in these areas, see Timothy Keller, *The Reason for God: Belief in an Age of Skepticism* (New York: Dutton, 2008).

ond and third positions converge in so far as religious zeal is seen to be *essentially* misdirected or excessive.

The first position, which sees all zeal as bad, is quickly dispatched, if zeal is understood as a disposition to fervent and diligent pursuit of what one takes to be good. On a classical philosophical understanding, the pursuit of what one takes to be good is just what ethics is about. To pursue that end with fervency and diligence, with the full alignment and employment of one's appetites, desires, and motivations, is exactly what *should* characterize one's response to what one takes to be good. Surely fervency and diligence in pursuit of nonmoral goods such as athletic or academic excellence, within moral bounds, is good; all the more so are fervency and diligence in pursuit of uncontroversial moral goods like the abolition of slavery or the establishment of civil rights. Even here, however, some may hesitate to endorse zeal, for the specter of fanaticism ever hovers in the background. For every example of good zeal, one is reminded of another, bad one.

Undeniably bad examples of zeal, however, do not establish that all zeal is bad, but only that not all zeal is good — which is not in dispute. The first position, we take it, has been dispatched: not all zeal is bad zeal. Let us turn to the second position: is all *religious* zeal bad zeal? Here we suppose a widespread suspicion that the answer is "yes": while zeal in some areas may be good, perhaps even very good, religious zeal is another matter. How strong is the claim that all religious zeal is bad zeal? Construed most strongly, the claim is that religious zeal is bad *as such:* in principle, essentially. More modestly, it may be held that, while religious zeal is not bad of necessity, it is bad as a *matter of fact* — given certain properties and tendencies of religion and religious belief, religious zeal tends, perhaps ineluctably, to go bad.

The third position is that what is determinative in cases of bad zeal is not the zeal as such, but rather its misdirection or excess. Our strategy in evaluating these positions shall be as follows. We take it as obvious and uncontroversial that, *at least,* zeal does go bad in the ways identified by the third position; zeal breakdown does result from misdirected zeal and/or excessive zeal. We start there, taking these as the central cases of zeal breakdown, and examine other possibilities in relation to them. The chief further question about religious zeal, then, is whether *all* zeal breakdown is the result of misdirected or excessive zeal (third position), or whether, in the case of religious zeal, there is something additionally and *specifi-*

cally problematic, so that religious zeal constitutes a *bad kind* of zeal (second position). Let us look more carefully at zeal breakdown, then, and consider its relation to religious zeal.

Misdirected Zeal

Zeal goes wrong in two clear ways: misdirected zeal and excessive zeal. Zeal may be *misdirected* with respect to the end that one (zealously) pursues, or to the means by which one pursues it, or to both. This implies four possible relations between end, means, (moral) goodness, and (moral) badness:

(A) Bad end, bad means. For example, the zealous Nazi, who pursues Aryan racial purity (bad end) by murdering Jews (bad means).
(B) Bad end, good means. For example, the zealous dictator who actively feeds the poor and nurses the sick in a refugee camp (good means), but only to gain their loyalty and lower their resistance in order ultimately to enslave them (bad end).
(C) Good end, good means. For example, William Wilberforce, who zealously works to abolish slavery (good end), through persuasion, acts of kindness, tireless campaigning, etc. (good means).
(D) Good end, bad means. For example, the zealous Crusader — assuming that his end is good (say, to honor God, protect innocent lives in Jerusalem) — who commits acts of murder and pillage in the service of that end (bad means).

In each example we have plausibly stipulated the agent as being zealous. We have also used religious examples in (C) and (D), representing not only putatively good and bad cases of religious zeal, but actual history. Which of these four examples constitute cases of bad zeal? (A), (B), and (D) are certainly *bad cases* of zeal (presumably (C) is a "good" case of zeal; we shall come back to that) — but do they constitute cases of *bad zeal?*

Consider (A), the zealous Nazi. What is the problem here? Is it the Nazi's zeal? His zeal certainly plays a negative role, in that it exacerbates the effects of his actions by making them more effective, helping him achieve his bad end. Zeal in the service of bad ends and means makes things worse for the world than were the agent less fervent and diligent.

But this is parallel to case (C), where fervency and diligence in the service of good ends and means makes things better for the world (plausibly Wilberforce would never have accomplished what he did without zeal). In each case, the distinctive issue — the fundamental problem — is not the agent's zeal as such, but rather his ends and means. Although we wish the Nazi were less zealous about his end and means, it is not his zeal that is at fault, but rather its employment in the service of a bad end. In a similar way, we may wish a Nazi were less competent in his efforts, but that does not denigrate the general value of competence.

Presumably (B), the deceptively benevolent dictator, does not present a specific problem for zeal. The exact moral nature of the case needs to be parsed further. On what we think is a plausible interpretation, *feeding the poor* is a good kind of action, all other things being equal. However, when other things are not equal, as when the agent's overall objective is to enslave them, the action of feeding the poor becomes a constituent of what is, *all* things considered, a bad action. The moral status of the complex act, including its constituent means, is ultimately determined by its overall end, and the badness of that end vitiates the goodness, otherwise considered, of the means.[34] *Qua* net moral status, on this understanding, (B) is indistinguishable from (A). In any case, whether or not one accepts this reading of the situation, it is not in fact the zeal of the agent in (B) that is determinative, but the end toward which the zeal is directed.

We are left, then, with (C) and (D). (C), the zealous pursuit of a good end, using good means, seems an uncontroversial case of good zeal. Our example of William Wilberforce, however, may well be considered problematic — not because there is obvious reason to doubt the goodness of Wilberforce's end or means but because his zeal was undeniably religious in nature.[35] This, of course, simply pushes us to the question of whether there is a specific problem with religious zeal, to which we return shortly.

The final case is (D), of the zealous crusader, where a good end is sought with bad means. Perhaps (D) provides the paradigm of bad zeal. But how exactly is the zeal implicated here? Again, the moral nature of the situation needs to be parsed. On our view, a plausible reading of it

34. This reflects a Thomistic understanding. See Aquinas, ST 1a2ae.18-21.

35. We take this to be uncontroversial. For a recent account, see Eric Metaxas, *Amazing Grace: William Wilberforce and the Heroic Campaign to End Slavery* (New York: HarperOne, 2007).

would be that, while a bad end vitiates even otherwise good means, as in case (B), even a good end would not justify essentially bad means, that is, essentially bad kinds of action. The overall moral status is a function of both ends and means, essentially related.[36] But in fact, *however* one parses this kind of case, it is not the agent's zeal that is the moral determinant. For if the end always justified the means, it would do so whether or not the agent were zealous. And if the end does not always justify the means, because some means are considered morally out of bounds, it is still not the agent's zeal, or lack thereof, that is morally determinative.

We have examined the four possible relations of goodness and badness of end and means of zealous actions, where three of the four possibilities constitute bad cases of zeal. In none of them is the zeal itself implicated as the bad-making constituent. In each case, the end ultimately sought, and/or the means employed toward that end, are defective, and this produces zeal breakdown. Each is a case of zeal misdirection.

How does this relate to religious zeal? As we have noted, (C) is a prima facie example of good zeal; as such it stands as a counter-example to the strong claim that *all* religious zeal is, in principle, bad zeal. In order to sustain the strong claim, one would have to hold either (a), that Wilberforce's zeal, while good, was not religious; or (b), that, even though it was religious and evidently good in all other respects, Wilberforce's zeal must nonetheless be considered bad, simply on the ground that it was religious — that the combination of religious belief and motivation with the end of abolishing slavery so degrades that end, and/or any means employed toward that end, that zeal for that end becomes, *ipso facto,* bad zeal.

It is difficult to imagine that either (a) or (b) could be sustained. That Wilberforce's zeal was religious in character is nowhere in dispute, and to reject in principle the goodness of *all* religious or religiously influenced ends, means, and motives would require a strong argument, indeed — much stronger than showing, for example, that the religion in question is factually false. It would need to show, a priori, that religious ends, means, and motives are morally bad, *as such,* and sufficiently so as to vitiate the goodness of all other ends, means, or motives to which they are attached.

Presumably this is a stronger claim than critics of religious zeal wish to make. The more plausible thought is that religious belief is defective in another way: while it may not *necessarily* vitiate the nature or quality of

36. See Aquinas, ST 1a2ae.20.2.

what are otherwise good ends or means, it *in fact* corrupts (or strongly tends to corrupt) the pursuit of those ends and the employment of those means. This weaker objection to religious zeal points toward the other form of zeal breakdown.

Excessive Zeal

Zeal goes bad, not only when it is misdirected, but also when it is excessive. The latter is *fanaticism.* Certainly fanaticism, including religious fanaticism, exists. It might seem, however, that our account of zeal in this chapter would make no allowance for this fact. After all, how could *any* degree of "fervent and diligent pursuit of what one takes to be good" be excessive?

Nothing in our account precludes understanding zeal to be excessive when its strength or intensity is not in proper proportion to the value or importance of the end that is sought. Bill's zeal for keeping his lawn well-groomed, an end that motivates and employs all of his powers throughout all of his waking hours, is excessive in this way. The end of a well-groomed lawn is not an intrinsically bad one, and the means employed (mowing, trimming, etc.) are not bad, as such. But the extent and intensity of Bill's commitment to this end is obviously out of proportion to its actual value and importance. Other goods competing for Bill's allegiance, related to his family's physical, relational, spiritual, and financial well-being, are far more important, but they are being sacrificed for this lesser good. Bill is a "fanatic" about his lawn, and this is not a good thing.

The appropriate level of zeal one expresses, then, is relative to the importance of the good one seeks. But how is this determined, and on what basis? Bill's case is obvious, but what about one's commitment to goods that are clearly (at least in retrospect) highly valuable and important? Was William Wilberforce's zeal for the abolition of slavery warranted or was it excessive? After all, there were other legitimate goods that he could otherwise have enjoyed, such as comfort and leisure; and there were other important moral aims to which he could have committed himself, but he sacrificed all of these for his single-minded pursuit of the abolition of slavery. Indeed, Wilberforce *was* seen by many of his contemporaries as a fanatic, and his zeal was widely criticized. One of his contemporaries, the popular poet, William Cowper, wrote a poem about Wilberforce, noting these criticisms explicitly:

> Thy country, Wilberforce, with just disdain,
> Hears thee, by cruel men and impious, call'd
> Fanatic, for thy zeal to loose th' enthrall'd
> From exile, public sale, and slav'ry's chain.

Similar charges of excessive zeal could understandably have also been leveled against Mother Teresa, who sacrificed even modest comforts and endured a lifetime of poverty and struggle in order to minister to the poor of Calcutta, or against Dr. Martin Luther King, who gave up his very life in pursuit of full civil rights for all Americans. In retrospect, however, most acknowledge the exceeding value of what Mother Teresa and Dr. King achieved, perhaps even the zeal without which they could not have done it.

It is evident that there is no simple, single scale for measuring appropriate levels of zeal in relation to ends. It is also clear, however, that some levels *are* appropriate, and others not; one may go wrong in the application of zeal, either by deficiency or by excess. As in much of philosophy, as well as in life, determining what is correct here requires wisdom and judgment. Zeal, in other words, operates as a virtue in that it both requires and expresses wisdom. Moreover, it does not stand simply on its own, but it is essentially related to and balanced by other virtues, including those described in this book.

These considerations relate to zeal in general. However, they may seem to pose a particular problem for religious zeal. Indeed, it is here, we think, that the central objections to religious zeal lie. Even beyond the charges that religion is essentially irrational (which, again, we do not address here), religious zeal may appear specifically problematic in this respect: religious ends, or religiously motivated and inspired ends, are seen by their adherents as requiring, by their very nature, a complete or absolute commitment, and this appears to eliminate the very possibility of proportioning one's zeal to one's end. In the service of religious ends, how could anything less than complete commitment be permissible? Moreover, in the pursuit of such overriding ends, how could one justify not employing any and all means, no matter how destructive or evil? For this reason, religious zeal appears to be *essentially* excessive — and thus to be, in fact, a *bad kind* of zeal.

We acknowledge the force of this concern: religious fervor certainly can, and often does, become unhinged from other concerns, overwhelming them. Historically, religious believers have confused other allegiances and values with their ultimate religious commitment, and have been all too willing to do terrible things in service to that "absolute" commitment. At least two things are important to note here, however. First, this phenomenon is not restricted to traditional forms of religion, but reflects a universal human tendency that rears its head in relation to *any* object of ultimate concern. It is strikingly evident, in fact, in explicitly antireligious movements such as the French Revolution and twentieth-century communism. Indeed, by far the most destructive expressions of excessive zeal in modern times have been in the service of secular, antireligious ends. While the excessiveness of "religious zeal" under discussion here rightly raises deep concerns, it should be understood as "religious" only in the more extended sense of "commitment to an ultimate concern," and so acknowledged as a universal human tendency, and addressed in those terms. Nothing about this phenomenon marks out problems that are specific to religious belief or practice, when the latter are understood in the narrower, traditional sense — and that is the sense that is needed for the objection to have force.

Second, once one looks specifically at actual religions and religious beliefs (in the narrower, traditional sense), one is faced with the fact that religions are not all created equal. Most critical discussions simply ignore the great differences between beliefs and behaviors as they are reflected within different, actual religions. Beyond the in-principle kinds of points we have already made, we are not interested here in defending a generic "religious zeal"; our concern is solely with the *Christian* virtue of zeal, on a biblical understanding. We do not claim (nor do we believe) that the kind of zeal advocated in biblical revelation is characteristic of, for example, Islamic terrorists.

On the other hand, of course, it is tragically true that there have been plenty of bad examples of zeal on the part of those who claim the name of Jesus. This is more than offset historically, we are convinced, by the positive expressions of Christian zeal that are reflected in William Wilberforce, Dr. King, and Mother Teresa, and in countless others.[37] Ironically, one example of the positive and pervasive moral influence of Christianity

37. See, e.g., Rodney Stark, *The Rise of Christianity: How the Obscure, Marginal Jesus Movement Became the Dominant Religious Force in the Western World in a Few Centuries* (San Francisco: HarperSanFrancisco/Harper Collins, 1996).

is that the very categories and values used by secular critics of religious zeal today are themselves profoundly shaped by the heritage of a biblical moral vision.[38]

In any case, it should be clear from our earlier account that irrational, unbalanced, and violent forms of zeal are simply and radically incompatible with biblical zeal. That there is ignorant and misdirected zeal is acknowledged in Scripture (Rom. 10:2; Phil. 3:6). What is advocated instead is, as we summarized it above, "a rational, fervent, and diligent disposition to pursue what is good, motivated by and expressed in love." The central text of Romans 12, we saw, stresses this pursuit as an essentially rational one, one that requires discernment in understanding what is good, what are one's own particular gifts and roles, and what are the needs of others. We also saw there that the love that motivates and expresses biblical zeal is characterized by, among other things: showing hospitality, meeting needs, blessing others (including enemies), identifying with the hurting and needy, and rejecting the seeking of vengeance for wrongs suffered. The biblical picture of zeal is not only a far cry from the behavior of terrorists and the caricatures of critics, but also from the actions of Crusaders and other Christian believers who have, tragically, fed the critics' worst fears. The problem with such believers, however, is not their zeal, but that theirs is not a fully biblical zeal.

Many are worried — rightly — about bad zeal, about fanaticism. We share their concern; we have personally encountered plenty of examples of unthinking, unbalanced fervor among Christian believers (including ourselves, at times), who find it difficult to distinguish between their ultimate commitment to God and the gospel, and their own projects, politics, or prejudices. In our view, however, an even more prevalent problem among Christians than excessive zeal, is the *lack* of zeal.

Sloth: Lack of Zeal

Having considered bad zeal in such detail, one might well be hesitant to include zeal in the catalogue of Christian virtues. As we have seen, however, zeal *is* a biblical virtue — a human excellence that is needed for the kind of flourishing life that reflects biblical values and aims. Yes, zeal can

38. See Keller, *Reason for God,* chap. 9.

go bad; but what are the consequences of its absence? We should ask, as followers of Jesus, "To what am I susceptible if zeal is *not* developed and demonstrated in my life?"

Within contemporary Christian life we observe a subtle but deadly spiritual condition, a disease of the soul whose effect is to undermine commitment to Jesus and his purposes and to thwart the aspirations of virtue. It is reflected in a variety of ways: absorption in trivia and personal comfort, but indifference toward the welfare of others; frenetic activity that is severed from larger, compelling purposes; aridity in worship, boredom in community life, lack of joy in obedience; and an orientation toward Christian discipleship that is timid, tepid, and minimalistic — a deadening of deep passion, feeling, aspiration, and ambition for a good that is bigger than oneself, and for giving oneself to needs that are beyond one's own immediate concerns.

This plague is not unique to our time. In Romans 12:11 Paul urges the Romans not to be *oknēros,* or sluggish and indolent in serving God.[39] The same term is used in the Septuagint to describe the proverbial sluggard (Prov. 6:6; 10:26), and to rebuke the unprofitable servant in Jesus' parable of the talents (Matt. 25:26). Medieval scholars, who thought extensively about the nature and depth of this condition, called it *acedia,* a Latin term that denotes moral lethargy and a lack of desire or indifference toward one's true good, namely one's spiritual good.[40]

Oknēros and *acedia* are rendered into English as *sloth.* Sloth is historically considered one of the "seven deadly sins" — deadly because the harm produced by these sins constitutes a fundamental obstacle to human flourishing, gradually producing death in the soul.[41] Some of these sins (actually, vices),[42] like lust, are well known and straightforwardly un-

39. "Not lagging behind" (NASB). It can also refer to what is difficult or troublesome, as in Phil. 3:1.

40. See Siegfried Wenzel, *The Sin of Sloth:* Acedia *in Medieval Thought and Literature* (Chapel Hill: University of North Carolina Press, 1960), p. 48.

41. While common idiom refers to these as "the seven deadly sins," medieval thinkers spoke of them as "the seven capital sins," as they are principal sources or "heads" (*caput* means source or head) of other sins.

42. Properly speaking, these are all *vices* rather than sins: they constitute, not so much acts or kinds of acts, as dispositions to act, desire, feel, and be motivated in certain ways. Just as virtues are good dispositions in these respects, vices are bad dispositions (cf. the definition of virtue in note 4, above).

derstood. This is no longer the case with sloth, which is part of its deadly, subtle power these days. In our acculturated naiveté about this condition, we focus entirely on sloth's external, behavioral features, such as laziness, idleness, and indolence, rather than on its internal, dispositional features, such as indifference and boredom.[43] Sloth is now seen as taking things easy, idleness in one's daily duties, and avoiding tension for the sake of relaxation. It has become synonymous with laziness.[44]

Kinds of Sloth

In Jesus' "parable of the talents," as recorded in Matthew 25:14-30, the master commends two of his servants as "good and faithful," for taking the money he entrusted to them ("talent" was a unit of coinage — its current meaning, indicating one's abilities or gifts derives from this passage), investing it wisely, and turning a profit. The third, however, buries his talent in the ground, fearing the master's judgment. The master rebukes him as wicked and *oknēros* (v. 26). English translations of the latter vary; older versions render him as "slothful," but most of the newer versions make the interpretive jump to "lazy." The difference makes a difference; while being lazy does involve the possession of certain characteristic attitudes and dispositions, it often connotes simply a lack of activity.

But this neither captures the essence of sloth, nor the point of the parable. By understanding the unprofitable servant's moral failing in solely behavioral terms (inactivity, not producing a profit), we lose sight of the intentions, motivations, and dispositions that constitute a more fundamental part of his moral failing. Sloth is more than laziness or inactivity. This becomes particularly evident when we notice, following the earlier tradition of thought on these matters, that sloth need not preclude fervent activity; indeed, such activity may well be a *form* of sloth. One of sloth's common masks is frenetic activity in the absence of a proper moral or spiritual aim, activity that is purposeless or engaged in trivial pursuits — whether to satisfy one's selfish pleasures or to fulfill penultimate or un-

43. Gabriele Taylor, "Deadly Vices?" *How Should One Live? Essays on the Virtues*, ed. Roger Crisp (Oxford: Clarendon, 1996), p. 161.

44. This is characteristic of Wasserstein's treatment in Wendy Wasserstein, *Sloth* (New York: Oxford University Press, 2006).

important duties.[45] According to Dorothy Sayers, one of sloth's guises is "to dissemble itself under cover of a whiffling activity of (the) body."[46]

If the target of the master's (and Jesus') rebuke is thought to be mere laziness (in the absence of other considerations), because inactivity alone has produced the servant's unprofitability, then an über-industrious or hyperactive-but-profitable servant would be someone to be commended. And in a Western capitalistic system that prides itself on industry, ceaseless activity, and profit, it is indeed tempting to approve of a hyperactive, profitable servant, without regard for the broader framework of dispositions and ends. But neither here nor elsewhere does Jesus commend work for work's sake, much less activity for its own sake. (Indeed, just a few chapters earlier is Jesus' famous invitation in Matthew 11:28: "Come to me, all who labor and are heavy laden, and I will give you rest.") He does oblige his disciples to be active and to work hard, but with particular kinds of aims or ends in mind (here, the end is to please the master, by stewarding his property faithfully and effectively), and this entails the disciples' having specific intentions, dispositions, and motivations. Activity as such, abstracted from its broader dispositional context, is not sufficient for "profitable" endeavor, in the right sense. (Activity is *necessary* to good action, of course; laziness or inactivity is *part* of what sloth comprises.) For one thing, as we saw earlier, activity (a fortiori, hyperactivity) in the service of the *wrong* end will likely make things worse for the world (the wrong sort of turning a "profit"). But we now see also that activity is insufficient because it may itself become a form of sloth — a distraction, diverting one from a proper commitment to what is the *right,* but perhaps much more *difficult,* end. (Indeed, although we usually assume that the servant was *in*active during his master's absence, it is equally possible that he was quite busy during that time — too "busy" to fulfill his charge.)

We do not wish to over-interpret this parable. Certainly, being productive is a central value here, one that Jesus is indeed charging his followers to fulfill, in light of his imminent departure and eventual return.[47]

45. Solomon Schimmel, *The Seven Deadly Sins: Jewish, Christian, and Classical Reflections on Human Psychology* (New York: Oxford University Press, 1997), p. 201.

46. Dorothy Sayers, "The Other Six Deadly Sins," in *Creed or Chaos?* (New York: Harcourt, Brace, and Company, 1949), p. 81.

47. See Michael J. Wilkins, *Matthew: The NIV Application Commentary* (Grand Rapids: Zondervan, 2004), pp. 819-20.

The third servant is judged in light of his nonproductivity in stewarding the master's goods. But, just as mere activity or inactivity is not in view here, so neither is mere productivity or profitability. For one thing, both of the prior servants were commended and rewarded as "good and faithful" servants, although one was more productive than the other. Obviously something more than mere profitability is in view, as important as that may be. Moreover, mere unprofitability hardly justifies the master's calling the third servant "wicked" in addition to *oknēros.* In context, Jesus tells this story among a series of parables that cast a vision for how his disciples are to live after he has left them, in anticipation of his return. The emphasis throughout, particularly in parables concerning servants and stewards, is on faithfulness and wisdom: being faithful in one's moral behavior in the master's absence (not being drunk, etc.), and being faithful, wise, and effective in fulfilling one's responsibilities to the master (cf. 24:45-51). The aim is to please the master, to represent him well — a task of great privilege, trust, and responsibility.

The behavior of the third servant is not merely an economic matter, but a matter of character; his failure is a moral one. Indeed, in the parable his failure is explicitly related to his attitude toward the master;[48] he viewed the master as unfairly demanding and harsh, and for this reason he buried the talent (verses 24-25). The master's reaction, as well as the broader context (especially given that these parables, ultimately, reflect Jesus in relation to his disciples), indicates that this was a false characterization, that it served as a mere excuse for the servant's unfaithfulness. The servant's picture of the master was a reflection, not of the master's character, but of the servant's. Indeed, that the master has entrusted his servants with such responsibility for managing his affairs suggests that significant personal relationships existed between them, and we may reasonably suppose that the master has genuine concern for the servants' welfare. But the third servant does not see the master *as* good, nor does he, in his intentions, identify *his* own good with the aim of pleasing the master. In fact he appears to be entirely uninterested in pleasing the master, even on a crabbed conception of the master's intentions, because he makes no attempt, even minimally, to honor the master or fulfill his responsibilities to him (vv. 26-27).

This points us toward the sorts of classical teleological considerations we introduced earlier, which emphasize action in terms of the end-

48. Wilkins, *Matthew,* p. 820.

directed pursuit of what the agent takes to be good. Understood in these terms, sloth may be expressed either in inert and lethargic behavior *(lethargic sloth)* that prevents an agent from realizing her end, or in fervent activity with an incorrect end in mind *(hyperactive sloth).* In both cases there is a failure of the kind of connection that should obtain between the structure of the agent's intentions, motivations, and dispositions, and the end that she pursues. In hyperactive sloth there is plenty of energy and activity, but it is not connected to an appropriate end. Note that this is similar, but not identical to its close cousin, discussed above: excessive zeal or fanaticism. Fanaticism is zeal, but unhinged from a proper end or a proper proportion of passion and activity toward that end. Hyperactive sloth also involves a wrong end and a wrong proportion of passion and activity toward the end, but it is not simply a misapplication of energy-toward-end. Rather, it is a derailing of energy-toward-end — away from a right, but more difficult aim, and toward some other, trivial end or to no clear end in particular. Lethargic sloth, on the other hand, involves an agent's having in mind what may well be a proper end, but not actually seeing it as good, and — because of this — not properly linking up his dispositional structure to the pursuit of that end.

Sloth and the Moral Life

Let us apply this conceptual framework to matters of moral transformation and Christian sanctification. As we saw in Romans 12, the end of such transformation and sanctification, for human beings, is seen as the *good* — the pursuit of what is supremely valuable. Moreover, it is a good in which the human agent *participates:* God's will is, for the believer, that which is the good, the pleasing, and the complete or perfect *(teleion)* (v. 2). This is classical teleological language. On the classical view, what the agent grasps as good to pursue is an end *(telos)* that is "perfective" of the agent — that is, it "completes" or fully realizes or actualizes her nature.[49] Seeing the end of her action *as* good in this way, seeing it as part of *her* good, as perfective of her nature, establishes an essential motivational link, for the agent, between intention and end.

49. *Telos* in Greek, and its Latin counterpart, *perfectio,* both mean end, goal, perfection, completion, and fulfillment.

Sloth, on this view, is an obstacle to human good, to what is perfective of human beings, and thus, a vice — by disconnecting the proper intentional, motivational, and dispositional links between our ends and our activity for the sake of our ends. Sloth obscures our vision of our true good *as* our good, and it fosters despair toward that good because it is difficult, or else it distracts from that good in the form of frenetic pursuit of other, lesser or counterfeit ends.

It is within such a teleological framework that Thomas Aquinas understands the vice of sloth.[50] He identifies the human good, that which is perfective of humanity, as: *becoming like Christ,* the one who is the very fulfillment and completion of human nature, who lived in perfect harmony with God. Sloth, then, is an obstacle to growth in virtue and transformation into Christlikeness — the human good.

For Aquinas, as a classical thinker, seeing the end *as* our good, as actualizing our capacities and completing us, involves our seeing it as desirable, and so desiring it — employing our will and its constitutive affections, orienting our intentions and dispositions, to achieve it.[51] Only God, who *is* ultimate goodness, can fully and definitively satisfy our desire for the good,[52] so that our completion or perfection is ultimately grounded in nothing less than God himself.[53] He is our good, and union with him is our deepest, truest longing. Thus Aquinas identifies the pursuit of goodness, for human beings, as that movement towards and transformation into becoming like the God-man himself, Jesus Christ. That end alone will ultimately fulfill, complete, and perfect those who bear the *imago Dei.*

The moral and theological virtues, as developed through the work of the Holy Spirit, are the primary means of this transformation, mobilizing us toward our good of becoming Christlike, and shaping our character into his image. The vices, on the other hand, deter us from this transformation. Like every other vice, sloth targets those dispositions that enable us to achieve Christlikeness. Sloth does this particularly by threatening our affections and passions — our motivational structure. Aquinas sug-

50. See Rebecca Konyndyk DeYoung, "Resistance to the Demands of Love: Aquinas on the Vice of Acedia," *The Thomist* 68 (2004): 173-204.

51. Aquinas, ST 1a2ae.1.6.c; Ralph McInerny, *Ethica Thomistica: The Moral Philosophy of Thomas Aquinas* (Washington, DC: Catholic University of America Press, 1982), p. 36.

52. Aquinas, ST 1a2ae.2.8.c.

53. McInerny, *Ethica Thomistica,* p. 30.

gests that sloth denotes sorrow toward, or aversion from, one's spiritual good.[54] It dulls our vision of the goodness of becoming like Jesus, or it deadens our affections for that good, or both. In either case, sloth disengages our affections and fervor of spirit from their proper relation to our end, rendering us indifferent to what is our true good.

The difficult good that is the aim of Christian discipleship and spiritual formation is no mere Sunday affair or tepid avoidance of sin. It is a difficult good, but it is *our* good; rightly understood, it calls out our deepest affections and excites our deepest passions. It requires zeal: a disposition to pursue what is good — rationally, fervently, and diligently, motivated by and expressed in love.

Developing Zeal: Some Suggestions

As Christians we are not only called in Scripture to pursue zeal, but we inherit a tradition of examples of faithful, arduous pursuit of the good — in Jesus and his disciples, in the early church, and in other faithful witnesses throughout Christian history, including William Wilberforce, Mother Teresa, and Dr. Martin Luther King. Following Jesus faithfully is indeed an arduous pursuit, and therein lies perhaps our chief challenge in developing zeal. Under the pressures of contemporary life, we have become a weary people and in our weariness we recoil at the call to arduous kingdom activity.

Our first suggestion for developing zeal is addressed to the challenge posed by busyness and weariness, and that is to *carve out space for rest.* We have seen that busyness can be, and often is, a form of sloth (hyperactive sloth), when activity and passion are derailed from a right end, and/or a right proportion to a right end. In any case, whether it masks sloth or not, excessive busyness and the weariness that results, *will* keep us from a proper, passionate, diligent, and joyful pursuit of what is good. I (David Horner speaking) know this from painful experience, as it took a recent, two-year-long struggle with debilitating chronic illness to help "cure" me of my addiction to work and busyness. The biblical antidote to this kind of lifestyle is rest: "Come to me, all who labor and are heavy laden, and I will give you rest" (Matt. 11:28). A practice that has become crucial, for

54. Aquinas, ST 2a2ae.35.1.c.

me, in developing a proper, sane perspective and discipline in this area, has been to begin to observe the "Sabbath": truly resting and refreshing, playing and praying one day each week, and trusting God to enable me to get done all that I truly need to get done.[55] Nothing has been more significant, for me, personally, in recovering and cultivating a proper zeal for God's call upon my life. A step like this is an important place to begin, for weary people, in developing biblical zeal.

Our remaining suggestions are drawn from Romans 12, the passage we have examined at length earlier. Recall that the entire passage is framed as a response to God's mercies, love, and goodness, and is structured teleologically, in terms of pursuing God and his will, motivated by seeing this as our true good. A second suggestion for developing zeal, then, is to focus our attention on what is Paul's focus: to *reflect and meditate on God's mercies, love, and goodness.* As the Old Testament worship leader, Asaph, concluded, after meditating on God's goodness in response to the evil and difficulty around him: "The nearness of God is my good" (Ps. 73:28, NASB). The wicked servant of Jesus' parable did not see his master and his master's will for him as his good, and as a result he was slothful and failed to be faithful and effective with what he had been entrusted. We saw that in Romans 12 Paul stresses the role of reason and the mind, specifically the "renewing" of our mind. Thinking hard and long about God's goodness and the goodness of his will for our lives, meditating on their reality and tracing their implications, is an important place to start in the renewing of our mind. Indeed, meditating on God's mercies, love, and goodness would be a good practice while observing the Sabbath!

Third, the context of Romans 12 is life within community, the body of Christ. A chief reason that zeal is difficult to sustain on our own is because we were never intended to do so. Paul calls his readers to identify with each other's conditions: "Rejoice with those who rejoice, weep with those who weep" (v. 15); so we may reasonably add, "Seek zeal with those who seek zeal, and encourage those who struggle with sloth to keep at the battle." We suggest that you *find others with like mind and pursue zeal with them.* Constantly remind each other of God's mercies, love, and goodness, as well as of his high, arduous calling upon your life, and pur-

55. A very helpful book is Mark Buchanan, *The Rest of God: Restoring Your Soul by Restoring the Sabbath* (Nashville: Thomas Nelson, 2006).

sue the cultivation of zeal together — praying devotedly for each other (v. 12), and holding each other accountable.

Our final two suggestions for developing zeal come from verse 11, where Paul explicitly exhorts believers to acquire and exemplify zeal. "Do not be slothful in zeal, be fervent in spirit, serving the Lord." Paul here identifies both a condition and an action related to zeal, each of which is suggestive for its development. The *condition* Paul identifies is the role of the Holy Spirit. Paul's specific imperative is: "be fervent in spirit" (literally: in spirit being fervent). The term "being fervent" *(zeontes)* may refer to burning (fire), to boiling (water), or to glowing (molten metal). The idea is to be "set on fire" — in this case, "in spirit." While the reference to "spirit" may refer to the believer's own spiritual nature or to the Holy Spirit, most likely it is the latter. "On this view, Paul is exhorting us to allow the Holy Spirit to 'set us on fire'; to open ourselves to the Spirit as he seeks to excite us about the 'rational worship' to which the Lord has called us."[56] The Christian moral life is not only a response to God's love and mercy, but it is a supernatural life in which his "divine nature" is produced in us by the Holy Spirit — the "fruit" of the Holy Spirit. The ultimate source of biblical zeal is not ourselves but God.

Unfortunately, the cultural pressures of our day instruct us to turn inward and draw upon "the self" to elicit "spiritual" fervency. Biblical zeal, by contrast, is not manufactured by human effort, but fanned into flame by the inner work of God's Spirit. As John Calvin said,

> It is the fervor of the Spirit alone which corrects our indolence. Diligence in well-doing, therefore, requires the zeal which the Spirit of God has kindled in our hearts. Why, then, someone may say, does Paul exhort us to this fervor? My answer is that, although this zeal is the gift of God, *these duties* are laid upon believers in order that they may shake off their listlessness and take to themselves the flame which God has kindled. It usually happens that we stifle or extinguish the Spirit by our own fault.[57]

56. Moo, *Romans,* p. 778.

57. Cited in C. E. B. Cranfield, *A Critical and Exegetical Commentary on The Epistle to the Romans* (Edinburgh: T&T Clark, 1979), vol. 2, p. 634.

Developing biblical zeal should begin with the Holy Spirit's work. Our fourth suggestion, then, is to *ask the Holy Spirit to kindle his fervor within our heart.* There is no special formula or practice to guarantee the flame of his presence: otherwise biblical zeal would be from us, not from him. We can only seek him and, in faith, ask him to intervene.

But, as Calvin points out, Paul situates this directive in the context of a list of duties, obedience to which becomes part of the development of zeal. Relatedly, not only does Paul identify a condition for biblical zeal in this verse, but also specifies an *action:* "but serve [literally, serving] the Lord." The proper expression of being fervent in the Spirit is serving the Lord: daily, deliberate obedience to Christ demonstrated in practical acts of service. Our final suggestion for developing zeal, then, is to *engage in intentional, regular acts of service,* as an expression of worship to Jesus. In service we use our abilities and resources to become the hands and feet of Christ to promote the good of others. "This reminder is the most effective antidote to weariness and incentive to ardor. When discouragement overtakes the Christian, and fainting of spirit as its sequel, it is because the claims of the Lord's service have ceased to be uppermost in our thought."[58] Ardor in serving Christ by loving others is cultivated by practice in serving Christ by loving others. According to St. John Chrysostom,

> Love by itself is not enough; there must be zeal as well. For zeal also comes out of loving and gives it warmth, so that the one confirms the other. For there are many who have love in their mind but do not stretch out their hand. This is why Paul calls on every means he knows to build up love.[59]

This picture of zeal expressed in practical love and service provides a needed, wise balance against counterfeits and confusions. It is the fervency of the Spirit, as the prior condition, that gives these practical acts of service their meaning and energy. And it is practical acts of service unto Christ that gives the fervency of the Spirit its proper expression. "The real proof of the presence of this fire of the Spirit would be not ef-

58. John Murray, *The Epistle to the Romans: The English Text with Introduction, Exposition and Notes* (Grand Rapids: Eerdmans, 1968), vol. 2, p. 131.

59. *Homilies on Romans,* cited in Gerald Bray, ed., *Romans,* Ancient Christian Commentary on Scripture (Downers Grove: InterVarsity, 1998), p. 315.

fervescent religious excitement but renewed energy and determination in the humble and obedient service of the Lord Jesus."[60] The pairing of condition and action addresses the vices of fanaticism and sloth. The burning of the Spirit has the effect of melting the callous scales of sloth, and the grit, austerity, and intimate proximity to others that often characterize practical acts of service tend to quell the kind of hunger for splashy episodes that characterizes fanaticism. Biblical zeal is expressed in a faithful life of service in Christ.

Questions for Further Reflection

1. Are you reluctant to develop the virtue of zeal in your Christian walk? Why? In what ways have the authors persuaded you to develop this virtue?

2. Have you ever been in a season of life where you felt like the slothful servant? What did you do, to whom did you turn, to wrest free of this condition? How would the virtue of zeal wrest you free from this condition?

3. In the discussion on Romans 12, the authors articulate the value of having a vision for life. Do you have a vision for life in the kingdom that presently guides your actions? Why is such a vision important for personal growth in Christlikeness? How much of this vision is grounded in Scripture? Do you find this vision inspiring? Why or why not?

4. What are the various ways in which zeal may go bad and become a vice? Why is wisdom important for preserving zeal and strengthening it as a virtue?

5. Which aspects of zeal do you still find uncomfortable? Can a biblical notion of zeal as described by the authors appease your uncomfortability? How so?

6. Why do you think zeal, moral living, and healthy Christian community are so intertwined in Scripture?

7. The virtue of zeal is an appropriate response to God's love and mercy. According to the authors, what is this appropriate response? How should this response inform and shape one's motivation for zeal? What are the characteristics of zeal when it is appropriated in the right way?

60. Cranfield, *Critical Commentary,* p. 635.

How does this appropriate response ward off vicious extremes, competitors, and confusions to this virtue?

8. Is the amount of time you allot to your activities appropriate? How much of your week contributes to what is important? Do you represent the Master and steward his resources faithfully and wisely? Would a wise and trusted friend agree?

9. In what ways do you see faith communities as a necessary part of your growth in Christlikeness? Are you part of a faith community? Is your faith community a place of mutual encouragement where members pursue Christlikeness together? In what ways do you contribute to the learning and growth of these communities? In what ways do other community members contribute to your learning and growth?

HOPE

Hope

William C. Mattison III

What does it look like to be a person of hope? Answering this question depends on explaining what hope is, and what sorts of actions the person of hope does. The task of this chapter is to address these questions.

"Hope" is a ubiquitous word whose prevalent usage can lull us into thinking that its meaning is obvious and uncontested. Who doesn't want to have hope, or better, to be hopeful? Isn't hope simply a desire for good things to come, even if obtaining them may be difficult? As this latter question reveals, determining whether or not we all value hope depends a great deal on what we think hope is. When understood in only this vague sense, of course everyone can appreciate it. But a moment's reflection reveals that hope can mean a whole range of different things. It can be an emotional response, as when we say "I feel hopeful about our prospects for success." It can indicate a fixing on a longer term goal, as when we say "I hope one day to be a teacher," or, "I hope they someday get married." In the Christian tradition hope is one of three theological virtues (the others being faith and love), and it directs us to yearn for God as our ultimate happiness. What is common to all these usages is that hope describes people in relation to good things that are not yet present, and that are difficult yet possible to obtain. But that does not say very much!

Efforts at further specification of hope reveal deep disagreement, both in terms of what sort of thing it is, and what it is properly directed toward. The first section of this chapter explains what Christian hope is. Far from a vague "desire for good things not yet present," we will find that hope in the Christian tradition is most properly a virtue, directed toward God's very self, and made possible only by the grace of God. It enables a person to long for union with God as constituting one's own complete fulfillment and happiness, and for God's help in attaining that fulfillment. Since this union is only complete in the next life, any Christian discussion of hope will also have to address eternal life, or "heaven."

We come then to a question that will govern the second section of this chapter. If hope seeks complete union with God, and this is not attainable in this life, what has hope to do with how we live our lives now? One simple way to answer is that hope "gets us through" this life, with all its difficulties given our state of not yet being where we are destined to be, where we will be ultimately fulfilled. Certainly, this is true in a sense. Yet does the hopeful person simply endure while awaiting union with God? Or does hope transform the way we act in this life even as it properly directs us toward the next? Section two attempts to answer these questions.

What Kind of Virtue Is Hope?

The purpose of this section is to explain what hope is. It identifies four characteristics present in any instance of hope. We will also see why it is important to understand hope as a virtue rather than simply a feeling. The section ends with an explanation of how Christian hope is a distinctive sort of virtue, one that entails radical claims about God's nature and God's plans for humanity.

Hope: More Than a Feeling

We often use the term "hope" to refer to a kind of feeling, or emotion, as in "I hope I pass the test" or "I hope we'll be served a tasty dessert after dinner tonight!" When we use "hope" in this manner, we're "saying" several things.[1] First, we are identifying something as *good,* since no one

1. The following analysis of hope closely follows the work of St. Thomas Aquinas, thirteenth-century Dominican friar and theologian whose theological work has had enormous influence on theology in the last eight centuries. For the following four characteristics of hope, see especially his *Summa Theologica* (hereafter ST), translated by the Fathers of the English Dominican Province (New York: Benziger

hopes for something they view as bad. Second, we're referring to something that is *future,* since we do not hope for things in the present or past. Third, we are acknowledging that the future good we hope for is not assured. Otherwise we would say something like "I can't wait for . . . ," indicating there is no question in our minds that what we long for will happen. Thus there is something *difficult* about the attainment of the future good. And yet, fourth, we're saying that attainment of the good is indeed *possible,* otherwise we would not "bother" hoping for it. Rather we would despair in not being able to attain it.

Our feelings of hope are conducive to living a good life only when these four characteristics are truly present in whatever prompts our hope. In other words, we hope well when we do not hope for things that are actually bad for us, or that are not truly possible. We see this also in the common ways we speak of hope. Consider someone saying, "I hope this essay is on the test," and a friend replying, "No you don't! That essay is actually the most complicated one there." The friend is implicitly saying that the good being hoped for is not actually a good — and so one should not hope for it! Consider another example, as when someone says, "I hope we'll get back together," and a friend replies, "You're wasting your time! You two will never get back together." What the friend is saying here is not that what is hoped for is bad, but that it is not possible, so one should not bother hoping for it.

These examples reveal that feelings of hope are natural and good, but that these feelings enable us to live well only when they are directed toward things that are actually worthy of our hope. After all, people who continually hope for bad things, or who hope for what can never be, are impeded in their ability to live a good life. Thomas Aquinas famously remarked that feelings of hope are particularly common in "drunkards!"[2] Those who are drunk are prone to see good things as more possible than

Brothers, 1948), esp. 1-2.40.1. St. Thomas also wrote about hope in a text called *On Hope,* in *Disputed Questions on the Virtues,* ed. E. M. Atkins and Thomas Williams (New York: Cambridge University Press, 2005), pp. 217-39, but esp. article 1. For more contemporary thinkers who have written on hope from a Thomistic perspective, see Josef Pieper, *Faith, Hope, and Love* (San Francisco: Ignatius Press, 1997), and Fr. Romanus Cessario, O.P., "The Theological Virtue of Hope (II-II, qq. 17-22)," in *The Ethics of Aquinas,* ed. Stephen J. Pope (Washington, DC: Georgetown University Press, 2002), pp. 232-43.

2. Aquinas, ST 1-2.40.6.

they are. Perhaps it is no surprise that some seek solace in "the bottle." Aquinas lamented this fact, writing that such people lack "steadiness in reality."[3] The moment we begin to speak about how our feelings can be shaped by a more or less accurate grasp of the world around us, i.e., how they can be more or less in accordance with "reality," we are speaking about how our emotions can be developed into (good or bad) habits.[4] Hope is a feeling, but it is more than a feeling when it reflects a deliberate way of seeing the world around us. Then it becomes a "habit," as we will see below.

Hope as a Virtue

As human persons we have all sorts of capacities. It is because each of our capacities may be developed in different ways that we have habits. For instance, we have a capacity to use our resources in service to others. In doing so, we can be stingy (vice of defect), extravagant (vice of excess), or generous (virtue — the mean). We also frequently face difficulties and dangers. In doing so we can be cowardly (vice of defect), foolhardy (vice of excess) or brave (virtue — the mean). Indeed there are seemingly countless capacities we develop, or "habituate" into virtues or vices throughout our lives. We develop a capacity into a habit (a virtue, if it is good; a vice, if it is bad) when we are deliberately inclined to consistently do acts related to that capacity in a certain sort of way. Although hope can be understood as a feeling, it is understood in the Christian tradition primarily as a virtue, or good habit. In other words, we can speak of hoping well or poorly; in the proper sense of the word, hope is a virtue possessed only by one who has a stable inclination to long for what is *truly* (rather than only apparently) good, future, possible, and not assured. Only one who hopes well has the virtue of hope.

How can we hope well? Since the virtue hope is a longing for a good that is future and possible yet difficult, we can begin by asking, what good do all people long for? The consistent answer to this question in the

3. Aquinas, ST 1-2.40.6 ad 1.

4. For an introduction to the more basic question of how it is intelligible to speak of having any emotion "well," see William C. Mattison III, *Introducing Moral Theology: True Happiness and the Virtues* (Grand Rapids: Brazos, 2008), pp. 75-94.

Western moral tradition (and beyond) has been "to be happy."[5] Ultimately we long to be fully and completely happy. Therefore, hope most properly concerns, or is directed toward, what will make us fully happy. What constitutes complete happiness must obviously be described further. And in order to be the target of the virtue hope, that full happiness must not yet be present, and it must be difficult but still possible.

Now we begin to see how the meaning of hope is not at all obvious and agreed upon by all people. How we hope reveals what we think life is all about, including whether complete happiness is possible and, if so, what it involves. For many, including famous twentieth-century existentialists such as Albert Camus and Jean-Paul Sartre, there is no complete happiness available for humanity, and thus no reason to hope.[6] For these people life is absurd, an occasion for despair. Others long for happiness in worldly things, such as pleasures or money or status or fame. Or they may place their hope in "higher" things in this world, such as a marriage relationship, a job, or a good cause. In these latter cases people place their hope for complete happiness and fulfillment in things of this world.

Here is where we see the radical nature of Christian hope. Christians have a distinctive understanding of the ultimate "good," a good that is future and possible yet difficult. The source and goal of Christian hope is God. Christians ground their hope in their faith in who God is, what God has done, and what God plans for us. Christians profess a God of love, who made all things out of love and in particular human beings in the *imago Dei* as uniquely capable of love. Despite human sinfulness, which is at root a human rejection of God's loving offer of fullness of life in pref-

5. For an account of how this is traditional yet eclipsed, see Servais Pinckaers, O.P, *The Sources of Christian Ethics,* trans. Mary Thomas Noble, 3rd edn. (Washington, DC: Catholic University of America Press, 1995). For examples of Christians and non-Christians alike who begin their ethical treatises by asking "what is happiness?" see Aristotle's *Nicomachean Ethics;* Cicero's *On Moral Ends;* Augustine's *On the Way of Life of the Catholic Church;* and Aquinas's *Summa Theologica.* Sadly, until recently this approach to morality had been out of fashion for centuries. For an influential philosophical account of the need for its resurgence, see Alasdair MacIntyre, *After Virtue* (Notre Dame: University of Notre Dame Press, 1981).

6. For a helpful comparison and contrast of Sartre and the twentieth-century Thomistic thinker Josef Pieper, as concerns the topic of hope, see Bernard N. Schumacher, *Une philosophie de l'espérance: La pensée de Josef Pieper dans le contexte du débat contemporain sur l'espérance* (Paris: Cerf, 2000).

erence for living on our own terms, God continually reaches out to humanity to reconcile us to himself. This culminates in God's becoming man in the person of Jesus Christ, the Incarnate Son sent by the Father to reconcile humanity with God (John 3:16) and enable us to have life, and have it more abundantly (John 10:10). Christians attest to God's plan to make all people friends of God, indeed to make us partakers in God's very divine nature (2 Pet. 1:4). This is a destiny of complete happiness and fulfillment that is beyond our imagination, let alone attainment, without the help of our loving God.

For Christians therefore, the virtue of hope enables us to long for the destiny of union with God as our complete happiness, and for God's help in attaining this destiny. Hope thus has a twofold "object," or target: in God who is our complete fulfillment and happiness, and in God who is our help in attaining that destiny. See how far we have already come from that vague meaning of hope that all can agree upon! Now let us note two further characteristics of the Christian virtue of hope.

First, Christian hope is a *theological* virtue, which means that it concerns God directly. As such hope is one of the three theological virtues recognized in the Christian tradition: faith, hope, and love.[7] In technical terms we say the "object" of these virtues is God, even though of course God should not be understood as an "object" in the sense of a thing to be used for something! God is the object of the theological virtues in the sense that God is the object of each of them used as a verb. We believe in God, we hope in God, and we love God (and all things in God). Virtues which are not theological are called moral virtues, since they directly concern not God but this-worldly activities such as eating, drinking, sex, making decisions, allotting our goods, facing difficulties, etc. The virtues which concern these activities (e.g., the cardinal virtues: temperance, prudence, justice, fortitude) may be exercised ultimately for the sake of God, but they immediately concern this-worldly activities. Hope, as a theological virtue, immediately concerns God.

Second, hope is an *infused* virtue. That means it is possible only with God's help, or grace. The Scripture tells us rather directly that "eternal life comes by the grace of God" (Rom. 6:23), and thus it is no surprise that

7. For lists of these three theological virtues in Scripture, see 1 Cor. 13:13 and 1 Thess. 5:8. For a definition and discussion of the theological virtues see Aquinas, ST 1-2.62.

the virtue whereby we long for eternal life, and God's help in attaining it, is possible only through God's grace. Some virtues can be obtained by our own good use of our God-given natural capacities. These are called acquired virtues. But the *infused* virtues, of which hope is one, are gifts of God's grace that direct us to our supernatural destiny of union with God.[8] Obviously all of the theological virtues are infused virtues.[9]

Before moving on to address the specifically moral importance of hope, one more question should be addressed. If hope inclines one toward ultimate happiness, in what way can it be said to concern something "difficult"? In other words, how can our ultimate happiness be difficult?

We hope wrongly when we hope in something that is not truly good, or future, or possible, or difficult. Recall how certain people like Camus and Sartre "hoped poorly" by thinking that complete happiness is impossible. This failure of hope is called *despair.* Others can hope poorly by seeking ultimate fulfillment in things which cannot fully satisfy, such as goods of this world. This failure of hope is actually rooted in the failure of faith called *idolatry,* since such a person in effect makes something "god" which is not God. Finally, people can hope poorly by regarding their eternal happiness as easy to achieve. They presume they can attain eternal life without God's help. Or even if they know God must help them enter eternal life, they do not think that help includes the grace of transformation in this life to make them fit for eternal life. So they go on living as they please, hoping poorly (or rather, presumptuously) that God will still grant them eternal life. This failure of hope is called *presumption.*[10]

Therefore, it is difficult to hope well. We are still very much beset by

8. For a definition and discussion of the acquired and infused virtues, see Aquinas, ST 1-2.63.

9. Though this is not a topic for this chapter on hope, note that moral virtues, which concern innerworldly activities, can be acquired virtues. But they may also be infused virtues, when we obtain them through the grace of God and they direct us to do innerworldly activities in a manner transformed by their being directed ultimately toward our supernatural destiny of union with God. For more on the important category of infused moral virtues, see William C. Mattison III, "Moral Virtue, the Grace of God, and Discipleship," in *Gathered for the Journey: Moral Theology in Catholic Perspective,* ed. David Matzko McCarthy and Therese Lysaught (Grand Rapids: Eerdmans, 2007), pp. 198-215.

10. Aquinas, ST 2-2.21, 1.

all the conditions that differentiate this life from the complete fulfillment of eternal life: sickness, death, ignorance, injustice, sinfulness, etc. These conditions can lead us to despair. Or we can be idolatrously sidetracked to seek complete fulfillment in things that are not God. Or we can presumptuously fail to acknowledge our need for God's grace, both to attain the complete fulfillment for which we long and to be transformed in this life so as to be made fit for eternal life. This is why yearning virtuously for complete happiness is difficult. Yet it is the virtue of hope whereby we keep our "eyes on the prize" and trust that the fullness of eternal life promised us by God is indeed possible with God's grace, even if not available in this life with all its brokenness. Such hope is not a fantasy, nor is it a delusional crutch for enduring hard times, but rather grows out of the radical claims of the Christian faith.

The Moral Importance of Hope

The previous section on the meaning of Christian hope raises a question that will drive this second section: If the infused theological virtue hope points one toward a destiny of complete happiness that is only fully possible in eternal life beyond this world, what does hope have to do with living in this world? Hope is a rather distinct virtue. As a theological virtue it concerns God directly, and inclines one to long for union with God as one's eternal happiness. That destiny is not attained in this life. Yet hope is a virtue only for those in *this* life. As St. Thomas explains, once eternal life is actually attained, there is no more reason to hope, since hope concerns a *future* good![11] So what does it look like for a person in this life to have hope?

Two Views of Hope Based on Two Views of Eternal Life

What does Christian teaching about the next life have to do with how we live in this one? Two responses to that question are offered here, with a clear preference for the second. It will then be noted how each answer engenders a distinct understanding of hope.

11. Aquinas, ST 2-2.18, 2.

One way of understanding the relationship between the next life and this one is labeled here an "extrinsic" relationship. This basically means there is no inherent continuity between life here and there. One version of this includes people who think only of heaven and neglect any involvement in this world, including a concern for justice.[12] For these people, activities in this life are only important to the extent that they directly impact their destiny in the next life. (In this claim they are actually right; but they have an inadequate understanding of the relationship between this life and the next.) Such activities would include prayer, worship, and anything they regard as directly related to God. Surely such a position is rightly criticized. Even if there have been Christians who lived this caricature, a brief perusal of Scripture would reveal that God is quite concerned with our love of neighbor, forgiveness of others, love of enemy, a just society, following the commandments, and many other things as well.

But there is a more subtle and alluring version of the extrinsic relationship between this life and the next. On this view, we are supposed to obey all the moral injunctions in the Scriptures, including those just mentioned. But the reason we do this is because God said so. (Presumably God could have instructed us otherwise!) And the reason this is related to our eternal destiny is that God clearly rewards or punishes us to the extent that we obey these ethical injunctions. The Scripture makes quite clear in passages such as the separation of the sheep and the goats (Matt. 25:31-45) that our eternal destiny is determined by how we act in this life. Perhaps God could have determined that destiny otherwise, but this is how we learn from the Scripture that he does determine it; so we better act rightly in this life!

There is much to be commended in this latter approach. After all, such people are interested in obeying God, living according to God's law, and going to heaven. Indeed, many people see this as a summary of the Christian life! But though one could have a lot worse understanding of the relationship between this life and the next, this understanding is less adequate than what is labeled here an "intrinsic" relationship between eternal life and this life. Explaining such an intrinsic relationship requires some brief words on the meaning of eternal life.

What is eternal life? Consider this enormous question through a story

12. See C. S. Lewis, *Mere Christianity* (San Francisco: HarperSanFrancisco, 2001), pp. 134-37.

from Scripture. There is a beautiful story in the beginning of Luke's gospel where Mary and Joseph present the infant Jesus in the temple (Luke 2:22-38). The holy family is greeted in the temple by a man named Simeon, who had been told in a dream that he would not die before seeing the Messiah. On the day he meets Jesus, he knows right away that this promise has been fulfilled. He lifts up the baby in his arms and exclaims, "Now Master, you may dismiss (in Latin, *"nunc dimittis"*) your servant in peace, according to your word, for my eyes have seen your salvation!" (Luke 2:29-30). Simeon had been promised to witness God's decisive act in history, and having witnessed it, he cries, "you may now dismiss your servant in peace!" He in effect says, "My life is complete; all that I have hoped for has been fulfilled, so there is nothing further to seek with my life."

Simeon's cry is a grateful response to the Lord's fulfillment of a promise that he would not die before seeing the Savior. Now he could die in peace. Yet the story is offered here for that beautiful phrase *"nunc dimittis."* Think for a moment about what would prompt you to utter Simeon's cry. What would satisfy all your desires? What state of affairs would have to exist in order for you to say, "That's it! I've arrived! I'm complete! *This* is fullness of life!"

Be careful how you answer! Even if you had that perfect job, would your entire life really be complete? Even if you were in that perfect relationship, would there be nothing else to long for? Even if the societal injustice, the fight you devote yourself to, were to be remedied, would there be nothing left to fight for? Even if a loved one who is near death were to be healed, would that occasion of great rejoicing give final and unceasing joy?

The true and complete answer to the question of what would fulfill all our desires is exactly what Christians call "heaven," or "eternal life," or "the fullness of life," or "union with God," or "seeing God face to face."

Eternal life is not just life as we experience it now but longer in duration, without suffering or injustice. It is *fullness* of life, which includes greater duration but much more. It is life without any of the longing for complete fulfillment which marks our current state, not because we cease to seek complete fulfillment but because it has been achieved. All the limitations that mark this life — sin, ignorance, death, sickness, injustice — are gone in that state, and thus there is nothing more to long for. In fact, even longings that are not even possible without guidance from God are fulfilled.

Of course, though it is helpful to understand our union with God as "the fulfillment of all our desires," one must be careful not to make "our desires" the basis for our understanding of eternal life. Union with God (which is eternal life) is the fulfillment of all our desires (and more) because such a state *is* true happiness, not because God wants to satisfy any desire we might have. What is offered to humanity in union with God is true fulfillment, not fulfillment on one's own terms. Our true and holy desires are fulfilled, even surpassed. For instance, we commonly hear people say they long to be with departed loved ones in the next life. It is a true and holy desire to be united with others in love. Such a longing will be fulfilled, and the communion with others enjoyed in the next life surpasses the loving union we can experience or even imagine here. (Christians call this belief the communion of saints).[13] We long to be free in the next life of our brokenness here: sin, sickness, and death. That longing, since it is a truthful and holy longing, is indeed fulfilled and surpassed.

Now we can begin to see what this understanding of eternal life has to do with the relationship between this life and the next. An understanding of eternal life as fullness of life means that even life on this side of death can be more or less full. If living most fully is having and attaining good, truthful, and holy desires, then we could even say that people are more or less alive while living this life. When Christ said that he came that we might have life, and have it more abundantly (John 10:10), he of course was referring to the way he made full union with God — something known only after death — possible. But life on earth can also be lived more or less fully. Though we commonly think of life in either/or terms — you are either alive or dead — life is also a qualitative state. Indeed, the virtuous life is a fuller life. That is why it leads to happiness. Full happiness (fullness of life) may only be achievable beyond the grave, when there will be no more suffering, sin, and death. But life can be more or less full, i.e., happy, even on this side of the grave.

It should now be clear how this understanding of eternal life is more intrinsically related to this life. Living according to the gospel in this life is not done simply because God commands it or because God has (seemingly arbitrarily) decided to reward such living with a blissful afterlife. The virtuous life is a foretaste of, a very participation in, eternal life. It is impossible to fully live heaven on earth due to ongoing sickness, suffering, death, and sinfulness (including societal injustices). But if the God of love

13. See *Catechism of the Catholic Church,* 2nd ed. (1997), 946-62.

is a Triune communion of persons who calls us into a fellowship of self-giving love with God and each other, then to the extent we heed that call even in this life, we live fully and eternally. To the extent that we love one another, forgive one another, participate in communities, and build institutions that are life-giving, help alleviate others' suffering, etc., we are living more abundantly even now in this life, actually tasting eternal life.

What has any of this to do with hope? Hope, we recall, inclines us to yearn for union with God as complete fulfillment and happiness, and to trust in God's help in achieving it. How one understands the relation between this life and the eternal life for which one longs will impact what it looks like to hope. Recall the extrinsic view of the relation between this life and the next described above. One who has such a view may through the virtue of hope long to be with God in eternity, and trust in God's help to get there. Her hope, therefore, enables her to "keep her eyes on the prize" of true happiness and not be sidetracked by seeking ultimate fulfillment in the goods of this life. Out of hope for eternal reward she will follow the guidance of Christ and the church. And since it is difficult to long for what is not yet achieved, her hope will sustain her in this life, helping her endure while not yet attaining her ultimate destiny and filling her with confidence that God will reward her at the end of the race.

Once again, in many ways such a person lives a good, virtuous life. Her hope concerns a genuine good (in fact the ultimate good!) that is future and possible yet difficult. Her hope inclines her toward the true source of ultimate fulfillment, and toward the grace of God in making that fulfillment possible. Yet since she sees no intrinsic relation between this life and the next, there is no way for her hope to have any intrinsic relation to how she participates in this-worldly activities.

Once the relationship between eternal life and this-worldly activities is understood more intrinsically, we see the impact this has on our understanding of hope. Hope inclines us to yearn for God, both as our ultimate happiness and our help in attaining such a destiny. As to the first, we only properly hope in God. Yet we can also hope in other things, not in themselves but as referred to our ultimate happiness who is God. As St. Thomas says, "hope regards eternal happiness chiefly, and other things, for which we pray to God, it regards secondarily and as referred to eternal happiness."[14] We *can* be hopeful in worldly activities such as our jobs, re-

14. Aquinas, ST 2-2.17, 2 ad. 2.

lationships, and good causes. We long for them, but not as ultimately fulfilling, and always in a manner transformed by our seeking them ultimately for the sake of God. As to the second, we not only trust in God's help in attaining eternal life beyond this world, but also trust in God's grace to help us engage in this-worldly activities in a manner befitting our ultimate destiny of eternal union with God. What does such a hope look like in this-worldly activities?

The Hopeful Life: Specific Examples

How is all of this relevant to daily life now? One of the main points of the previous section was establishing an intrinsic connection between our actions in this life and our eternal destiny. In other words, the "content" (if you will) of eternal life as self-giving, loving communion of persons — with God and others — dictates that precisely such self-giving, loving communion is what the hopeful person desires as truly fulfilling even in this life, to the extent that this is possible. But how does being hopeful for that eternal destiny concretely shape our actions in this life?

Pleasures, Temperance, and the Virtue of Hope The virtue of temperance most properly concerns (especially sensual) pleasures such as eating, drinking, or sexual activity. The temperate person enjoys these activities in whatever manner best contributes to (rather than impedes) the person's overall human flourishing, or happiness. What, then, does hope have to do with how we enjoy these activities?

How often do we turn to alcohol, or food, or sexual intimacy to seek solace, to fill the restless longing we feel for happiness and completion? Doing so is not only a failure in temperance, but also entails a lack of hope. Recall some of the vices opposed to hope. One who has the vice of despair acts as if the complete fulfillment constituted by union with God is either non-existent or not possible for him. Unsurprisingly, he "settles." He may sadly think that the best he can do is find solace in the bottle, bedroom, or refrigerator. Of course, rarely do people consciously say this to themselves! But their actions with regard to these pleasurable activities reveal their vice of despair.

Another vice against hope is presumption. Unlike the person afflicted with despair, the person with presumption thinks that true fulfillment is not only possible but assured. She fails to see any relationship (or intrinsic connection) between her actions in this life and that eternal destiny, since she assumes — really presumes — that the latter is guaranteed. Therefore she goes on doing as she pleases with regard to pleasurable activities. We find such people mentioned in 1 Cor. 6:12-20, where Paul addresses those who think that their sexual activity, like the kind of food they eat, has nothing to do with their salvation. Paul is quite clear this is not the case.

How does the person of hope act in matters of direct concern to temperance? The person of hope enjoys pleasurable activities, but knows they do not offer complete happiness or fulfillment and so does not seek that in them. She engages in these activities, all the while understanding how they are intrinsically related to her final destiny. Thus how she eats, drinks, or has sex will only be in a manner that helps her continue on the journey toward union with God. (If engaging in any of these at all or in some way is a detour off of that journey, then she does not do so!) In one sense, the person of hope is "detached" from the activity, not needing it since she knows it is not her "be all and end all." In another sense it is the person of hope (and of course temperance) who can most fully enjoy the activity, because she does not expect it to "save" her, and it is engaged only in a manner that it serves as part of her journey toward union with God.

One more observation is warranted about the impact of hope on one's sensual pleasures. At times, despite one's faith and hope and love, the flesh is weak. One is tempted to drink or eat too much, or engage in sexual activity that is not part of one's path to genuine union with God (and others). Though these temptations (and any ensuing failures) are first and foremost matters of temperance, the virtue of hope can be of crucial assistance here. Despite not "feeling" that way at the moment, we people of hope can remind ourselves that the pleasure at hand will not fulfill the longings we have. That one more drink, another sweet, or another sexual encounter is actually not what we are ultimately longing for — even as we are in the moment longing for them! Hope can help us here. Hope fixes our eyes on the true prize, on what will truly fulfill us. Recall also that hope not only fixes us toward God as our fulfillment, but also as the one who makes it possible to be with him. And thus in such moments when we feel powerless to resist, hope also assures us that God's grace is indeed available and can enable us to resist our temptation. Such resistance is difficult for sure. In such moments we are acutely aware that we are still travelers on the way to full happiness. But the virtue of hope not only points us to our true destination but is also given graciously by God to sustain us on the way. Hope is a potent virtue indeed in the moral life!

Relationships with Others, Justice, and the Virtue of Hope It is the cardinal virtue of justice that disposes a person to good relations with others. Often when we hear the term "justice" we think of law and the courts, and these are indeed one arena of justice. But the virtue of justice has traditionally been understood to include any interpersonal relations, including friendships, family, and romantic relationships as well as more broadly societal ones. What does hope have to do with our relationships with others, which are first and foremost a matter of justice?

Perhaps it is easiest to start with romantic relationships since the dynamics are most obvious there. How often do we place all our hope in those with whom we are in love? Particularly in our culture, romantic love is so often regarded as the source of true happiness. We hear young people saying, "She's all I need," or "He's all I could ever want." Or, as the protagonist of the movie *Jerry Maguire* famously says to his love-interest, Dorothy Boyd, "You complete me."

Well what is wrong with all this? Are Christians opposed to romantic love? Of course not. But the Scriptures warn us clearly against placing all our hopes in man (Jer. 17:5). And the attitudes described here seem to idolatrously place the beloved as one's "be all and end all," in effect, as one's god. What has this to do with hope? For whatever reason (a lack of faith? shame at one's brokenness?), the person does not think the true complete happiness constituted by union with God is possible for her. So she seeks it in a substitute that is not bad in itself, but surely not up to the task of complete fulfillment. And when the relationship does not completely satisfy her (as even the best marriage cannot), there is further reason to despair, or even foolishly seek that elusive complete happiness in another relationship with someone else.

What does the hopeful person look like in such relationships? First and foremost, she does not expect her romantic relationship to "complete her." The relationship is part of her path toward union with God, otherwise she would not be in it. It is a part of the journey, and not the goal. The hopeful person is therefore in one sense detached, or put more colloquially, not as "needy" in the relationship. This is not because she is apathetic in the negative sense of uncaring and distant. To the contrary, the hopeful person is actually free to be engaged in the relationship, fully present in each moment, simultaneously knowing it need not meet the impossible demand of providing complete fulfillment, *and* that nonetheless the relationship is intrinsically related to her final destiny and not something simply to "endure" until that destiny is reached. The hopeful person also knows she has in the virtue of hope the gift of God's grace to sustain her during those inevitable difficult times, whether they be failures on the part of her spouse (neglect, cruelty, unfaithfulness) or unfortunate circumstances that befall the couple (sickness, job loss, death in the family). Ironically, by not desperately (as in "despair") and idolatrously placing all her hope in a relationship, the person of hope is more free to love the other and find true (even if not ultimate) fulfillment in the relationship.

The influence of hope can also be seen on relationships of justice on a far larger scale, as in the political arena. Consider briefly the example of Martin Luther King, Jr. Anyone who has read his writings knows how he regarded his work in pursuit of social justice and racial equality as intimately intertwined with his Christian faith and desire for the establishment of the kingdom of God. For King, God's kingdom was not merely some "otherworldly" affair. His hope (and faith and love) were the engines that drove his pursuit of justice. How was he hopeful? King surely was not presumptuous, by assuming (again, really presuming) that all would work out fine in the next life regardless of what happened in this one. Nor did he desperately regard this life as the last "hope" for humanity. Instead, by both recognizing God's kingdom as our ultimate destiny and recognizing the intrinsic connection between this life and that kingdom, King was free enough to be fully engaged in his cause. He could commit himself wholly to the cause without burning out, or becoming hateful out of impatience with those who were resisting his changes. He could also trust in God's grace not only to bring people — black and white — to eternal life beyond this world, but also help transform their existence in this world to better conform to God's kingdom.

Facing Difficulties, Fortitude, and the Virtue of Hope Fortitude (which is synonymous with courage and bravery) enables people to face difficulties well, and the paradigmatic difficulty in life is death. The brave person faces death well, be it a death on the battlefield, martyrdom, or death as a result of a ravaging illness. How does hope assist someone during occasions requiring bravery? Though it is not the paradigmatic case of fortitude, which would be having one's own life threatened, let us examine how people endure the loss of a loved one to see what difference hope makes. It is a topic infrequently treated and yet of crucial importance. It is also one where what is commonly assumed to be Christian hope might actually not be the fullness of hope described here.

When a loved one dies it takes great fortitude to go on. This virtue enables one not to be crushed by the loss while mourning the loved one. The brave person sees accurately the real loss that has occurred, but is not overcome by that loss. What role does hope play in one's grieving? The person of hope knows that ultimate fulfillment is not available in this life. One of the main reasons for this claim is the reality of death. Though true and beautiful fulfillment can indeed be known in this life such as in our relationships with loved ones, one of the reasons such joy is not complete in this life is the fact that people die. And the complete fulfillment we long for has no end.

Of course, central to Christian faith is the belief that death is not the definitive end of a life. And so it is common to hear Christians who lose a loved one — or Christians speaking to those who have lost a loved one — assuring others that they know their loved one is just fine, and remaining "all smiles" after such a loss. It is as if the destiny in which they hope eclipses all sense of loss and suffering in this life. This seemingly powerful hope, however, is often a mask for a deeper lack of hope. Or better, it is a hope that reflects an extrinsic relationship between eternal life and this life.

The person of hope does indeed trust that God conquers sin and death, and that what the church has witnessed in Christ is also God's plan for each of us. The person described in the previous paragraph agrees with this, and thus has true hope. Yet our God of life is not just a God of life beyond this world, but of all life. And death is antithetical to life, even if God in his love and mercy brings new life out of death. The hopeful person does not fail to recognize that death is evil (even in the "best" of circumstances, such as a heroic death or an end of suffering). Grief at the loss of life is not only excusable but perfectly appropriate, and also compatible with hope that the beloved will enjoy eternal life. Indeed, the death of a loved one is a reminder of the void that could lead us to despair, but also of the unimaginably gracious and beautiful promise of eternal life. Furthermore, the person of fullest hope trusts in God's grace not only to bring the beloved to eternal life, but also to sustain the grieving as they experience one of the most painful reminders that life on earth is not the complete fulfillment for which we long.

Conclusion

We have indeed come a long way from this chapter's opening words on the simple and obvious goodness of hope. A deeper inquiry into what exactly constitutes hope reveals that Christian hope is radical. It is a virtue, and not just a passing feeling. But even more radically, it is rooted in extraordinary truths of the Christian faith about the nature of God and what God has in store for us. The person who possesses what Christians understand to be the infused theological virtue hope stands as a witness to who God is and to what a life of discipleship to Jesus Christ looks like. As should now be clear, though hope most properly concerns a destiny achieved only in the next life, hope is indeed a virtue for this life. People of Christian hope not only "endure" this life while awaiting the next, but also live this life in a manner that is transformed by hope. In doing so, they witness to and experience a foretaste of eternal life in the here and now, "having life, and having it more abundantly."

Questions for Further Reflection

1. Think about all the various occasions where we use the word "hope" in everyday life. How would the vision of hope presented in this chapter change, if at all, what you mean when you say you "hope" for things?

2. The Scripture famously teaches us that cursed is the one who hopes in man (Jer. 17:5), but blessed, or happy, is the one who trusts in the Lord (Jer. 17:7; Ps. 37:3). How do you understand these passages in light of this chapter?

3. Why is it important that hope be understood as a habit (in this case a virtue) and not simply a feeling? What are some of the important characteristics of a habit?

4. Think of some examples of how Christians may speak or act that

(perhaps unwittingly) reveal the belief that there is an *extrinsic* relationship between this life and the next. How would an *intrinsic* understanding of that relationship lead them to speak or act differently?

5. Give several examples of how hope transforms everyday activities in this life.

Contentment

Steve L. Porter

Introduction

For quite some time a particular passage in St. Paul's letter to the church in Philippi has been lodged in my mind. In thanking the Philippian church for providing for his needs while he was imprisoned in Rome, Paul puts forth the following:

> I am not saying this [that is, "thanks"] because I am in need, for I have learned to be content whatever the circumstances. I know what it is to be in need, and I know what it is to have plenty. I have learned the secret of being content in any and every situation, whether well fed or hungry, whether living in plenty or in want. I can do everything through him who gives me strength (Phil 4:11-13, NIV).

This passage has remained with me because Paul's claim seems so "out-of-this-world." Has he really learned to be content in whatever his circumstances? What would life be like for someone who could honestly say that? As I reflect on my own experience, discontent abounds and contentment often goes unrealized. Whether I am discontent with traffic on the freeway, with my financial situation, with my neighbor's parking habits, with a lingering cold, with my inability to shed a few pounds, with the amount of work I accomplish in a day, I find myself hardly able to imagine what it would be like to possess an inner peace or contentment in the midst of troubling circumstances. And yet, that is exactly what Paul is suggesting. He is not suggesting that with Christ things always go his way, but that whether or not things go his way, he has learned to respond with a peaceful repose towards them. This has brought me to wonder what Paul learned regarding contentment. Assuming that contentment is part of the good life, how is it that contentment can be more fully realized?

I argue in this chapter that contentment is not only a dimension of the good life but that it also qualifies as a virtue — and that there is a peculiarly Christian way to bring it about. In fact, if Paul is right, ultimate contentment can only be found through the strengthening presence of Jesus Christ. I first turn to the nature of contentment, then deal with contentment as a virtue. Lastly, I focus on the manner in which contentment may be spiritually formed.

The Nature of Contentment

As with many complex psychological states, the nature of contentment is difficult to pin down. Our intuitions about and experiences with what might be called "contentment" vary considerably.[1] As a rough characterization, consider the following: contentment is the psychological state or disposition of being at peace towards one's circumstances. Contentment is a *psychological state or disposition* in that it is an inner attitude or frame of mind either occurent at a point in time or prone to arise at any given point in time. Contentment is a psychological state or disposition of *being at peace* in that the attitude is one of tranquil acceptance or peaceful repose. And contentment is a psychological state or disposition of being at peace *towards one's circumstances* in that in the case of contentment the attitude of being at peace is always directed towards some specific situation. We are content with *this* or *that,* even if the object of contentment is our life as a whole. So, to put it more fully, contentment is an inner attitude or frame of mind, either occurent at a point in time or prone to arise at any given point in time, of tranquil acceptance or peace-

1. I completely agree with Thomas L. Carson: "In view of the extreme vagueness of the concept of contentment (how much less than perfectly contented must a person be before we say that he is discontented with something?) it would be foolish for me to try to make this account any more precise than it is." Thomas L. Carson, "Happiness, Contentment, and the Good Life," *Pacific Philosophical Quarterly* 62 (1981): 380.

ful repose towards some specific situation.[2] Once contentment is characterized in this manner, discontent can be thought of as an inner attitude of frustration or agitation towards one's circumstances.

To sharpen our focus on the nature of contentment, let's explore the relationship between contentment and satisfaction.[3] Let's suppose that a person is satisfied with *x* when that person's desires about *x* are fulfilled. I am satisfied with my financial stability when my desires for financial stability are realized and I am *dis*satisfied when my desires for financial stability go unfulfilled. On this understanding of satisfaction and dissatisfaction, the contented person is not necessarily the satisfied person. And perhaps more often than not contentment is called for in the face of some amount of dissatisfaction. We struggle to find contentment (that is, an inner, peaceful repose) precisely when our desire is for things to be other than they are (that is, we are dissatisfied). The contented soul is able to accept calmly the otherwise unsatisfactory state of affairs. I may not be satisfied with my financial stability, but I may nonetheless be content regarding this undesirable instability. My spouse, on the other hand, may not only be dissatisfied but also discontent (that is, frustrated and agitated about it).

Further, it seems that contentment is not always present in satisfying circumstances. The usual case, no doubt, is that when we are satisfied with *x* we are also content with *x* (that is, our desires for *x* are fulfilled and we have a peaceful repose towards *x*). But it is also conceivable to be satisfied with *x* and nonetheless discontent with *x*. That is, our desires for *x* are fulfilled but we do not have a peaceful repose towards *x*. Certainly we have the experience of getting what we desire, finding that there is something further we lack, and then experiencing discontent with the newly realized dissatisfaction. But it also seems possible to be completely satisfied in certain respects and yet still discontent in those very same respects. I am thinking, for instance, of the billionaire on his luxury yacht in the Mediterranean who can't sit still and enjoy the pleasures that surround him. Servants cater to his every whim, and yet he is discontent. Apparently, his discontentment is not due to some unsatisfied desire. His

2. On a rough distinction between "peace" and "contentment," see Robert C. Roberts, *Spiritual Emotions: A Psychology of Christian Virtues* (Grand Rapids: Eerdmans, 2007), p. 166.

3. I depart here from Carson, who seems to identify the concept of contentment with being satisfied ("Happiness," pp. 380-82).

discontent is directed solely upon his present satisfying circumstances. He lacks the peaceful repose, the calm acceptance of his current, satisfied state of being. My intuition is that just as one can be dissatisfied with *x* and yet content with *x*, the opposite relation also holds: one can be satisfied with *x* and yet discontent with *x*. With contentment we are looking for something beyond mere satisfaction with our circumstances: we are looking for the ability to possess an inner peace towards those circumstances. Whatever the ingredient of contentment that makes it possible in unsatisfactory circumstances is, presumably, the same ingredient that can be missing in satisfactory circumstances.

But whatever we conclude about whether discontent is possible in times of satisfaction, the case of greater interest is the experience of contentment in times of dissatisfaction. Dissatisfaction with various features of our lives is typically a frustrating experience and so the attainment of contentment in these times is both appealing and in need of explanation. Of course, this assumes that contentment is a good worth pursuing, which leads us to examine the notion that contentment is a virtue.

Contentment as a Virtue

The claim that contentment is a virtue gets one into all sorts of trouble. The nature of a virtue and what traits count as virtues are much disputed.[4] The case of contentment is all the more troubling because contentment is not found on any standard lists of virtues. There is very little historical presumption in its favor. The weightiest authority on all matters virtuous, Aristotle, does not countenance anything like contentment on his standard lists.[5] Not even Hume, who famously has the most generous list of virtues, finds room for contentment.[6] Indeed, the best I could

4. For a discussion of some of these issues, see Daniel Statman, "Introduction to Virtue Ethics," *Virtue Ethics: A Critical Reader*, ed. Daniel Statman (Washington, DC: Georgetown University Press, 1997), pp. 19-20.

5. While patience may be akin to contentment, it is distinct from contentment. I can be discontent with traffic but nonetheless patient as I sit through it. It is often the case that a content person will also be a patient person. Here, I would suggest, patience emerges under the influence of contentment. We can be patient when we are content but it is difficult to be patient when we are discontent.

6. See, for instance, James Fieser, "Hume's Wide View of the Virtues: An Analysis

come up with is that "tranquility" appears as virtue number eleven on a list of thirteen virtues developed at age 20 by Benjamin Franklin. Franklin's maxim regarding tranquility is: "Be not disturbed at trifles, or at accidents common or unavoidable."[7]

With all due respect to Franklin, something else must be said in favor of categorizing contentment as a virtue. Much depends on whether one regards a virtue as a teleological or a non-teleological reality. Rosalind Hursthouse has a teleological conception of the virtues. She understands a virtue as "a character trait a human being needs to flourish or live well."[8] Under such a teleological account, a trait counts as a virtue only if it is a constituent of or means to a preconceived notion of the good life. On a non-teleological account of the virtues, a virtue is good in and of itself, whatever connection it may have to human flourishing.[9] For instance, Robert Adams offers such an account, identifying virtue with "persisting excellence in being for the good."[10] Without the *telos* of human flourishing operating as a criterion of what counts as a virtue, some other means is required to determine whether a particular trait is a virtue. While I think there are good grounds for maintaining that there is a concept of what it is for human persons to flourish and that the virtues are partly constitutive of that flourishing, this teleological conception of human nature does not entail a teleological account of the virtues. That is, it does not follow from the claim that human nature has a *telos* (which includes virtuous living) that a virtue is only good because it contributes to the *telos.* Rather, a virtue can be intrinsically good and, for that very reason, be partly constitutive of human flourishing. But whichever account one prefers, the shared conception is that a virtue is an excellence of human

---

of His Early Critics," *Hume Studies* 24 (1998): 295-311. Contentment or tranquility would be, for Hume, considered a "monkish virtue." See Elizabeth Dimm, "Hume and the Monkish Virtues," *Philosophical Investigations* 10 (1987): 212-25.

7. Benjamin Franklin, *The Autobiography of Benjamin Franklin,* Touchstone edition (New York: Simon & Schuster, 2003), p. 60.

8. Rosalind Hursthouse, "Virtue Theory and Abortion," *Philosophy and Public Affairs* 20 (1991): 226. Reprinted in Statman, ed., *Virtue Ethics Reader,* pp. 227-44.

9. For a helpful discussion of teleological and non-teleological accounts, see Linda Tinkaus Zagzebski, *Virtues of the Mind* (Cambridge: Cambridge University Press, 1996), pp. 78-84.

10. Robert Merrihew Adams, *A Theory of Virtue: Excellence in Being for the Good* (Oxford: Oxford University Press, 2006), p. 6.

character, either intrinsically so or due to its connection with some larger vision of human excellence.[11]

On this minimal understanding of a virtue, contentment counts as a virtue: it is a human excellence. The content person is ready to face circumstances of any kind with a peaceful repose. All else being equal, wouldn't we prefer to go through life with contentment rather than discontent, and don't we admire those who are able to be at peace in the face of difficult circumstances? Consider the following two cases:

> Case #1: Two graduating seniors are both applying for Ph.D. programs in philosophy. Both are uncertain about whether they will be accepted into the programs to which they have applied, both are diligently doing everything in their power to gain acceptance, and both are hopeful that they will receive some acceptance letters. But one of the two students does all this out of a place of contentment, while the other is discontent. That is, the content student is at peace with the uncertainties and is calmly open to whatever the outcome will be, while the discontent student is frustrated by the uncertainties and ponders the possible future outcomes with great agitation.
>
> Case #2: A father is waiting for his three-year-old son to get into his car seat so that he can buckle him in and get on with the drive to the store. But before settling into his seat, the boy collects a few books, rolls up the window on the opposite side of the car, and dilly-dallies in numerous other quasi-ritualistic ways before sitting down in his seat. Rather than experiencing agitation and frustration towards his son's behavior, the father calmly accepts the inefficiency of life with a three-year-old.

It seems quite clear that contentment is a good in both cases — that the content student and the content father are both better persons precisely because of their contentment. Notice, contentment is consistent with the student's diligent efforts to get accepted to her preferred school. And contentment is consistent with the parent's act of encouraging his son to hurry along or even setting consequences for further delays. The difference contentment makes is that the attempts to change one's circum-

11. Zagzebski writes that, "The central idea that virtue is an excellence has never been seriously questioned." *Virtues,* p. 85.

stances are not fueled by inner frustration and agitation. In other words, contentment is not apathy and does not endorse passivity. The content person can be actively involved in bettering her own life or the lives of others, all the while experiencing contentment (that is, inner tranquility) in those very circumstances. What motivates the pursuit of change is not discontent, but rather a vision that things could or should be better.

This brings up an important objection to the notion that contentment is generally a good. Allowing that in some situations contentment is good, we might wonder: what about contentment in the face of some sort of injustice? Shouldn't we be *dis*content with child abuse, racial discrimination, drug addiction, extreme poverty, our own vices, and the like?

The easy thing to say is that we should not be content with morally bad states in the same way that we should not be patient with injustice, generous when it comes to supporting immoral causes, or courageous in wrongdoing. We might say that these kinds of traits are only morally virtuous when they are exercised in the right situation. But when it comes to contentment this response is particularly problematic, for contentment in the midst of morally bad circumstances (for example, an injustice towards one's self) stands out as a paradigm case of the goodness of contentment. St. Paul, for instance, had learned the secret of being content in the poor conditions of an unjust prison sentence. He was not agitated or frustrated by his lot, but was able to be at peace with his situation all the while making efforts to better his situation (that is, to correct the injustice). Would he have been better off to be in these conditions *and* experience agitation regarding them? Recall what is meant by contentment. We should not be content with child abuse, for instance, if what we mean by contentment is a passive resignation to that situation. But it seems to me that such resignation is better called apathy or indifference than contentment, and such a response would be vicious, not virtuous. But actual contentment is compatible with caring deeply about and working passionately to change one's own or others' circumstances. Indeed, we might be morally outraged about an injustice, have trouble sleeping at night until the injustice is remedied, expend all of our energy in seeking justice, and nonetheless experience a peaceful repose towards that circumstance. We might think here of the Sister of Charity who has inner peace regarding her work with the impoverished conditions of thousands in Calcutta, though she works tirelessly to improve those conditions. Again, would it be better for the Sister of Charity to work to improve poverty with an attitude of agitation and frustration? There is much to be said for the contented social reformer (such as Mahatma Gandhi) over and against the frustrated and agitated social reformer.[12]

The putative goodness of contentment in morally bad situations sets in relief the question as to the moral nature of contentment. For while it may be granted that contentment is a human excellence in at least some circumstances, we are interested in whether it is a distinctly *moral* virtue. While distinguishing moral values or qualities from non-moral ones is no simple task, perhaps we can surface the moral quality of contentment by considering character traits psychologically connected with contentment and discontentment.[13] For instance, the inner frustration and agitation of the discontent heart would be a state of the soul that would engender worry, envy, jealousy, and malice. When we are frustrated with our own circumstances we do not tend to think favorably about others nor desire to further their good, especially if they are responsible for our unfavorable circumstances. Discontentment is not a morally neutral response but rather is a frame of mind from which various vices flow. Alternatively, contentment appears to be the breeding ground for such qualities as patience, gratitude, generosity, compassion, and kindness. The content heart does not get caught up in the undesirability of its own lot and consequently is more able to look to the good of others. This is not to say that the moral quality of contentment is due to its utility, but rather that the connection between contentment and various identifiable virtues as well as the connection between discontent and various identifiable vices helps demonstrate that contentment is a moral attitude. For whatever virtuous states tend to flow

12. Consider the example of Jesus driving out those buying and selling in the temple courts and overturning the tables of the moneychangers (Matt. 21:12-13). The text says nothing about Jesus' emotional or attitudinal state when he did this. We might imagine he was angry as he sought to make a point regarding the corrupt spirituality of first-century temple worship. But was he discontent with his situation? It seems fair to say that he was content within himself regarding his own role in purifying the temple, but he was angry and stood against what was happening in his Father's house. Perhaps his inner peaceful repose is evident when immediately following the clearing of the temple (according to Matthew's narrative), the blind and the lame move towards him to be healed (Matt. 21:14).

13. For a discussion of the distinction between moral and non-moral values, see Harold N. Lee, "The Differentia of Moral Value," *International Journal of Ethics* 41 (1931): 222-29.

from contentment or vices from discontentment, a pervasive attitude of peaceful acceptance of the vagaries of life (particularly during difficult times) is a morally admirable and preferable state of being.

The Formation of Contentment

This brings us to the final and really most crucial issue: the unique resources that Christians possess for the formation of contentment. Our analysis of contentment suggests that the virtue of contentment is particularly commendable in the face of unfulfilled desires. While the satisfaction of all one's felt-desires may not guarantee contentment, contentment is certainly more of a struggle when one's felt-desires go unsatisfied. The challenge is to be content when things are not going the way we want. The question for the formation of contentment is: how can one remain content even in the face of unfulfilled desires — even unfulfilled desires that are rather central to a one's well-being?

Perhaps the most prominent theory of virtue formation, stemming from Aristotle, is what might be called formation by emulation. Daniel Statman presents the theory as follows:

> appealing to some paradigmatic personality who exemplifies the virtues in an extraordinary way appears to be the only available way to understand and apply the virtues. . . . Becoming a good person is not a matter of learning or "applying" principles, but of imitating some models. We learn to be virtuous the same way we learn to dance, to cook, and to play football — by watching people who are competent in these areas, and trying to do the same.[14]

But how exactly is emulation supposed to bring about change? At times it might be suggested that merely being with persons of virtuous character over time (either in-person or through writings) "rubs off" on the one in need of formation.[15] Certainly role-models have some sort of impact, but

14. Statman, "Introduction," pp. 10, 13.

15. For a critique of this conception of moral education, see Kristján Kristjánsson, "Emulation and the Use of Role Models in Moral Education," *Journal of Moral Education* 35 (2006): 37-49.

in terms of *formational* power, simple exposure to paradigmatically virtuous persons seems only to reflect the general sociological pattern that we tend to believe and behave in ways similar to those around us. This emphasizes the importance of community in formation, but we might reasonably wonder whether there is something more to emulation than just role-modeling.[16]

Indeed, a second way of understanding formation by emulation (which is more faithful to Aristotle) is that we ask, witness, or imagine what the virtuous person would do in a certain situation and *attempt to do likewise.* By the intentional practice of virtuous actions, we become habituated in the virtues. As Aristotle puts it: "For the things we have to learn before we can do them, we learn by doing them . . . we become just by doing just acts, temperate by doing temperate acts, brave by doing brave acts."[17] Harold Alderman puts the point this way: "The ordinary moral agent, not possessing paradigmatic character, must emulate the *actions* of some moral exemplar in order to acquire that character."[18]

But what are the actual dynamics of this "practice-habituation" model of formation by emulation? On Myles Burnyeat's reading of Aristotle, through the repeated performance of the virtuous act we: (1) learn how to do the act; (2) perceive the goodness of the act (that it is indeed virtuous); (3) experience appropriate pleasure in doing the act; and (4) develop the desire to do the act for the sake of the goodness of it.[19] The key point is that in perceiving the goodness of the virtuous act we

16. This is not to say that the sole or even main role of community in formation is role-modeling. For instance, various psychological theories would propose that the manner in which parents relate to their children (consistently, warmly, compassionately) has far more impact on their emotional, intellectual, and, therefore, moral and spiritual development than whether the parent is a paragon of virtue. Of course, it is difficult to parent in the way suggested if the parent is lacking in certain virtues, but the point is that the role of community in virtue formation might have far more to do with emotional attachment than moral modeling. For an example of such a theory, see Daniel J. Siegel, *The Developing Mind: How Relationships and the Brain Interact to Shape Who We Are* (New York: Guilford, 2001).

17. Aristotle, *Nicomachean Ethics* 2.1.

18. Harold Alderman, "By Virtue of a Virtue," in Statman, ed., *Virtue Ethics Reader,* p. 160.

19. M. F. Burnyeat, "Aristotle on Learning to Be Good," *Essays on Aristotle's Ethics,* ed. Amélie Oksenberg Rorty (Berkeley: University of California Press, 1980), pp. 74, 76-78, 87-88.

consequently experience an appropriate pleasure in doing the act — the pleasure that comes from doing a virtuous act in a virtuous way. This enjoyment of the act leads to a habituated desire to do virtuous acts and we eventually do them for their own sake. In other words, by doing virtuous acts in a virtuous way a settled, virtuous character is formed. Burnyeat states that the ultimate goal of practicing the virtues is that the practitioner "should become the sort of person who does virtuous things in full knowledge of what he is doing, choosing to do them for their own sake, and acting out of a settled state of character."[20]

Unfortunately, the proposed mechanism by which practice and habituation is supposed to bring about virtue is problematic. The overarching problem is the connection between doing virtuous acts without a fully formed virtuous character and the supposed subsequent formation of such a character. That is, we can do virtuous acts for non-virtuous reasons/motives/desires and what becomes habituated, then, is not a virtuous character but a non-virtuous one. For instance, I can do brave acts, look outwardly brave, and become habituated to respond in brave manners and all the while possess a deep cowardice. Even though I am sincerely intent on becoming brave, my habituated brave acts continue to be the result of my attempt to overcome my cowardice rather than the result of an inner proclivity to respond bravely. Or, I can do kind acts towards my wife, look outwardly kind, and become habituated to respond to her in kind ways and all the while be thinking about how she owes me kindness in return. I am not in possession of a kind character. Rather, I have a self-absorbed character that nevertheless manifests itself in acts that appear kind. As these examples suggest, the outward practice of virtuous acts does not always (or even regularly?) translate into the inner reality of virtuous character. The outward practice of virtuous acts without virtuous character can just as easily habituate non-virtuous character as it can virtuous character.[21]

Burnyeat would no doubt respond, on behalf of Aristotle, that what habituates virtuous character rather than non-virtuous character is the

20. Burnyeat, "Aristotle," p. 73.

21. Robert Adams has a similar concern about this Aristotelian view. Such a view of formation, Adams states, "relies heavily on incentives less clearly virtuous" and for this reason he is pessimistic about "engineering" virtuous motives. See his *Theory of Virtue,* p. 219.

proper enjoyment that accrues from a virtuous act done in a virtuous manner. Burnyeat writes:

> the delight of the temperate man who is pleased to be abstaining from overindulgence, or that of the brave man who is pleased to be standing up to a frightful situation, is not the same or the same in kind as the pleasure of indulgence or the relief of safety. The character of one's pleasure depends on what is enjoyed, and what the virtuous man enjoys is quite different from what the nonvirtuous enjoy. . . . What the virtuous man enjoys . . . is the practice of the virtues undertaken for its own sake.[22]

This is to say that the proper enjoyment of a virtuous act is dependent on that act being done in a virtuous manner — that is, its being done for its own sake. The proper enjoyment of the virtuous act done out of a virtuous character is what brings to light the pleasure of the act and the resultant desire to do the act for its own sake. So it is only when a virtuous act is done out of a virtuous character that it becomes habituated for virtuous reasons.

But now we have a more serious problem with the practice-habituation theory of formation. It appears that this purported process of virtue formation requires that the virtue being sought is already present in the practitioner. Needless to say, the whole point of this model of formation is that the practice of virtuous acts without the requisite virtuous character is supposed to bring about virtuous character. But such practice can only do so when the virtuous act already proceeds from virtuous character. That is, on this view one already needs the virtue in place in order to bring about that very virtue. Obviously, the repeated performance of virtuous acts out of a virtue already possessed would reinforce and habituate that virtue, but it is unclear how such a process could form virtue from scratch. Howard Curzer makes the point that this view not only requires virtue to already be in place in order for it to be habituated, but that in cases when the virtue is not already in place, proper enjoyment of the virtuous act does not occur. Therefore, virtuous acts are not reinforced. Curzer puts the critique as follows: "learners [of virtue] do not learn that virtuous acts are pleasant by performing and enjoying them,

22. Burnyeat, "Aristotle," p. 77.

because learners do not enjoy them. Indeed, virtuous action is painful for learners. It certainly does not positively reinforce the desire to perform virtuous acts. . . . Virtuous acts are typically not even overall pleasant for these less-than-virtuous people."[23]

It appears that practicing virtuous acts will only habituate virtuous character if the character is already present. But if the virtues are not already present then there is no guarantee (or perhaps even likelihood) that the practice of virtuous actions will form virtuous rather than non-virtuous character. What the practice of virtuous action does is to habituate whatever characterlogical state is already present, whether that state is virtuous or non-virtuous.

A further problem for Aristotle's practice-habituation model (at least as interpreted by Burnyeat) is that the theory is strained in cases like contentment. How do we practice acts of contentment when contentment is more attitudinal than behavioral? Is there such a thing as content acts without the attitude of contentment? In order to practice contentment, do I simply bite my tongue or take a deep breath when I am actually frustrated with my circumstances? Those actions may help, but is that the practice of content acts or is that engaging in certain practices that are meant to bring about certain states that lead to contentment?

The general difficulty with Aristotle's practice-habituation theory of emulation is that undertaking virtuous behavior in order to bring about virtuous character puts the cart before the horse. A central feature of virtue ethics is that virtuous character is foundational to and motivates right action. So it appears odd to commend right action unmotivated by virtuous character as a means to bring about virtuous character. Instead, what is needed is a theory of virtue formation that shows us how to develop the psychological states and dispositions (thoughts, beliefs, feelings, desires) which give rise to virtuous acts in the paradigmatically virtuous person so that we too can perform those acts in the way that the virtuous individual does. In other words, we don't practice the virtuous acts of the moral exemplar in order to get the exemplar's character. Rather, we practice the

23. Howard J. Curzer, "Aristotle's Painful Path to Virtue," *Journal of the History of Philosophy* 40 (2002): 149, 150. Curzer goes on to argue that Burnyeat's reading of Aristotle has a more serious fault as an account of virtue formation because "virtuous acts are *not* typically overall pleasant *even for the virtuous,* let alone for the learners" (p. 150).

lifestyle that made the exemplar the kind of person he or she is, in order to develop the same kind of virtuous character that the exemplar possesses.

Indeed, practice and habituation bring about virtue when an activity is engaged in that brings about the psychological states and dispositions which form the characterlogical basis for the virtue in question. For instance, the person who wants to have courage when facing the threat of physical assault could take a self-defense class. Notice, we do not recommend that the person practice courageous actions. Learning self-defense moves is not in and of itself a courageous act. It takes no courage to experience in a self-defense class that when the class instructor grabs you from behind there is an easy way to break free from such a grasp. But we can certainly see how courage may be fostered through such an activity. Presumably the person lacks courage (at least in part) because there is some doubt about his abilities to deal effectively with a physical assault. Once that doubt is relieved through the experience of becoming competent in self-defense, courage of a certain sort naturally begins to blossom. What has been practiced in this case is an activity that fosters a degree of confidence in one's self that sets the stage for courage. The courageous act would be performed out of a courageous character that was fostered through an activity which directly facilitates the production of such character. This is a quite different process than performing a virtuous act without virtuous character with the expectation that behavioral imitation will set in motion a process of character formation.

On this alternative view of virtue formation there is a practice-habituation process, but the practices are activities that are meant to give rise to certain psychological states and dispositions (thoughts, beliefs, feelings, desires) and what is habituated are these activities along with the resultant inner states and dispositions. Sounding a similar note, Curzer writes, "Aristotle cannot simply mean that people acquire [the] desire and ability [for virtuous action] merely be repeatedly acting rightly. The thoughts and feelings of the learner are a crucial part of the process."[24]

While much more needs to be said, the proposal is that what needs to be intentionally practiced are not the virtuous acts themselves but the activities of mind and body that foster the inner states and dispositions

24. Curzer, "Painful Path," p. 158. While I think Curzer is on to something and may have the correct interpretation of Aristotle (*pace* Burnyeat), I am not committed to Curzer's claim that fear and shame *(aidōs)* bring about virtue.

which give rise to virtuous acts. On this theory of virtue formation, we need to understand the inner resources that make a virtuous person virtuous and then seek to discover what activities that person engaged in or what activities could be engaged in to develop those inner resources. The crucial question is: what experiences and activities have made this person who he or she is and how might I engage in these sorts of experiences and activities such that I develop a similar type of character?

With this theory of virtue formation before us, how might such a modified view of emulation be applied to contentment? The key question will be: from whence does contentment arise in the contented soul? On one natural understanding of the psychological states and dispositions which give rise to contentment, contentment with an undesirable *x* is a product of being satisfied with *y*, where *y* involves one or more other valuable realities. In other words, we are psychologically able to be content with dissatisfactory circumstances when we are satisfied in other important ways and we struggle with contentment precisely when our overriding life experience is one of dissatisfaction. One writer helpfully puts it as follows: "When we go through life cultivating the ability to be grateful that it's not raining, that we are not sick, that we have good friends if not a lot of resources, and that we have found things we like to do, we are rich enough inside to sustain whatever we might lose around us."[25] The general idea is that the realization of certain fulfilled desires balances out or even outweighs one's unfulfilled desires so that one is able to remain content in times of dissatisfaction. For instance, I may have an unfulfilled desire to be married but remain content with my singleness because I have other relationships in my life (other fulfilled desires) that counterbalance that dissatisfaction. Perhaps another way to think about this is historically. I may have an unfulfilled desire for physical health (I have an incurable disease) but remain content because I have experienced good health for many years.[26]

Hence the formation of the virtue of contentment would involve practices of realizing, appreciating, and internalizing the various dimensions of goodness in one's life. This is why we often say in response to some dis-

25. Joan Chittister, *Becoming Fully Human: The Greatest Glory of God* (Lanham, MD: Rowman & Littlefield, 2005), p. 107.

26. This suggests that there is a deep interconnection between gratitude and contentment.

appointment: "it's not the end of the world," "it could have been worse," "look on the bright side," or "consider all the things that have gone well." Of course, it will not be enough to merely speak these types of sayings or even to simply reflect on these goods. One must actually *feel* the goodness of them such that the areas of discontent begin to pale in comparison.

The immediate problem with this view of the formation of contentment is that the putative countervailing goods (the fulfilled desires) are finite and unstable: they come and go, they can come into conflict with the attainment of other goods, and they may be outweighed by unfulfilled desires. Contentment attained in this way will always be dependent on the ups and downs of human life. It will be difficult to sustain a settled, unchangeable disposition of contentment when the goods of one's life are subject to the instability of human existence. This is especially so in those times when it *is* the end of the world, when things could *not* have been worse, when there is *not* a bright side, and when *nothing* has gone well. In such scenarios there are insufficient fulfilled desires to overcome one's unfulfilled desires. St. Paul's notion of contentment in all circumstances would certainly be out of reach.

This is where a distinction between natural contentment and Christian or supernatural contentment comes into play. Supernatural contentment, much like Aquinas's "infused virtues," is rooted in the infinite goodness of God.[27] Having one's ultimate desires fulfilled in the goodness of God is infinitely valuable and, at least on some views, unceasingly constant. If one begins to realize, appreciate, and internalize this greatest good, contentment in whatever circumstances would follow — even in circumstances in which there are little, if any, other satisfied desires. This realization, appreciation, and internalization is not just a cognitive process, but involves an in-depth experience and appropriation of the reality of God's goodness in one's life.[28]

This is, it seems, the natural interpretation of St. Paul's earlier cited text (Phil. 4:11-13). The "all things" that Paul can do through Christ's strength is precisely the ability to be content in all situations. The

27. Thomas Aquinas, *Summa Theologica* 1-2, q. 63, a. 3; and *Disputed Questions on Virtue,* a. 10. See Thomas F. O'Meara, "Virtues in the Theology of Thomas Aquinas," *Theological Studies* 58 (1997): 254-85.

28. On our need for God and the connection of realizing that need with virtue formation, see Roberts, *Spiritual Emotions.*

strengthening presence of Christ (that Paul elsewhere describes as being "rooted and established in [God's] love" [Eph. 3:17, TNIV]) makes up for any loss that Paul might experience. The writer of Hebrews makes much the same point: "Keep your lives free from the love of money and be content with what you have, because God has said, 'Never will I leave you; never will I forsake you'" (Heb. 13:5, TNIV). The same sentiment can be also found in Psalm 23:1-4: "The Lord is my shepherd, I lack nothing. He makes me lie down in green pastures. He leads me beside quiet waters, he refreshes my soul. . . . Even though I walk through the darkest valley, I will fear no evil, *for you are with me*" (TNIV, emphasis added). Once again, it appears to be the experience and appropriation of the presence of God in one's life — the fulfillment of those chief desires — that enables one to respond peacefully to otherwise troubling events.

Similar to the formation of natural contentment, the relevant practices for forming supernatural contentment will be disciplines that foster the realization, appreciation, and internalization of the many ways in which God is "for us."[29] The discipline of meditating on one's own life, the lives of other believers, spiritual readings, and biblical passages will be central, as will a discipline of conversational prayer which habituates one's orientation to the abiding presence of God in one's life. Since the goal of such disciplines is to form a deep confidence in and experience of God's loving presence in one's life, especially in the midst of difficult circumstances, some thoughtful reflection on the problem of evil may also prove helpful. And since there will be various cognitive, emotional, and spiritual obstacles to understanding and living in the fullness of the reality of God's "I will never leave you nor forsake you," the means of growing into such a place will be varied. Some might require therapy, dramatic experiences of answered prayer, prolonged times of solitude, fasting, intense theological study, experiences of God in worship, spiritual mentoring, and so on.[30] The immediate aim of

29. For more on spiritual practices, see Dallas Willard, *The Spirit of the Disciplines* (San Francisco: HarperCollins, 1989); and James Gould, "Becoming Good: The Role of Spiritual Practice," *Philosophical Practice* 1 (2005): 135-47.

30. Robert Adams is suggestive along this vein: "Excellence in being for the good involves having feelings and desires that respond appropriately to the good. . . . It is reasonable, I think, to seek resources in practices that are not purely intellectual; various forms of psychotherapy and of religious meditation come to mind." Adams, *Theory of Virtue,* p. 222.

these practices will not be to bring about the virtue of contentment but to bring about a deepening receptivity to the goodness of God, the realization, appreciation, and internalization of which brings about contentment in all circumstances.

Conclusion

In conclusion, it has been argued that the persisting disposition to remain content in undesirable circumstances is a dimension of virtuous character that can be brought about in both a natural and supernatural manner. The natural formation of contentment involves practices which help one realize, appreciate, and internalize the aspects of one's life that are satisfying so that the aspects that are unsatisfying are not as bothersome. The supernatural formation of contentment involves practices which help one realize, appreciate, and internalize the ultimate satisfaction of being rooted and grounded in God's love so that any other unsatisfying elements of life pale in comparison. The great good of "contentment in all circumstances" is possible only through satisfaction in a supernatural good that would outweigh dissatisfaction in all else. St. Paul's virtuous contentment was not a stoic *self*-sufficiency, but rather the sufficiency of the strengthening reality of Christ in his life. The degree to which this kind of contentment is available to us is dependent upon the degree to which we are able to practice means of receiving more deeply God's gracious operation in the human heart. What is habituated on this practice-habituation theory of formation is not contentment itself, but the practices that direct us to God's gracious and loving presence. As we live more and more in the fullness of that presence, contentment becomes the natural response to even the most undesirable of circumstances.

Questions for Further Reflection

1. What makes "contentment in all circumstances" a good worth pursuing?
2. What were the two main problems with Aristotle's practice-habituation model of change?
3. Explain the difference between the natural formation and super-

natural formation of contentment. Why are both important for the Christian?

4. Consider one or two specific practices that would foster contentment according to the theory of virtue formation presented in this chapter?

Courage

Rebecca Konyndyk DeYoung

There is probably no virtue that enjoys broader recognition across cultural and historical boundaries than courage. From ancient Greek and Eastern warriors to medieval knights, from the cowboys of the Wild West to American soldiers in overseas conflicts, in real life, myth, and film, courageous individuals are held up as heroes and bravery is valorized as a moral ideal. How should we think about these pictures of courage? What implications do different models of courage have on who we validate as having courage — e.g., the weak or the strong? In particular, who might we look to for examples of Christlike courage?

Courage is the virtue most directly concerned with strength and weakness, power and vulnerability, life and death. What will count as courage depends on what kinds of things ought to be feared, and feared most. Handling these concerns well is an essential task of the moral life; it is also a central issue in Scripture and in biblical injunctions about faithful living. Today, courage is perhaps better known as an American value than a Christian virtue, since it epitomizes qualities that Americans idealize: strength in adversity, believing in yourself against the odds, tough self-reliance. Developing a Christian conception of courage in conversation with these cultural ideals will require us to examine the dominant paradigms and definitions of courage, to explore links between fear and love as deep human motivations, and to sort through different views of human fear and power, to determine what may be considered virtuous and what vicious.

How do we learn what virtue is, and how do we learn to become virtuous? Often, we turn to a person who has the virtue, a person who embodies courage. We observe his or her character to learn what the virtue is like, and we imitate that person to become more virtuous ourselves. Christians take Jesus Christ as their model of the perfectly virtuous person. For centuries, Christians have understood moral formation as the imitation of Christ (Eph. 5:1).[1] Learning to become virtuous involves, among other things, trying to become more Christlike in our character. The apostle Paul describes this process as "taking off" our old sinful practices — the vices — and "clothing" ourselves with the virtues (Eph. 4:22-24; Col. 3:5-14).

Does taking Jesus Christ as our exemplar of courage make the Christian conception of this virtue different or distinctive? How does the courage of Jesus compare to the heroic ideals of courage found in ancient Greek epic poetry or in contemporary American films? If the courage of Christ is not the "heroic warrior" courage we are so familiar with, then what sort of courage would it be?[2] What sort of strength does Jesus embody, and how does it compare with human and worldly ideas of power? Our conclusions about courage as a virtue will depend on who we take to be our guiding patterns and ideals, and how these people practiced and embodied courage in their own lives.

In this chapter, I will describe a form of Christian courage that is different from the traditional heroic model. Although this alternative picture of courage affirms some things about conventional views of the virtue, it also challenges them and provides a warning about trusting human power to conquer evil, fear, and death. Drawing on the thought of Thomas Aquinas (1224/5-1274), I will first explain the different expressions of courage found, respectively, in the conventional action-adventure hero and in the Christian martyr. Aquinas's treatise on courage is a good place to think through various models of this virtue. Like us, Aquinas had to evaluate dominant cultural conceptions of courage he in-

1. Among many possible examples, we find that the title of Thomas à Kempis's well-known work, *The Imitation of Christ,* and the three traditional vows of those in religious orders (poverty, chastity, obedience) reflect just this conception of the moral or spiritual life. All biblical references are to the NRSV unless otherwise noted.

2. Early Christian desert ascetics commonly referred to themselves as "athletes" and "soldiers" of Christ, trained to fight in the arena; however, these terms designated spiritual contests with inner temptations and the demons standing behind them, not with other people. See, for example, John Cassian, *The Institutes,* trans. B. Ramsey, O.S.B., Ancient Christian Writers 58 (Mahwah, NJ: The Newman Press, 2000), Book V.

herited from the Greeks and Romans and decide what courage might look like from a Christian point of view. Aquinas argues that endurance and patient suffering — especially that of martyrdom — can be as courageous as the daring battlefield heroics typically lauded by Greek culture (and that are echoed in our own action-adventure films). As we will see, the key to his picture of courage is love, not human power. What unites the aggression of the hero and the endurance of the martyr as courage is their willingness to risk death for the sake of something they love. Section two of the chapter is thus devoted to explaining the connection between courage and love.

Using Aquinas's two forms of courage and their link to love as a foundation, I will then consider how courage looks in practice. How is the virtue of courage, as defined by the Christian tradition, embodied in a person and a life? To answer that question, I will offer three "character studies." I will consider J. K. Rowling's portrayal of Harry's death in *Harry Potter and the Deathly Hallows* as an expression of courage.[3] I will argue that her depiction of Harry fits within a long moral tradition which envisions courage as endurance. Comparing Harry to the conventional action-adventure hero and also to Voldemort — the antithesis of courage — gives us a more concrete and "fleshed out" picture of the relevant models of character and their strengths and weaknesses. In the end, it will be clear that both Aquinas's and Rowling's accounts of courage make fruitful test cases for the ways ancient and contemporary conceptions of courage must be transformed in order to capture a Christian view of this virtue, and that they agree on the fundamental character of courage.[4] I will conclude by answering a brief objection about the scope of courage's practical application in everyday life.

3. J. K. Rowling, *Harry Potter and the Deathly Hallows* (New York: Arthur A. Levine/Scholastic Books, 2007).

4. Aquinas's account of courage is found primarily in the *Summa Theologica* (hereafter ST) 2a2ae.123-40, especially qq. 123-24, a passage traditionally known as the treatise on courage. He also discusses fear in the treatise on the passions, ST 1a2ae.40-48 (on the irascible passions), and fear of God in ST 2a2ae.19. All translations are by the Fathers of the English Dominican Province (New York: Benziger Brothers, 1948; repr. Christian Classics, 1981).

Courage and Fear

The virtue of courage is most often defined by its regulation of fear. Courageous people need not be fearless, but they are not overcome by their fear. Rather, they have mastery over it — at least enough to persevere in doing some good or noble deed. To understand courage, therefore, we have to know something about fear. Aquinas first discusses fear as a reaction of the "irascible appetite." The irascible appetite is, roughly, our power to respond to obstacles, difficulties, and pain when they stand in the way of our attaining something good we desire. For example, I desire security, but a threatening noise in my house at 2 a.m. arouses fear. I desire that my children be treated with justice, but a playground bully sends them home bloodied and crying. To satisfy my desires for security and justice, to gain or regain my hold on those goods, I first have to face some evil or difficulty that stands in my way. My previous attachment to these goods — my love for my children and my desire to live in a home that is safe and secure — drives my perception of certain things as threatening and my visceral reactions to them.

Natural reactions like fear presuppose a world in which the things we want and need are threatened or blocked, or in which trying to acquire and hold onto good things involves struggle, hardship, and pain. Fear is one of several possible reactions to these evils that complicate our pursuit of the good; anger at the bully's threat to my children's well-being is another. In understanding and evaluating a reaction like fear, then, we must hold together in mind both the evil obstacle *and* the good it threatens.

How we respond to difficulty or evil depends on what that evil is, and what we care about, therefore, but it also depends on our character or virtue, since human beings can direct and train their fears and desires to follow reason. Aristotle calls the process of cultivating patterns of thought and feeling "habituation," that is, habit-formation.[5] The courageous person — as a person of virtue — is not someone who merely *happens* to handle fear well; she is someone who has been *trained* to handle fear well. How she reacts to fearful situations, what she fears, and how she expresses her fear can be deliberately shaped over time through practice.

To put it another way, human fears and desires arise in us naturally, but fearfulness in danger is more than a mere instinct, just as the desire for

5. Aristotle, *Nichomachean Ethics* 2.1–2.4, 1103a15-1105b15.

pleasure is not something we are compelled to give in to every time it is aroused. With the virtues — good habits or character traits — we can direct and perfect the expression of fear, desire, and other such reactions in ways that help us to flourish fully as human beings. For this, we need to use practical reason's "big picture" view of how this particular situation fits into our overall pursuit of the human good. An important part of formation in virtue, a life of cultivating Christlike character, is engaging in the sort of practices and disciplines that gradually align our initial reactions to accord more and more with this big-picture view of our good. Rather than letting fears interfere with our pursuit of what we love, then, we can with courage discipline them enough to enable that pursuit, or even see the good more clearly and pursue it more wholeheartedly and faithfully.

Think about Peter Pettigrew's fear in contrast to that of Harry Potter. Peter's fear leads him to betray those he loves. Peter does love his friends, but his fear of Voldemort overcomes that love. So he betrays his friends to save his own skin. Harry, in *The Deathly Hallows,* also experiences intense fear of death at Voldemort's hands. But his love for his friends leads him instead to face that fear and not to let it interfere with what he knows he must do to preserve what he loves. Fear can overwhelm us and our judgments about what is good. When left unchecked, fear can even reshape our vision of the world and the good. Pettigrew shows us the damage cowardice can do over time to a person and the quality of his life. Harry shows us how courage is the power to withstand fear for the sake of protecting what is good.

When something dangerous or evil threatens, Aquinas says that two reactions are typical: we fight or take flight. Daring is the fight response; fear prompts us to flee. Both responses are prompted by an evil that threatens some good we love, but they are opposite reactions. One moves us to strike back; the other urges us to run away.

When do we fight, and when do we run? The key difference between fear and daring is whether we judge it *possible* for the threat to be overcome and the good attained. "Daring is aroused by things that make us think victory is possible," according to Aquinas.[6] Daring causes us to fight against whatever is threatening us because we believe we can get rid of it or hold it off. A reaction of daring depends on the judgment that it is possible for us to do something about what threatens — we can fight it or

6. ST 1a2ae.45.3.

overcome it.[7] Fear, on the other hand, makes us want to flee, because we judge that whatever we face is something with the power to overcome *us*.[8] We are afraid when we know we are vulnerable and perceive the danger to be overwhelming. So daring makes us want to attack or fight because we think we can win, while fear instinctively inspires flight to cut our losses.

For Aquinas, courage concerns fear *and* daring. Its task is to hold fear in check, so that it does not interfere with or prevent our pursuit of a worthy good, and to "moderate" daring, so that we are properly cautious with the good of our own life. Like Peter Pettigrew, the cowardly person is too cautious. The rash person, on the other hand, is not cautious enough.[9] (Thus the virtue of courage lies in Aristotle's "golden mean" between the extremes of deficiency and excess, too little and too much.)[10] Fear moves us to withdraw from dangers, and daring prompts us to strike out against them. The virtue of courage is necessary because each of these passions can interfere with protecting or pursuing the good. Fear is the passion that most needs moderating when we must bear with an overpowering difficulty or danger. Aquinas calls this act of withstanding fear "endurance" (an act necessary to avoid the vice of cowardice). Daring is the passion that needs moderating in the act of attacking some evil or obstacle in one's path. This virtuous act is aptly named "aggression."[11] When moderated by reason, it should be distinguished from heedlessly rushing in (the vice of rashness). Most of the Harry Potter books end with Harry, Ron, and Hermione engaging in an act of aggressive courage, en-

7. ST 1a2ae.45.1.

8. ST 1a2ae.41.2 and 4.

9. In Rowling's novels, Sirius Black sometimes tends toward rashness and excessive risk-taking.

10. In Aristotle and Aquinas, parsing the virtue and vices involved is slightly more complicated, since courage concerns both fear and daring. So the vices might be characterized as an excess and deficiency of fear (cowardice and rashness, respectively), or they might be characterized as an excess and deficiency of daring (excess daring being something like rashness, again, and a deficiency of daring being something analogous to cowardice). See, for example, ST 2a2ae.126, *Nicomachean Ethics* 2.7 (1107b1-5). Aquinas thinks that the case of excessive daring doesn't arise much because fear for one's life (a natural inclination) serves to restrain daring and increase fear (ST 2a2ae.123.6). Having too much fear is the usual moral problem, and the one I will concentrate on in this chapter.

11. ST 2a2ae.123.6.

tering the fray to fight Voldemort and the Death Eaters, risking injury or possible death in attempting to overcome the threat and defend the good. This is what makes Harry's willingness to simply lay down his life without fighting back at the end of Book 7 so striking by contrast.

Although it concerns both fear and daring, Aquinas argues that courage is primarily concerned with restraining fear.[12] Why? Because the danger that threatens usually serves as a natural check on excessive daring and aggression, but at the same time it increases our fear.[13] Yet if fear is the main passion courage moderates, then endurance — bearing with difficulty and standing fast against our fear of danger — must be its paradigmatic act.

Aquinas consistently emphasizes that fear is our natural emotional response when some evil threatens and resisting or aggressively attacking the evil is not an option. Sometimes endurance is required because we *cannot* avoid or attack the threat. Aquinas says that sometimes courage is necessary because evil comes from a cause which is stronger than we are and outside our control: "Fear regards a future evil which surpasses the power of the one who fears, so that it is *irresistible.*"[14] In these cases, we are forced to stand firm from a position of weakness.[15] Our helplessness and vulnerability make facing the threat inevitable and escape impossible. This is one reason we need courageous endurance. Other times, however, endurance is required because we *ought* not avoid or attack the threatening evil. In these cases, to fight back will also compromise the good we love and are trying to protect, or to compromise our moral integrity. Even if we do have greater power, or the power to fight back, faithfulness to what we love — not (just) the greater force of what threatens — requires that we lay down our power of aggression and endure what comes. Because this is a choice, and not something forced upon us, it can make these instances of courageous endurance even more difficult yet.

In an interview, J. K. Rowling describes the difference between

12. ST 2a2ae.123.6; *Nicomachean Ethics* 3.9, 1117a30.

13. ST 2a2ae.123.6. Aquinas's point here also relies on the natural inclination of all beings toward self-preservation. See ST 1a2ae.94.2.

14. ST 1a2ae.41.4, emphasis added. It might be more accurate to say the threat "appears to be" irresistible, because it is the agent's perception and judgment of such that prompts the passion to arise. See ST 1a2ae.42.2, where Aquinas quotes Aristotle to make this point.

15. ST 1a2ae.42.3.ad 3; ST 1a2ae.43.2.

James's and Lily's reactions to Voldemort in terms of the distinction between aggression and endurance.[16] Voldemort arrives at their home with intent to kill. James reacts with daring and aggression; Lily with fear mastered in an act of endurance. Rowling says, "I think there are distinctions in courage. James was immensely brave. But the caliber of Lily's bravery was, I think in this instance, higher because she could have saved herself . . . [For James it was] like an intruder entering your house. . . . You would instinctively rush them. But if in cold blood you were told, 'Get out of the way' [so Voldemort could kill your child] . . . what would you do? . . . [Lily] very consciously [laid] down her life. She had a clear choice." She can't fight Voldemort — she doesn't have her wand. But she will not sacrifice her child to escape, out of fear. Instead, she courageously chooses to stand firm and endure, even to the death.

Aquinas's defense of martyrdom as an exemplary case of courage depends on this picture of fear and daring, endurance and aggression.[17] Both his and Rowling's pictures of courage serve to challenge the dominant "aggressive" paradigm of this virtue, or at least to expand our conception of courage to new and perhaps less familiar expressions of it. Aquinas inherited Aristotle's definition of courage as paradigmatically displayed on the battlefield, and Aristotle's account reflects the brave Greek warrior from the epic poets before him. Contemporary moral imaginations and ideals track a similar aggressive type. In fact, not only do most action-adventure heroes in film — from John Wayne to Rocky to John McClane — fit this model, but so do Harry and his friends in the first six books of the Harry Potter series. Each book ends with a climactic scene in which Harry and company battle against Voldemort. Courage is the virtue of fighting off evil, getting into the fray and defeating what threatens, risking one's life in a battle to protect and save others. Privileging martyrdom — an act of suffering and *enduring* an evil that we cannot or should not overcome by attack or a show of force — therefore radically changes our view of courage and the type of strength it requires.

Examples of aggressive courage are inspiring and noble, without a doubt. Why does Aquinas argue that these cases typically depict a lesser

16. Interview by Emerson Spartz et al., July 16, 2005, Edinburgh, Scotland. Full text available at http://www.Mugglenet.com. All quotations from Rowling in this chapter are from this interview.

17. See ST 2a2ae.124.

degree of courage than martyrdom, which seems to be a more resigned *reaction* to threats from others, in contrast with courageous *acts* which combat great evils and protect great goods? If we are looking for an *action* that best embodies courage, why settle for this apparently passive model — especially in our age, in which *doing* is valued more highly than (indeed thought almost utterly to eclipse) *suffering?*

Earlier, we saw Aquinas distinguish our reactions of fear and daring based on our perception of whether the danger was overwhelming or possible to overcome or avoid. In acts of daring aggression, our attack of daring is based on the belief that it is possible to avoid or conquer the evil that threatens. Thus there is a sense in which the courageous person still has some control over the situation: he acts courageously because he believes he has sufficient power to gain or protect the good; to that extent, he still trusts his own power to overcome the threat.

In an act of endurance, on the other hand, the courageous person can only avoid danger or death if she renounces or betrays the good at stake. That means, *given her love for and faithfulness to that good,* she is powerless to evade the threat. She must stand firm against it and take what comes. Her deepest loyalties demand it, and the sacrifice of her own life that comes with it. Her intense fear signals that her control over the safeguarding or protecting of her life is gone. In this position, her only means of resisting the evil is to stand fast and not give up on the good she loves while she suffers.[18] As Josef Pieper puts it, "fortitude . . . is nothing else than to love and to realize that which is good, in the face of injury or death, and undeterred by any spirit of compromise."[19]

18. Notice that it is the protection of her own life that she forfeits. Aquinas's definition of courage does not require that we sacrifice the lives of others, especially those for whose well-being we are responsible. Courage *serves* justice; it does not undermine its demands. Rather, he is thinking of situations when the only remaining way to preserve the integrity of the self and one's relationships to others (human or divine) is to lay down one's life.

19. Josef Pieper, *The Four Cardinal Virtues* (South Bend: University of Notre Dame Press, 1966), pp. 130-31. It is interesting that as Harry himself matures and his character deepens, he turns from aggressive courage to endurance and moves away from an attempt to remedy his situations of suffering to realizing that his suffering is not to be alleviated or avoided, but borne with steadfastness. He also moves from a suffering that is not chosen to the need to choose it voluntarily. This requires greater courage from him as well.

The fact that the aggressively courageous person — like our familiar action-adventure hero — is active, rather than forced into a position of suffering, implies that he is in a position of greater control over both the situation generally and his own physical well-being. It is a common experience that in the face of dangers and threats of pain, a greater sense of powerlessness also increases one's fear.[20] The aggressively courageous person thus has physical and psychological strength to draw upon which the one who must endure lacks. The martyr must stand firm from a position of greater weakness and greater fear.[21]

There is a sense in which the aggressively courageous person's aim and efforts are directed at still trying to avoid death, while the challenge of the one who courageously endures is to face and accept it.[22] So it makes sense that Aquinas takes martyrdom as his paradigmatic picture of endurance. The martyr is threatened with death unless she renounces her faith. Unless she is willing to betray Christ, she will be killed. Her position is one of weakness, of being required to suffer and undergo death. But her resistance is not a merely passive, "doormat" type response and is not to be confused with merely giving up. It is a deliberately chosen resistance to the temptation to bail out and betray the one she loves most in order to save herself, and it is a resistance that requires her to stand firm against fear, even fear of death.

Thus in the act of endurance, physical strength, brute force, better weapons, and human power are not what make the martyr strong. These things have either been stripped away or laid aside. To endure the danger that threatens and her own fear, the martyr needs strength of soul — and this is the heart of courage. Courage, for Aquinas, is a power that can be perfected even, and perhaps especially, in weakness.

20. This has been observed and documented among those with terminal illnesses that render them unable to care for themselves. See, for example, those cited in "Severe Mercy in Oregon," *Christianity Today,* June 14, 1999, p. 66.

21. See my "Power Made Perfect in Weakness: Aquinas's Transformation of the Virtue of Courage," *Medieval Philosophy and Theology* 11 (2003): 147-80.

22. This is not to deny that there are opportunities for and acts of endurance comparable to martyrdom on the battlefield.

Courage and Love

It is evident from the examples of Lily and the martyrs that the virtue of courage does not stand by itself. Love's role as the source and end of all we do is essential for understanding the nature of courage in Aquinas, as in Rowling, and they are right to make this strong connection. To put it simply, rightly ordered love is, and should be, the ultimate motive for any act of courage.[23] What makes the courageous person stand firm is not confidence in her power, but love. Without love, all the bravery in the world is mere gritted teeth — or, more darkly, it is idolatrous reliance on human strength to save the day.

For Aquinas, if a courageous person endures persecution to the death, that action should be characterized *primarily* as aiming at some good that her endurance of death safeguards, *not* as aiming at dying bravely, as if this were in itself something good (see also 1 Cor. 13:1-3). In fact, to see courage as requiring one to face death or suffering stalwartly for its own sake would be to miss its main point. Aquinas writes, "endurance of death is not praiseworthy in itself, but only insofar as it is directed to some good."[24] G. K. Chesterton once said of courage, "The true soldier fights not because he hates what is in front of him, but because he loves what is behind him."[25] Likewise, I face the intruder at 2 a.m., not because I crave risk or danger, but because my family's security depends on my protection. My love for them is my deepest motive. To be a virtue, courage must point beyond itself to love as its source and to love's end as its goal.

Augustine defines courage as "love readily bearing all things for the sake of the object beloved."[26] For courage to point beyond itself, for love to "endure all things," there must be some good we love even more than the suffering and pain we fear. The good we love, which motivates us to stand firm against fear, is an essential part of courage, for, as Aquinas ex-

23. ST 2a2ae.124.2.ad 2: "Charity inclines one to the act of martyrdom, as its first and chief motive cause, being the virtue commanding it, whereas fortitude inclines thereto as being its proper motive cause, being the virtue that elicits it." For the more general claim, see also ST 2a2ae.23.8, where charity is described as the efficient cause, foundation and root, end and commander of all the other virtues.

24. ST 2a2ae.124.3.

25. *Illustrated London News,* Jan. 14, 1911.

26. *De Eccles. Morib.* 15.25, quoted in ST 2a2ae.123.4, obj. 1 and 123.7, obj. 3.

plains, "fear is born of love."[27] In fact, not only fear but all human reactions presuppose an underlying love of some kind.[28] This means fear is a derivative emotion. Our love for something makes us fearful when it is threatened, lest we lose it. The loss and fear are greatest in cases involving a good that is loved naturally by everyone, such as our own bodily life and its preservation.[29] And yet love of an even higher good can motivate risking great loss, even as our fear acknowledges the loss as itself something evil — a *loss* of something good. In the case of courage, while love of the good of our own life causes fear, love of something even greater than ourselves can enable us to face its loss and withstand our fear of death.

The more we love something, the more sacrifice and suffering we can endure for its sake.[30] Nothing less than love for her own child moves Lily to lay down her life and put herself between Voldemort's killing curse and her beloved son. Likewise, Aquinas says it is the martyr's great love for God that enables her to withstand her fear of losing her life. Love makes courageous self-sacrifice possible.[31]

Courage: A Character Study

So far we have set out Aquinas's descriptions of courage and its various forms. The virtues, however, are meant to be an integral part of human character and the practices of the moral life. In this section, then, we will consider concrete cases of courage and courageous characters in more detail, using our own action-adventure heroes and Rowling's characters. The pictures of moral character we draw here will put flesh on the contrast between aggressive courage and the courage of endurance seen in Harry Potter and his ultimate act of self-sacrifice in *The Deathly Hallows.* We will also draw a character sketch of the antithesis of courage, using the character of Voldemort. These character studies will help us to see

27. ST 2a2ae.123.4.ad 2; 2a2ae.19.3; 2a2ae.125.2; and 1a2ae.43.1, quoting Augustine's *83 Questions,* 33.

28. ST 1a2ae.27.4.

29. ST 2a2ae.123.4.ad 2; 1a2ae.94.2: We share this inclination with all substances.

30. ST 2a2ae.124.3.

31. As I discuss in "Power Made Perfect in Weakness," the martyr needs divine assistance (grace) for this.

more clearly the different views of power underlying different moral ideals, and the way that love grounds true courage.

Our first character study is the aggressively courageous hero. Our most familiar models of courage — action-adventure heroes — are inspiring, noble, and fun to watch on the big screen. From the Lone Ranger to Rambo, from Tom Cruise in *Mission Impossible* to Bruce Willis in *Die Hard* to Toby Maguire in *Spiderman 1* and *2,* we love to cheer these heroes on as they rush in and rescue others from danger and distress. They fight the bad guys and win. They use aggressive means, even violence, to achieve just ends. They are rescuers, problem-fixers, fighters, individuals who can *do* something about evil, and do it with their own power and ingenuity. Their sort of courage exemplifies human power triumphing over evil. And the "power" in question is usually physical or military power — it involves the use of force, whether brute strength, bigger guns, or both. Not coincidentally, the action-adventure hero is almost always male. This picture of aggressive courage easily trades on our desires to solve our own problems and save the world on our own terms and in our own strength. Note that the action-adventure hero is never a conventional citizen but a maverick, authority-defying rather than inclined to play by the rules; he steps in when the government fails and the police are found inept, and overcomes the enemy himself. He is autonomous: he "goes in alone."

Now there *is* something admirable about this model: the action-adventure hero loves justice and fights for a good cause, and he is willing to risk his life (but not others' lives) for the sake of that good cause. As is true of all courageous people, our action-heroes are willing to suffer, put up with injury, risk death, and face their fears in order to achieve a good end. But there is a danger here. We should be wary of the way this model tends to glorify human power and its ability to overcome all evil. We should be cautious of heroes who never need others, and who expect to be able to conquer evil and evade death by their own strength and on their own terms.

Taken to extremes, these action-hero tendencies and temptations can produce a character like Voldemort. Rowling deliberately depicts Voldemort as one who has great power, but not love. This explains why it is impossible for Voldemort — unlike the action-hero — to have courage. Courage is the virtue that enables us to stand firm against our fear of injury, difficulty, and ultimately, death, for the sake of some good that transcends us — that is, for something other than ourselves or our own good. Courage requires that we recognize and care about some good greater than ourselves, a good that facing danger and risking death can — in some cases — protect or preserve.[32] Courage is a safeguarding virtue — standing fast against our fears (even our fear of death) is good only as it enables some great good to be safeguarded or protected.

Why can't Voldemort have courage? Because for him, his life *is* the greatest good. He loves nothing but himself. There is nothing in Voldemort's universe worth risking his own life for, nothing and no one worth dying for. He cannot recognize any good that transcends himself. That means death is the greatest evil for him. As Rowling says, "He regards death itself as ignominious. He thinks that it's a shameful human weakness. . . . His worst fear is death." Because his own life is the greatest good, he must protect and preserve himself at all costs, and for that he needs the power to defy death.

Voldemort's quest is not courageously to stand firm in the face of fear, but rather to *eliminate* fear, especially the fear of dying. To get rid of fear entirely means that we have to accumulate enough power for ourselves to overcome everything that threatens us, including death. Ultimately, the way to get rid of all fear is to become invincible, all-powerful — godlike. When asked what Voldemort would see if he were in front of the Mirror of Erised (the mirror which shows you your heart's greatest desire), Rowling answers, "[He sees] himself, all-powerful and eternal. That's what he wants." Voldemort is infatuated with power, his own power, because he seeks to be above death, immortal, beyond the possibility of fear. Ideally, he won't need courage, because he will have eliminated his own vulnerability to death and any possibility of his own weakness or suffering.

32. We note here the following important caveats. For Aquinas, you may (and in some cases you ought) to lay down your physical good if by doing so you can protect the good of another person. This is an act of love. (Although it would take more argument than I offer here, this position does *not* imply that it is virtuous or morally required to endure just any form of injury to the body or that certain forms of suffering — domestic abuse for example — are either morally required or praiseworthy.) You may not, however, lay down your spiritual good (that is, you may not commit a sin) for the sake of protecting another. The virtue of courage regards risks to one's physical safety and preservation. For a discussion of fear as it pertains to spiritual risk and self-preservation, see my chapter "Holy Fear" in *The Intellectual Legacy of John Paul II*, ed. Laura L. Garcia (forthcoming, Crossroads Press).

Through the Sorceror's Stone, the Horcruxes, and the Elder Wand, Voldemort's quest for power is motivated by his desire to be beyond fear.

It is easy for aggressive, action-hero courage to slide toward a Voldemort-like agenda. As John Paul II once said, we live in "a cultural climate which fails to perceive any meaning or value in suffering, but rather considers suffering the epitome of evil, to be eliminated at all costs."[33] Viewing death and suffering only as weaknesses to be overcome fuels our search for power and control over them. We are often tempted to use military might, genetic engineering, medical treatments, and physical force to try to eliminate our vulnerabilities, even to try to place ourselves above death, invulnerable, superhuman. Suffering is certainly not something to be gloried in for its own sake. Sometimes, however, courage requires it, because to try to overcome evil instead of suffering it will cost us our integrity and everything we love. As in Dumbledore's search for the Hallows and his mistaken quest for the "greater good," or in our culture's pursuit of more and more control over life and death, the worry is that we will increase and use our power to try to overcome our vulnerabilities in ways that deny our humanness and trample others. Dumbledore's power-driven agenda as a young man justified (in his mind) controlling Muggles and not acknowledging their fully human status.[34] This is not courage, but a perversion of it. This is a selfish, worldly view of power and what power is for. It makes us less human, not more fully human.

Human power to overcome evil and death is so inadequate. Perhaps this is why we are so often tempted to go to extremes, and why our action-adventure heroes often have to be superheroes — with superhuman powers or power-enhancing props like the Elder Wand. As Dumbledore says, "[Voldemort] believes the Elder Wand removes his last weakness and makes him truly invincible."[35] But he also confesses that in his own pursuit of the Hallows, "I too [like Voldemort] sought a way to conquer death, Harry."[36] The "Hallows" of course is another name for the "Holy" — that is, the powers reserved only for God. Thus Harry's choices and character are not defined by a search for the Hallows and their god-

33. *Gospel of Life: Evangelium Vitae* (New York: Random House, 1995), 15.

34. Rowling, *Hallows,* p. 716. For similar themes, see C. S. Lewis, *The Abolition of Man.*

35. Rowling, *Hallows,* p. 721.

36. Rowling, *Hallows,* p. 713.

like powers, but by a sacrifice of himself for the sake of love. Our action-hero model of courage can tempt us, as it did the young Dumbledore, toward an obsession with our own self-sufficiency and power.[37] Even when we are engaged in the fight against injustice, like an action-hero, how often do we want to rely on ourselves to save the day, and assume we are able to secure justice by ourselves? The danger of the action-hero model of courage is that it can easily slide into a Voldemort-like choice to place our confidence in our own power, and to seek to enhance human power to reach superhuman, or even divine, levels.

We turn now to Harry Potter himself. What makes Harry's case of courage different from the action-adventure hero's aggression and Voldemort's plan to eliminate the possibility and the fear of death altogether? We have seen that the courageous person does not seek death, and he does not glorify it. In fact, he naturally fears it. He recognizes and values the life he lays down; his sacrifice is *not* a suicide.[38] Nor is it an attempt to escape suffering. What enables him to face his fear and endure death is not confidence in his own power, but in the power of love. The good he loves enables him to face his fear. To be courageous, your love has to be greater than your fear of death: there has to be something or someone you love more than your own life. True courage is rooted in self-giving love, not prideful self-assertion.

When Augustine defined courage as "love bearing all things *for the sake of the beloved*," he could have been writing about Lily Potter.[39] Or about Harry in *Deathly Hallows*. While his definition also applies to the true action-adventure hero — including Sirius or James or Lupin — Harry's sacrifice is importantly different.[40] Harry endures death because

37. As he says to Harry, "I had learned that I was not to be trusted with power" (*Hallows*, p. 717).

38. Harry neither kills himself nor wills his own death by the hand of another (the definition of active and passive suicide, respectively). Unlike the perpetrator of suicide, he wants to live. The difference between the suicide and martyrdom cases can be seen by running the following counterfactual: How would the agent react if he or she did not die after all? The suicide will feel her intentions thwarted; Harry and the martyr will be glad to be alive.

39. See note 26. Emphasis added.

40. It is also greater than Lily's. As Rowling notes (see note 16 above), Lily is acting according to a mother's natural love for her child, and does not have time to back out. While her choice is more voluntary and deliberate than James's, Harry's is even

it is the only way to preserve and stay faithful to the good he loves. For Harry, to choose to live, rather than to face Voldemort in the forest, would have compromised the good of everyone he loved — as Pettigrew's failure to stand firm against fear caused Harry's parents' death. For Harry, to choose to live would have betrayed everything he was and everything his parents' died for. To give up his life was a choice demanded by his love and faithfulness to the good.

Harry's courage to lay down his life, to endure death, is similar to the kind of courage Aquinas says the martyr has. And the martyrs were imitating Christ. It is no accident that Aquinas describes this courageous act of self-sacrifice first and foremost in terms of love: "Now of all virtuous acts, martyrdom is the proof of the perfection of love." It is "a sign of the greatest love, [because,] according to John 15:13: 'Greater love has no one than this, that one lay down one's life for one's friends.'"[41] This picture of courage is a picture of a love for others which is powerful enough to keep our fear in check so that we can lay down our lives out of love. It is not (as in the first two models) a picture of conquering evil or eliminating fear on the basis of our *own* power, whether physical, technological, or magical. Harry puts away his wand so that he will not be tempted to use it to fight,[42] just as he deliberately chooses to pursue the Horcruxes,[43] not the Hallows. Harry intentionally follows Lily's example — her courageous choice to lay down her life, to endure death, for the sake of love. And thus Rowling's picture of virtue stands in this tradition of thinking about courage in terms of the power of love, not the power of human force or the quest for power over death. This is why Lily — a woman — and Harry — a teenager with inferior wizarding power — can be a picture of this sort of courage. And so can we. Because the only power courage ultimately

---

more voluntary and deliberate than hers (see Aristotle's *Nicomachean Ethics* 3.1, 1110a5-1110b5 for a discussion of the voluntariness of acts done under threat). Harry, on the other hand, acts on behalf of friends he has voluntarily pledged loyalty to, and has time to weigh his choice, put away his wand willingly, and renege on his decision. In my judgment, that makes his act of courage more difficult than hers.

41. ST 2a2ae.124.3. It is important to note that her sacrifice of her life does *not* have salvific significance; like the martyrs, she bears witness to a self-giving love for others. Catholic theology acknowledges something redemptive even in the suffering of the martyrs, insofar as the martyrs willingly participate in the sufferings of Christ.

42. Rowling, *Hallows*, pp. 703 and 704.

43. In Latin, "the dreaded cross."

needs is the power of love. Only a love that is stronger than death has the power to "bear all things" (1 Cor. 13:7). As Rowling's Dumbledore wisely observes: "Of house-elves and children's tales, of love, loyalty, and innocence, Voldemort knows and understands nothing. Nothing. That they have a power beyond his own, a power beyond the reach of any magic, is a truth he has never grasped."[44] Voldemort cannot have courage because he "has not love" (1 Cor. 13:3).

Virtuous courage of the kind we are celebrating in this chapter is not self-sufficient or autonomous. As we have seen, the aggressive action-adventure hero tends to be a rugged individualist: he works alone, and depends on himself, his ingenuity and physical strength. Voldemort goes even further, acting only for himself and even using others as disposable means to his own good. Harry, by contrast, relies essentially on his friends throughout the books, and in his death, claims the power of the communion of the saints by using the Resurrection Stone to surround himself with those whose love has made him what he is. Laying down his life is Harry's own decision and act, but as Rowling writes, "Beside him, scarcely making a sound, walked James, Sirius, Lupin, and Lily, and their presence was his courage."[45] Love binds us together in community; love recognizes that we are not meant to be self-reliant. We flourish in solidarity, not solitary self-sufficiency. Again, it is not our own power that makes us courageous.

Aquinas says that "fear is born of love"; what we fear most depends on what we love most. Voldemort fears death most because he loves his own life more than anything else. His fears are rooted in selfish self-love. Harry can face death courageously because he loves something beyond himself and his own life. His love of others and their good, and his desire to protect them, is a love that is stronger than his fear of death. This is nothing less than a Christian love, the greatest of the virtues.[46]

44. Rowling, *Hallows,* p. 710.

45. Rowling, *Hallows,* p. 700.

46. To be clear, I am not arguing that Harry is a Christian or has grace, or that Rowling intends this part of the tale allegorically to represent Christian martyrdom. I merely mean to say that Harry — like characters in a Flannery O'Connor novel — gives us a true picture of what Christian love looks like in his character and his practice, even if it is one that he himself is not aware of or would define in those terms. Harry Potter is not a story about Christian characters; it is a story about virtues that Christians recognize as fitting in their tradition of moral practice and perhaps only fully articulable within it.

In the end, it is a power that transcends him — the power of his mother's love — that enables Harry to endure. It is not his own wizarding skill or intestinal fortitude that saves the day. Lily's love for Harry and Harry's love for others ultimately defines his view of power and therefore also his courage. And this picture of power and courage and love is one that itself echoes through many centuries of the Christian moral tradition. The martyrs, too, found the grace to endure by looking to Christ, who chose love, not force, as the way to defeat evil and death.[47] As a model of this sort of courage, Harry's defining name should perhaps have been not "The Boy Who Lived" but "The Boy Who Loved."

Courage as a Christian Practice

If we find compelling this picture of courage as endurance, even in the face of death, for the sake of love, we might still object that choosing martyrdom — an act as rare as it is exemplary — as the paradigm makes this view of courage highly irrelevant for ordinary people trying to live courageously amidst more mundane difficulties. After all, most of us can't compete with Harry Potter when it comes to chances to save the world, and in the contemporary United States, opportunities for martyrdom are fairly rare. Nonetheless, Aquinas's picture of courage was meant to instruct ordinary Dominican friars in the imitation of Christ. If the model of virtue he offers is too far removed from ordinary experience and too remote a possibility for practical imitation, then he will have failed to meet his own pedagogical aims.

Does the paradigm of martyrdom make courage too inaccessible for ordinary people? In fact, I think the opposite is true: the aggressive/action-hero paradigm of courage actually narrows the range of the virtue more than the endurance/martyrdom paradigm. The main point of making martyrdom the paradigm of courage is to show that this virtue can find expression as much or more in suffering and weakness as it can in striking out against a threat. The aggressive paradigm has, until very recently, been

47. Aquinas is clear that the ultimate expression of this type of courage requires setting *human* power aside in favor of reliance on divine power and grace. Thus Aquinas transforms this Aristotelian virtue in ways Aristotle would neither have dreamed of nor approved.

largely restricted to males, and even further restricted to those males who meet certain requirements for ability and physical strength. To make martyrdom the paradigm, on the other hand, enables *anyone willing to endure suffering for the sake of love* to echo this supreme example of courage in their own lives, and leaves physical power, with its attendant gender, health, and age limitations, out of the picture.[48] It also provides a necessary check on our temptations to rely too fully on our own power. *Anyone* who is unable or unwilling to use force when love demands this is a candidate for practicing courage — and this included, perhaps especially, the vulnerable: women, children, the elderly, the economically and socially disempowered, and the disabled. Civil rights leader Martin Luther King, Jr. defined his non-violent resistance — again, a form of courageous endurance — by this guiding belief: "I believe that unarmed truth and unconditional love will have the final say in reality."[49]

As fallen and vulnerable human beings in a world marred by sin and death, the endurance of suffering and death is necessary for us all, and courageous endurance is an answer to the question, "What is left for me to do when my own strength is exhausted, my burdens can't be lightened by human resources or power, or when faithfulness to the good demands that I suffer rather than betray what I love most?"

Moreover, for Aquinas's intended readers, as for us, the moral life is coextensive with the process of sanctification — becoming more and more like Christ in our character. This process requires the death of the old self and the coming to birth of the new, dying *with* Christ in order also to rise with him. This is another form of laying our lives down for the sake of love. This is not a rare opportunity but a daily discipline. So martyrdom, in an analogical but no less important sense, is a task for all of those who claim Christ as their own and seek to love him above all else.[50]

To understand courageous endurance as an exemplary expression of

48. Analogously, superior technological power (of the sort that can trump the limitations mentioned in the text) usually comes with economic privilege, which is another way of restricting the exercise of power to a few.

49. Rev. Martin Luther King, Jr., Nobel Peace Prize acceptance speech, Dec. 10, 1964.

50. Although I do not make this point here, I have argued elsewhere that the usefulness of an exemplar is not limited to its direct imitability; an ideal can teach in other ways as well. See chap. 2.1.1 and chap. 5 of my "Virtues in Action" (Ph.D. diss., University of Notre Dame, 2000).

the virtue of courage, we first have to understand the ultimacy of love in the moral life. This form of courage shows us how rightly ordered fear must be grounded in love, not a reliance on human strength or power. Courage requires that love be the center of the moral life, shaping our hopes and fears. And for Christians, it demands that we be not afraid to take Christ's love — a love powerful enough to endure suffering and the ultimate self-sacrifice — as a model of virtue worth imitating.

Questions for Further Reflection

1. What are you most afraid of? When do you feel most vulnerable? List three of your deepest fears, or three moments when you were most fearful. How are these fears expressed in your habits of thoughts and actions or reactions? When you examine your response to threatening evils, do you find that you are overly fearful or overly confident?

2. How do your fears reveal what you love? Is your love primarily focused on yourself, temporal things, other people, a greater cause? Is the love your fears reveal a healthy self-love or a selfish one?

3. Who are your heroes? Do they typically express courage as endurance or aggression? What have you learned, and what can you learn, about courage through their example? Think of one act of courage they've performed: What pain do they endure, what evil do they fight against? For the sake of what do they endure and fight?

4. In what ways are you trying to be a superhero, seek eternal youthfulness, and deny your own vulnerability and mortality? In what ways does our culture encourage this (e.g., by overvaluing safety/security, beauty as youthfulness, human strength, military prowess)? How might the stories of the Christian community offer counterexamples of a healthy and honest view of death and its meaning (e.g., the Eucharist, Jesus weeping at Lazarus's tomb, martyred saints)? How might Christian practices embody that view (e.g., hospice care; welcoming and including the aging and terminally ill, rather than isolating them; Christian funeral practices; the refusal of extraordinary medical treatments, or cosmetic surgeries)? How do these practices teach us that love is stronger than our fears?

5. Set aside time to reflect on your own death. This practice of "memento mori" has been used for centuries to clarify for people what is truly

important and worth living for. What does this reflection help you discover about yourself, your fears, the way you are living out your priorities? Mother Teresa, working amidst great suffering and death, famously said that God did not call her to be successful, but to be faithful. What sorts of things can you practice daily and in small ways to help you become more faithful to what you truly love, even when this is difficult or requires self-sacrifice?

LOVE

Love

Charles Taliaferro

Christianity makes extravagant claims about love: "Whoever does not love does not know God, for God is love" (1 John 4:8). The two commandments that characterize the Christian life are both commands of love; the very reason for God's redemptive action through Jesus Christ is defined by love (John 3:16). Augustine taught that there is a proper order of love *(ordo amoris)* in creation and that sanctity consists in loving well, whereas to love badly is to be estranged from the Creator. Augustine proposed that love is not a stagnant state, but dynamic: it is the best way for the soul to travel toward and in God.

In light of these extraordinary claims, I propose that in this chapter we take on board a set of interrelated questions: Are there different kinds of love? What might it mean to claim that "God is love"? Would it make sense to claim that "love is God"? Is there an order of love and why would love be seen by Augustine (or anyone else) as a means of divine travel? Can you love a person too much? Can loving someone or something create values or make somebody or something valuable? In other words, can love be a source of value so that, for example, you are valuable, in part, *because you are loved by someone?* Augustine warned us about the danger of loving love. Why would that be dangerous? Does Christianity have any distinctive resources for assisting us in the practice of love?

I am deeply grateful for conversation and comments by Clifton Nesseth and Cody Venzke, and a wonderful dialogue about love with Jil Evans and Christine Baeumler while driving their artwork from Minnesota to New York City.

Any one of these questions is enough for a book on its own, so my goal in this chapter is more to stimulate inquiry and suggest some promising lines of reasoning, rather than to attempt a definitive philosophy of love.

Defining Love

Let us grant at the outset that there may be vast differences between the ways people define or picture what they refer to as "love." Be that as it may, there is a serious tradition — including Augustine and Thomas Aquinas, the Florentine Academy in the Renaissance, the Cambridge Platonists in early modern philosophy, and many twentieth- and twenty-first-century philosophers — that argues that for a person to love something or someone (I will refer to the thing or person loved as "Mike"), that person in some sense affirms or approves the good of Mike.[1] This amounts not just to preferring that Mike exist rather than not exist; in a case of authentic love there is also an actual pleasure in Mike or a disposition to take pleasure in Mike. So, if I love you, then I must in some sense affirm the good of your being and take some pleasure that you exist. Love of a person will (one hopes!) differ from the love of consumption and use, as when I love walnuts (which amounts to my loving to eat or taste something) or an automobile (which amounts to my loving to drive). Love of persons for their own sake rather than use, then, may be treated as nonconsumptive love. This initial demarcation of love puts the stress on *goodness,* for in loving a person one approves not merely of a person's being but of their well-being.

The definition of love is the contrary of a plausible definition of hate. For a person to hate Doug, the person disapproves of Doug's existence and prefers that Doug not exist rather than exist. There is also some sense in which hatred involves displeasure in Doug. So, if I hate Doug, and this hatred is absolutely thorough in that I truly despise him, then Doug's be-

1. This tradition might be called Platonic Christianity, though I hesitate to define the view of love presented in this chapter as Platonic love because "Platonic" in ordinary English can mean a relationship in which there is no sexual intimacy. In this chapter I am identifying a form of love that can include (but need not have) a sexual dimension.

ing gives me no pleasure whatever. (If I merely hate Doug's annoying voice, on the other hand, his voice fills me with displeasure and I might prefer that Doug had a different voice.) On these accounts, love and hate turn out to be contraries rather than contradictions. A is contrary to B if it is the case that if A is the case, then not-B is the case. So, the contrary of day is night; if it is day, it is not night. But day and night are not contradictions, for you can have a time of day that is neither day nor night, namely dusk. Similarly, if someone thoroughly loves Mike, they cannot simultaneously hate Mike, but it is possible to be in a state of complete indifference and neither hate nor love.

Before moving on, let us see how these definitions work in terms of some problem cases. What of a case when you love another person who is suffering horribly from some incurable disease? Could it be that a loving person would prefer that the person cease to suffer (and thus desire that the dying process not be extended) and, as a consequence, the lover actually might prefer the nonexistence of the beloved? This seems plausible, but I suggest that a loving person would always prefer the well-being and flourishing of the beloved to her nonexistence. As a result, it would *only be when such well-being and flourishing is not (short of a miracle) possible* that a lover would grievously desire the death of the beloved. The definition would still hold, however, insofar as the lover has the opportunity to have faith and hope that the beloved will find well-being and flourishing in God on the other side of death. If, on the contrary, you are at the deathbed of Skippy and you not only hope that Skippy perish in this life, but you also hope for Skippy's annihilation and hope that Skippy will not find any redemption after death, then I suggest that you actually hate Skippy.

The definitions involve pleasure and displeasure, but can't you love someone and yet feel no pleasure in their well-being? Could it be that this is even a higher love of love because it does not rest on the coming and going of feelings? Arguably, love is a more sturdy virtue than passing feelings. When good feelings accompany love, this is all for the good, but feelings should not be seen as part of the definition of love itself.

In reply, I am going to make what might be an unpopular suggestion that insofar as you claim to love a person or thing *and take no pleasure whatever in the good or well-being of X,* then that love is either incomplete or tarnished in some way. Recall that the definition of love posits that there is either an actual pleasure in the beloved or a *disposition* to take pleasure in the beloved. Times may arise, for example in moments of stress or in a crisis of some kind, when there is simply no opportunity for any pleasure of any kind. This does not undermine the fact that if you truly love Skippy, you are disposed to take pleasure in him. While rescuing Skippy from drowning out of love you are not thereby feeling such pleasure, but if, after the rescue when Skippy and you have recovered, you have *no disposition whatever* to feel pleasure in Skippy's well-being, then I suggest your love is incomplete or it has been compromised or eclipsed.

Aren't our best and most precious cases of love those cases when we want to enjoy (and hence feel joy about) the beloved? Short of actual joy, however, I propose that love involves at least a movement toward and openness to pleasure. There is a telling example of a failure in love in Charles Williams's great novel, *Descent into Hell.* The final damnation of a main character happens, not when the professor fails to honor or take pleasure in a rival's receiving honor, but when he fails to try to take pleasure. I suggest that this case is illuminating: perhaps you love another person during periods of personal emotional sterility and exhaustion, but if there is no effort even to make an effort to make an effort to feel pleasure in the beloved, then the so-called love of the beloved may be merely mechanical or habitual and not full. I think something similar is true with hate: imagine someone truly hates another person but feels no displeasure at all about the person. I suggest this would *not* be a central case of hatred, but a kind of routine disapproval of someone rather than hate.

The importance of pleasure in love will emerge briefly when we address the question of why some Christian philosophers think of love as a means of travel toward God.

Consider a different puzzle about the proposed definition: what about love-hate relationships? Can't I love you but hate the fact that you are a smoker? I suggest that a close look at love-hate relationships must differentiate the objects of love and hate. Yes, you might love someone as they are and yet *because you desire their well-being* you disapprove or take displeasure in their smoking. This might be a case in which your hatred of their smoking habit stems from your love of the person. (Arguably, this would be a case of loving the sinner but hating the sin, or at least hating an unhealthy habit.) But I do not think you can love and hate the same thing or person in the same way or the same respect at the same time. If I truly love your sense of humor, I cannot truly hate it simultaneously. I might love the humor but feel envy (I want to be funnier than you) or jealousy (why is it that you are funnier when you are with her rather than me), and so on, but none of this changes the fact that if I truly love your humor there is a sense in which I must approve or desire to take pleasure in it.

In what follows, I seek to refine the definition of love in addressing the series of questions raised at the beginning of this chapter.

If God Is Love, Is Love God?

In the classic, twelfth-century work, *Spiritual Friendship,* St. Aelred of Rievaulx raises the possibility that love or friendship is God, though he does not endorse this view.[2] One reason he does not endorse such a thesis is because, in classical theology, love is an activity or practice whereas God is a substantial reality, a Trinity of Persons. An activity (by definition) cannot be an individual, substantial Person or Persons and so it cannot be the case that love is (literally) the very same thing as God. Still, there are deep reasons in Christian theology for claiming that, in God, love is fulfilled in a complete and super-abundant form, and that, because it is love that is behind both the creation and re-creation of the cosmos through Christ, love is in some respects divine.

There are different accounts of the Trinity historically. The one that I commend, propounded by the Cappadocian Fathers like Gregory of Nazianzus and Basil of Caesarea, tends to stress the Father, Son, and Holy Spirit as distinguishable centers of consciousness that are mutually interrelated in the highest form of unity. This view has been defended recently by Stephen Davis as *perichoretic monotheism* in which God is not a homogenous being but three Persons existing in mutual penetration or coinherence.[3] As articulated by Davis as well as Richard Swinburne and, before them, in the work of Richard of St. Victor, in God we find the three

2. St. Aelred develops his philosophy of love in both *Spiritual Friendship* and *The Mirror of Charity,* both classics in the history of writing on friendship and the love of God.

3. Stephen T. Davis, *Christian Philosophical Theology* (Oxford: Oxford University Press, 2006), chapter 4.

highest, most fitting forms of love. There is self-love, the love of another, and the love of two for a third.

There are ample ways to illustrate such loves; consider only one, the early love between the Romantic poets William Wordsworth and Samuel Coleridge. When they were young each had proper self-love (without vanity), love of the other, and they together loved a third: English language and literature. Only in old age, when Wordsworth's self-love faded into vanity and Coleridge became awash with personal insecurities, did their love for each other falter and at least Coleridge's poetry suffered. Unlike the many cases of our failures at either proper self-love, love of others, and the love of a third, the Trinity actually images or portrays an ideal convergence of love.

Given a perichoretic account of the Trinity, the creation itself is seen as stemming from the great love within the Godhead and then brought into being for the sake of its goodness and for itself to be a reflection of divine love. The love and joy that exists in God's inner life (what the theologian Jonathan Edwards called God's inner glory) leads God to create outside of God's being (and thus to create an arena for external glory or *gloria ad extra*). On this view, when created persons engage in proper self-love, the love of another, and then the mutual love for another or others, they are acting in ways that are in the image of God. In perichoretic theology, malicious hatred and other sins become doubly grave as they both mar the goodness of creation and dishonor and violate the great love that defines the Godhead. A person made in the image of God who yields to hatred violates the original ground of that person's being and ruptures God's intent that persons mirror back the love that underlies the creation itself. So, while it would be theologically tenuous to think that "love is God," there are grounds for thinking that proper loves can reflect and (as I shall argue in a last section of this chapter) participate in divine love.

The Order of Love and Divine Travel

Augustine's notion that the created order includes "an order of love" is a dramatic statement of what we routinely recognize as common sense. Arguably, we all have an implicit understanding of the degrees of love that befit persons, goals, and events. If someone found childbirth uninteresting (not worthy of any interest) or they were in sustained, uninterrupted ecstasy every time they realized that squares have four right angles we might well assume brain damage or rather strong drugs are involved. Philosophers from Aristotle to Spinoza built their ethical systems on accounts of the degree and kinds of pleasures and displeasures, loves and hates, that different events call for. Christian theologians have similarly conceived of virtues and vices in terms of ordered or disordered love. Humility or proper pride has been identified in terms of taking a balanced, fitting affirmation of the good of the self while avoiding vanity (an inordinate desire for preeminence) and severe self-deprecation (self-humiliation). Paradoxically, intense self-deprecation (e.g., "I am the worst sinner *ever*") can actually be a sign of vanity (e.g., rather than lamenting your plight, you are actually bragging).

As for divine travel, I believe that one of the reasons that Augustine thought of love in dynamic terms is because of the nature of pleasure itself. Perhaps drawing on Plato, Augustine realized that when you take pleasure in something there is a bond (whether this is very faint and tenuous or strong) between the lover and the object of love. One can see this in our use of possessive language in English. If you really love something, whether this is a romantic relationship with Skippy, the love of a baseball team, or a favorite fruit, it makes sense to refer to *your* Skippy, *your* Boston Red Sox, *your* strawberries. By loving God or loving other persons as part of your divine vocation, there is a sense in which the pleasure you are taking in God and others will extend or move you beyond the confines of who you would be if you lacked such love. There is a further use in English that signals the way in which loving another person can (as it were) take you outside of yourself. Compare these two sentences:

A. I take great pleasure that you won the race!
B. I take great pleasure in your winning the race!

I suggest that B signals a greater identity with the race-winner, and it would be a natural way in which a lover would express pleasure in the beloved's victory. Similarly, the practice of taking joy or delight in God (through worship, for example) can be a means of becoming increasingly closer to God.

Because of this order of love and goodness, I shall briefly argue for what may seem like a paradoxical thesis: *there is a sense in which you can-*

not love another person too much. What, after all, might loving another person too much involve? Some plausible cases in which it appears (initially) that you might love someone too much include: you take great pleasure in a person and desire to be with them romantically but this would be illicit (one of you is married, for example); you love another person so much that you neglect your own well-being and others around you; you love your children so much that they find themselves suffocated by your attention. But are any of these cases of actual love?

In the first case in which someone appears to love another too much, imagine that divorce is out of the question ethically and that the "beloved" is happily married. How might your desire (much less your acting on that desire) for an illicit relationship count as approving of or taking pleasure in the good of that person? Assuming that an affair is unethical and not for the good of the beloved (involving the breaking of vows, compromising integrity, deception and so on), a persistent desire to consummate an illicit relationship does not seem to be a *bona fide* case of love. Terms like "lust" or "passion" or "obsession" or simply the term "desire" would fit the case better than "love." The tradition of love defended in this chapter, going back to Plato on up through the Cambridge Platonists and so on, holds that love has to focus on the good of the beloved, and insofar as the good is truly respected it is not in the nature of love to harm the beloved. Put another way, this form of love calls for loving wisely and it rejects the idea that is hinted at, at the end of Shakespeare's play *Othello.* In the final act, Othello claims he has loved "too well" but not wisely his wife Desdemona. Is it plausible to believe Othello loved his wife too well or too much? Not at all. Even if Othello was correct in his deluded belief that his wife had been unfaithful, killing her cannot plausibly be seen as a loving act or something that stemmed from love. The tragedy is that Othello (through the manipulation of Iago) came to hate the one whom he loved.

The second case, when someone loves another so much that it leads "the lover" to self-neglect or even self-destruction seems like a plausible case of loving someone too much. After all, drawing on Shakespeare again, didn't Romeo and Juliet love each other so much so that each elected to commit suicide rather than to live without the other? According to the tradition I am defending in this chapter, no. Certainly, there is a familiar tendency in friendships and romantic relations to put the beloved at a higher level of loyalty and value than oneself (Montaigne recognized this in his famous essay "On Friendship"), but when this is taken to certain extremes questions arise about whether "love" has itself wound up being distorted. When Romeo thinks that Juliet has died, and kills himself, he may be seeking to immortalize their love or testify to his all-absorbing passion but (absent the idea that death is a doorway to reunion with the beloved), Romeo's death is the killing of his love for her. You cannot continue loving Juliet when dead. And when Juliet kills herself, she likewise removes the possibility of continuing to love Romeo (perhaps in the form of grief or mourning). Their suicides seem to me (like Othello's murder of his wife) not so much a matter of too much love, but of not loving wisely, and certainly not retaining sufficient self-love so as to resist a perhaps natural urge to die with the beloved. It is hard to see how the good of either Romeo or Juliet is served or respected by a self-killing. In Act 2, scene 2, Shakespeare seems to hint at the nature of Juliet's passion for Romeo when she refers to him as "the god of my idolatry."[4] Idolizing someone is not the same as loving them.

Consider, finally, the case of the over-bearing, all-controlling parent. In reply, wouldn't such cases sometimes be described in very different terms than love? For example, extreme cases might involve a parent's fear or perhaps even hatred for a son or daughter's independence. Recalling again the lines from *Othello,* I suggest that parental love must aspire to loving wisely (or as wisely as one can). Insofar as the love of a parent is used in a way that causes genuine, evident harm, then it appears that the loving itself is not being done well.

In sum, if the above reasoning is correct, *you can love a person less than you should, but you cannot love a person more than you should.* As mentioned at the outset, this chapter is designed to stimulate your own reflection, so I make no claim to have *proven* this thesis. (I will count it a success, if I have simply made the claim sound interesting for you to engage!)

The Creativity of Love

Can loving someone or something create values or make somebody or something valuable? In other words, can love be a source of value so that,

4. For further support of this critique of *Romeo and Juliet* and other classic cases of when it appears that romantic love leads to death see *Love in the Western World* by Denis de Rougemont (Princeton: Princeton University Press, 1983).

for example, you are valuable, in part, *because you are loved by someone?* Princeton University philosopher Harry Frankfurt thinks so. He proposes that loving another person can provide reasons why you value the person. He thinks that the reason why he values his children is because he loves his children rather than vice versa. In *The Reasons of Love,* Frankfurt writes:

> It is true that the beloved invariably is, indeed, valuable to the lover. However, perceiving that value is not at all an indispensable *formative* or *grounding* condition of the love. . . . [Loving another] is not necessarily . . . a *result* of recognizing their value and of being captivated by it. . . . Rather, what we love necessarily acquires value for us *because* we love it. The lover does invariably and necessarily perceive the beloved as valuable, but the value he sees it to possess is a value that derives from and that depends upon his love.[5]

Is that plausible? I suggest there is some truth in his claim, but that his thesis needs to be highly qualified.

What I suggest may be right about Frankfurt's claim is that once you are in a reciprocal relationship of love, there can be great additional goods such as all the goods that comprise a friendship. In a healthy friendship or romance (or both) there can be the great good of taking joy in the relationship itself, a kind of savoring of the good of the bond of affection. If you truly love Skippy there can be a sense in which her or his good is magnified in the sense that Skippy's acts and adventures meet with heightened pleasure and joy. And a good relationship may generate a host of goods whose value consists only in the fact that these goods were created through love (e.g., a sentimental collection of some kind may become a treasure to the lovers but be of zero interest to an outsider). But I suspect that something has gone wrong if the beloved is believed to have value chiefly because (to use Frankfurt's term) the beloved is infused with value through our love. Frankfurt claims: "It is by caring about things that we infuse the world with importance."[6] But in human relationships, isn't this more reasonably described in terms of you recog-

5. Harry Frankfurt, *The Reasons of Love* (Princeton: Princeton University Press, 2004), pp. 38-39.

6. Frankfurt, *Reasons,* p. 23.

nizing the wonderful (full of wonder) value of the beloved? You respond to her or his courage, wit, intelligence, physical looks, history, modesty, or sense of fairness, and on and on, and on. One hopes that in a case of mutual attraction and shared love there might then come to be the new value of something that did not exist earlier: the good of friendship or romance or marriage (or all three). But the ground floor or foundation is not the idea that the beloved is found to be valuable because of the love bestowed upon the beloved. This thesis becomes important when it comes to Augustine's warning about the danger of loving love, which we will address after a brief look at love and control.

Is Love under Your Control?

Because the view of love developed in this chapter involves pleasure or a disposition to pleasure it may appear that love is not under one's control, for how might one decide to be pleased by someone or something? This seems very hard to control directly. Even so, I suggest that love may be *indirectly* under one's control through the use of focused attention and the imagination. Certainly it appears that we can come to hate people by focusing on properties that appear mildly irritating until this irritation metamorphoses into spite; people can nurse ill-feelings until they become more than passing feelings. And the imagination can, of course, be used for ill purposes. There is an amusing line in Evelyn Waugh's darkly comic novel, *A Handful of Dust,* when two characters who come to commit adultery realize that they have each fantasized about an illicit relationship: "In the week they had been apart, each had, in thought, grown more intimate with the other than any actual occurrence warranted."[7] If focused attention and the imagination can fuel hatred and illicit passion, surely these instruments may be used to enhance opportunities and the practice of love.

Two obstacles that may hamper one's control of love should be noted: self-hatred and the failure to appreciate the opportunities for dynamic change through forgiveness and hope.

Selective, mild forms of self-hatred need not completely eclipse the

7. Evelyn Waugh, *A Handful of Dust* (Boston: Little, Brown and Company, 1962), p. 58.

love of others (you might value other people and yet think of yourself in general abject terms) but thorough and radical self-hatred appears to undermine the very capacity of love. To love another person you have to be able to affirm the good of such love or at least recognize the good of such love. If your self-malice is so deep that you can hardly tolerate or recognize any good coming to pass in your life, then it is hard to see how you might be able to sustain a sense of the good of loving others. Paradoxically, without some self-acceptance or modest self-love, love of others will be impeded. Self-acceptance or self-love can enhance one's ability to love.

I suggest that one's ability to love others may also be hampered to the extent that one does not place a high value on forgiveness, fails to recognize when a person who has done wrong apologizes and reforms, and fails to cultivate a spirit of hope that genuine reform and moral renewal is possible. There may be cases when forgiveness is not fitting, but a steadfast resistance to consider forgiveness as an option and a tendency toward resentment rather than hope can surely limit one's capacity to love.

The Danger of Loving Love

Why would anyone, let alone Augustine, have a problem with loving love?[8] The problem here is that if your central love is love itself, then you may not be loving the person you claim to love *for her or his own sake.* You are, instead, engaging in a self-centered practice because you are actually loving the love rather than loving the person who is loving. This may not be perceived as a problem so long as the mutual love endures. But consider a case when there is a breakdown of mutual love. If when we are together I largely love your love for me and then you stop loving me, then *the object of my love* has ceased to be. Arguably, one of the distinguishing marks of a robust love for another person is that such love does not depend fully on reciprocation. Emotional trauma, profound physical injury, betrayal, or death can end such reciprocation. And yet don't we think that part of the glory of a person truly loving another is that such love will not always end under those conditions? Of course the kind of

8. Augustine wrestles with the dangers of loving love in his masterpiece *The Confessions.*

love and the expression of love may change. After a divorce, continued longing for being united with the beloved is (presumably) merely frustrating (at best), but continued love in the sense of desiring the well-being of the beloved and perhaps even (if possible) taking pleasure in the accomplishments of the beloved may still be fitting and good. If, however, the object of love is simply the return of love itself then such enduring love is not feasible. Returning to Frankfurt's proposal, I think his philosophy of love would have a harder time explaining the value of enduring love even after a breakdown. After all, if I think my value or worth is partly derived from the fact that someone loves me (my value is infused or bestowed by another person's love), and that love ceases, has my value or worth ceased? It may certainly feel that way, but I suggest that, ideally, a philosophy of love should recognize that the beloved has value whether or not she or he returns your love.

While I endorse Augustine's warning about the danger of loving love, I suggest that there is still good involved in loving (or appreciating or savoring or relishing) being loved as well as in the activity of loving. While this may seem especially true in romantic or marital relations, I think this has a worthy place in friendship as well as in less intimate relations, whether at school or in a workplace. Augustine's warning comes into play (from my point of view) only when, instead of the beloved, you make the object of your love the love itself. But assuming you truly love the beloved, loving her or his love is an additional good.

In the last section, let us consider briefly the extent to which Christianity offers a distinctive contribution to the practice of love.

Christian Love

As noted above, Christians can see earthly love between persons and the love of the creation itself as a reflection of the very inner glory of the Godhead and of the very purpose of God in creating the cosmos. This background conviction about love can inform and provide a basis for taking delight in the opportunities for love in this life. It can likewise sustain the hope that the loves and persons we love will not cease at death. The Christian teaching that God first loved (and loves) us before we love God also provides a deep view of love as having an antecedent, foundational role in our lives. Christianity is also able to address two of the factors noted earlier that can inhibit our ability to love: For the Christian who faithfully believes that she is created by God (and is thus good) and also that she is the object of Christ's redeeming love, self-malice or self-hatred are not live options. Also, for a faithful Christian, refusing to forgive others or becoming entrenched in hopeless resentment is also out of the question.

Christian faith offers at least three further offices or opportunities for the practice of love. These may be called participatory love, agape love, and redeeming love.

Participatory love: Some Christians have worried about how to balance the two chief commandments. If you are to love God with all your heart, mind, and soul, how can you (in addition to that) love your neighbor as yourself? Aelred of Rievaulx and many Christian philosophers approach this paradox by appealing to the way in which one can love God through loving other persons, just as one can love other persons by loving God. There is a sense in which the love you have of another human being can participate in God's love for them. Although some ascetic, austere Christians regard loving God and loving "the world" as incompatible, this robust alternative concept allows one to have a richer love for the world *because of* and not despite one's love of God. Christianity also provides an extraordinary arena in which to engage in lovingly affirming and participating in the lives of others through petitionary prayer. Such prayers cannot take the place of actual, material contributions to others (what Roman Catholics used to call corporeal acts of mercy), but they provide an important means by which to express love for others and to intercede for their well-being.

Agape love: In the definition of love used in this chapter there has been no distinction between different categories of love. In ancient Greek, "erōs" was used of love that involves desire for the beloved. "Erōs" may or may not involve sexual or erotic desire, but it does involve a desire to be united or in the presence of the beloved (sometimes called unitive love). Then there is "phileō" love which may fittingly describe more general objects of love as in the love of wisdom. Then there is "agapē" love which has a distinctive Christian origin, referring to love that is selfless and unconditional. I believe that all three kinds of love fit the definition of love defended earlier, but in Christian terms agape love is often identified with divine love. Agape love does not necessarily accept or delight in everything about the beloved. It can involve redeeming love (to be discussed next), but it is not conditioned on what the beloved does or has done. This is a kind of love-no-matter-what state. It is also selfless in the sense that the love is not contingent on the beloved returning the love or the lover getting some kind of personal benefit or gain from the loving. More on agape after a brief look at redeeming love.

Redeeming love: At the heart of Christianity is the conviction that one can find in Christ the opportunity for a renewed life, dying to the old self and being regenerated in the image and likeness of Christ. This process of redemption is brought about because of the love of Christ, but it also sets before each person the ideal of finding fullness of life (and thus fulfillment) in relationship with Christ. What may be called "redeeming love" is the loving engagement in this renewed redemption whereby persons pursue and long for a redeemed (or unitive) life with God in Christ. This speaks practically to one of the puzzles that arises in the philosophy of love. When you love another person, do you love him simply as he is? What if you do not think the person in his present position is very healthy or redemptive? Can you love another person by not loving who he is now, but loving who you hope he will become? I suggest that this is where agape love and redeeming love can work together. Agape love involves affirming the person's good and desiring to take pleasure in his good selflessly and unconditionally; it involves loving who he is now. But redeeming love can be dynamic, for it is the kind of love that longs for the beloved to come to a life of true fulfillment in a redeemed identity in Christ.

I close by looking back, from a distinctively Christian point of view, at the danger of loving love. I still think that Augustine was right that there can be a danger of loving love, because of the risk that such love could not survive a state of unrequitedness or a failure of returned love. One of the beauties of the Christian understanding of love is that the love of God for you and me does not depend upon our loving God. Biblical history is filled with many narratives (principally the story of Christ's crucifixion) in which divine love goes unrequited (to say the least) and yet this divine love for us is undiminished. Even so, if Aelred of Rievaulx, St. Bernard of Clairvaux, and so many other Christian thinkers are right, there is a sense in which God does love our love and desires it. This is especially apparent in the Old Testament Song of Songs, which has been traditionally interpreted as a picture of the love between the soul and God. Some Christians have been scandalized that such an erotic text is even in the Bible at all, but most Christians have relished it as both an affirmation of the good of erotic love and an allegory of God's deep and searching love and desire for the love of the soul.[9] It is that extraordinary vision of a generous, overflowing, immutable, divine love which seeks our love in return that has led so many Christians over the centuries and in different cultures to affirm the line that began this chapter: Whoever does not love does not know God, for God is love.

Questions for Further Reflection

1. Loving another person seems to involve having an accurate understanding of the beloved. If, for example, you think you love Skippy because Skippy is a great adventurer, a poet, a philosopher, and a superior athlete, and yet Skippy is none of these things (Skippy is cowardly, hates poetry and philosophy and lives on a sofa in front of a giant television), it appears that you do not really love Skippy but only your image of Skippy. But if this is right, how are we to understand loving a person whom you have not been in communication with for years? She may have changed completely since you last met. In this case, if you claim to love her, aren't you loving the image of who she was rather than the person she is today?

2. Can you love others if you do not love or respect yourself?

3. What do you think of the claim that you can love persons less than you should, but you cannot love a person more than you should?

4. In what concrete ways might Christians enhance the practice of love amongst themselves, with the world, and with God?

9. St. Bernard of Clairvaux wrote and delivered eighty-six fascinating sermons on The Song of Songs, available in a four-volume translation by Kilian Walsh (Kalamazoo, MI: Cistercian Publications, 1976).

Compassion

Michael W. Austin

Unlike many of the virtues described in this book, compassion is *in*. Celebrities champion compassionate causes. Bono, U2's lead singer, has been instrumental in bringing attention and aid to those in Africa who suffer deeply due to grinding poverty, AIDS, and unfair trade policies. Other celebrities such as Julia Roberts, George Clooney, and Tom Brady have joined in this fight through their involvement with the ONE campaign.

Compassion pops up seemingly everywhere. At the beginning of the new millennium, in the realm of politics, we heard a lot about compassionate conservatism. The federal government has a Compassion Capital Fund, and there are numerous corporate forms of compassion. There is a child welfare organization called Compassion International, an order of nuns called the Sisters of Compassion, a group called Animal Compassion, and even one called Compassion for Greyhounds. Many of the virtues discussed in other chapters of this book such as faith, humility, and zeal have fewer devotees proclaiming their merits in our culture. Compassion, however, appears to have wide support as a worthwhile and desirable character trait.

A Christian understanding of the virtue of compassion is the main focus of this chapter. And our moral exemplar in this regard is of course Jesus himself, who was moved with compassion at the suffering of those he encountered in his earthly ministry (e.g., Matt. 9:35-37; Mark 6:30-44).

Bob Morrin provided several very helpful comments on a previous version of this paper, for which I am grateful.

In what follows, I will clarify what compassion is, drawing from both classical and contemporary sources, and also discuss compassion as a Christian moral virtue. In addition, I will offer some practical advice and questions for reflection aimed at assisting in the acquisition and practice of this important virtue. The ultimate aim of this chapter is therefore not only to develop a deeper understanding of compassion, but also to help us become more compassionate people in our everyday lives.

Virtue, Happiness, and the Good Life

The points raised in this chapter depend on the conviction that the possession and expression of certain moral virtues, including compassion, are essential to a good, flourishing, and abundant human life. Moral philosophers in the tradition of Aristotle often define virtue as an excellent state of character that is conducive to human flourishing. Christian theism has the resources, as a worldview, to explain why the intellectual and moral virtues are conducive to our flourishing, and why they are excellences of character. Virtues are conducive to flourishing because God designed human beings such that they function best when possessing and exemplifying the virtues. Virtues are excellences because they reflect the perfect character of God.

Jesus Christ is the ideal person, the moral exemplar we should endeavor to imitate. In this chapter, I will address the virtue of compassion as a trait we should seek to possess and display in our efforts to imitate Christ. In this imitation, we will be better suited to both exemplify and experience the abundant life Christ came to give (see John 10:10).

The Nature of Compassion

As followers of Christ, seeking to take on his character, we should be committed to compassion. But what does such a commitment involve? In his discussion of the nature of commitment, philosopher Roger Trigg says that

> the fact of commitment logically entails certain beliefs and precludes certain others. One must believe what one is committed to. . . . Any

> commitment, it seems, depends on two distinct elements. It presupposes certain beliefs and also involves personal dedication to the actions implied by them. Each element can occur without the other, but if someone is truly committed, both elements will be present.[1]

The points raised by Trigg are relevant as we seek to understand and embody the virtue of compassion. If we are truly committed to being compassionate people, we must have certain beliefs about the nature of compassion as a moral virtue. We must also possess a dedication to doing the acts that the virtue of compassion inclines us to perform. Additionally, at least when discussing the embodiment of a moral virtue, we should include certain emotional states as well. The upshot is that a commitment to and the embodiment of compassion involves belief, emotion, and action. In this section, I explore these three different aspects of compassion: cognitive, emotional, and active. The cognitive aspect of this virtue has to do with the beliefs associated with its possession. What beliefs are involved when one exercises compassion, about oneself, those who suffer, and reality as a whole? The emotional aspect of compassion has to do with the feelings and desires involved in compassion. When we feel compassion, what is it that we feel? What do we want, when we have compassion for others? Finally, the active aspect of compassion relates to the actions that the relevant beliefs and emotions should produce. What sorts of actions does compassion lead us to perform?

The Cognitive Aspect of Compassion

When speaking of the cognitive aspect of compassion, I am referring to the relevant beliefs one has when exemplifying this moral virtue. The example of Jesus is instructive, as illustrated in Matthew 9:35-36:

> Jesus was going through all the cities and villages, teaching in their synagogues and proclaiming the gospel of the kingdom, and healing every kind of disease and every kind of sickness. Seeing the people, He

1. Roger Trigg, *Reason and Commitment* (New York: Cambridge University Press, 1973), p. 44.

> felt compassion for them, because they were distressed and dispirited like sheep without a shepherd.[2]

It is noteworthy that Jesus felt compassion for the people, and I will discuss this in the next section. It is also important that the compassion of Jesus led him to act. At present, however, I will focus on the beliefs that Jesus possessed relative to compassion. It is evident from the passage that Jesus believed that the people were genuinely in need, given their distressed and dispirited state. From the context, the diseases and sicknesses were one source of this distress, but the passage also points to the people's need for a "shepherd." They needed someone to heal them, as well as guide, protect, and care for them as a shepherd does for his sheep. And this is precisely what makes the gospel of the kingdom good news. We are able to live under the rule and reign of God, who is the good shepherd. Implicitly, we can also see that Jesus believed that the people were worthy of compassion, not in the sense that they deserved his compassion, but in the sense that they were valuable and so proper objects of compassion as humans made in the image of God. It is safe to assume that if the people were neither in need nor valuable, there would then be no reason to have compassion on them. These beliefs are crucial insofar as they form an important cognitive basis for the appropriateness of compassion.

Philosophers have noted the importance of the cognitive aspect of compassion as well. Contemporary philosopher Martha Nussbaum provides insightful commentary on this aspect of compassion in her discussion of Aristotle's treatment of this virtue.[3] According to Nussbaum, Aristotle offers three cognitive requirements of compassion. First, one must believe that the suffering endured by the sufferer is serious, not trivial. Second, one must believe that the suffering in question is undeserved. Third, one must believe that the same sort of suffering could happen to him or her.

Let's first consider the belief that the suffering in question must be *serious.* Much of the so-called suffering of everyday life would fail to fulfill this cognitive requirement. That is, even though we might believe that

2. For this and subsequent biblical references, unless otherwise noted, I am using the New American Standard Bible (NASB).

3. See Martha Nussbaum, *Upheavals of Thought: The Intelligence of Emotions* (Cambridge: Cambridge University Press, 2001), pp. 304-27.

certain routine difficulties represent a kind of "suffering," that belief is unjustified. Traffic congestion, computer glitches, minor physical discomfort, and waiting more than two minutes for one's fast food meal are fairly trivial instances of suffering. In fact, they are better thought of as mere inconveniences. It would be counterintuitive to say that we should have compassion on those who have been inconvenienced. But what sorts of experiences are serious enough to merit compassion? According to Aristotle,

> All unpleasant and painful things excite pity if they tend to destroy, pain and annihilate; and all such evils as are due to chance, if they are serious. The painful and destructive evils are: death in its various forms, bodily injuries and afflictions, old age, diseases, lack of food. The evils due to chance are: friendlessness, scarcity of friends (it is a pitiful thing to be torn away from friends and companions), deformity, weakness, mutilation; evil coming from a source from which good ought to have come; and the frequent repetition of such misfortunes.[4]

Death, injury, illness, loneliness, and betrayal are all occasions for compassion. When we encounter someone who is undergoing one or more of these occasions of suffering, we should have compassion on that person. And there is no shortage of such instances of suffering in our world, even if we are fortunate enough that no one in our immediate circle of family and friends is going through such serious suffering. For example, 24,000 people die every day from hunger and hunger related illnesses, and 75 percent of these deaths are children aged 5 and under. 6,000 people die every day from AIDS in Africa alone. Thousands of children are forced to become child soldiers in many parts of the world. Children are emotionally and physically abused and neglected, genocide is a recurring problem, the young and old suffer from cancer and other debilitating and fatal diseases, deep and lasting friendships are becoming a rarity in our society, and animals are treated inhumanely in factory farms. Instances of "evil coming from a source from which good ought to have come" abound, as children are preyed upon by parents, teachers, pastors, and others entrusted with their care. Clearly there is an abundance of serious suffering in our world, and so an abundance of opportunities for compassion.

4. Aristotle, *Rhetoric* 1836a-b.

Regarding the seriousness of any particular case of suffering, Nussbaum rightly points out that our determinations of the seriousness of the suffering of others is fallible. Given this, we should at least sometimes defer to others' judgments. For example, if members of a group in society have suffered in ways that I as a member of a more privileged race, class, or gender have not, then it may be the case that I should defer to the evaluations made by qualified members of that group.

Before moving on to the second requirement of the cognitive aspect of compassion, I would like to add one further qualification. Sometimes, the seriousness of the suffering in question will be a matter of perspective. This is not to endorse any sort of relativism about truth or morality, but rather to note that sometimes suffering that is not serious in Aristotle's sense can still merit compassion. For example, if one of my children doesn't perform well in a soccer game, this is not serious suffering, all things considered. My child might feel pained at her athletic performance. While she is neither suffering from a debilitating disease nor in excruciating pain, she is still undergoing suffering. From her perspective, that she suffers is understandable and a perfectly reasonable way to feel, as long as the intensity and/or duration of the suffering is proportional to its cause. Given this, it is fair to say that I should have compassion on her.

I fear that in these sorts of instances, we are too quick to judge the suffering of others as trivial (and often we are too quick to judge our own suffering as serious!). This might have even more force as a temptation for those of us who are followers of Christ, because many of us tend to make strong distinctions in our minds when assigning value to particular pursuits. So we might think of going on a mission trip to Haiti as being quite significant, and of playing soccer as being insignificant. If we have such a view, then we find it easier to dismiss the emotional pain that a child might experience on the soccer field because of our broader view of the overall significance of athletics. Even if this view of the relative insignificance of sport is an accurate one — which it is not, in my view — to disregard and dismiss the pain of one's child in such a situation as trivial would be callous. The upshot is that there are cases when we should still feel and act with compassion towards another person, even when the suffering she is experiencing is not "serious" in an Aristotelian sense.

The second cognitive requirement of compassion for Aristotle is that the suffering in question must be *undeserved.* According to Aristotle, if the one who suffers deserves to suffer, then we should not have compassion on that person. For example, Aristotle holds that the good human being rejoices at the suffering of the murderer, because justice is being done. In less extreme circumstances, this thought also seems to ring true. If a person who suffers brought the suffering on himself in some way that he then deserves to suffer, compassion seems to be a misguided response. A person might build up significant financial debt, and then begin to suffer the consequences in his financial life. We might think that such a person deserves this hardship, because he created it for himself by his own unwise choices.

My view, by contrast, is that we can and should extend compassion to others, even when the suffering in question is both deserved and appropriately proportioned. For example, in the film *Dead Man Walking*, Sister Helen Prejean shows compassion towards the convicted murderer played by Sean Penn, and I think that she is right to do so. She also shows compassion to the families of his victims. A person who is guilty of murder may deserve to suffer and perhaps in some cases to die, but it need not follow from this that we should not have compassion on him. We may have compassion for him because of the character that he possesses. We might feel sorry that someone could be in such a wretched state, and have compassion on those grounds. In more everyday circumstances, we may still have compassion on those who suffer in small or large ways because of their unwise choices. We need practical wisdom here, but there are times when compassion is the right response, even to deserved suffering.

Aristotle's third requirement of the cognitive aspect of compassion is the belief that the same thing could happen to me. Given human frailty, we must realize that the suffering others endure could also happen to us, or one of our loved ones. In the movie trilogy *The Lord of the Rings*, Frodo's attitude towards Gollum exemplifies this aspect of compassion. Gollum is despised by nearly everyone he comes into contact with, but Frodo has compassion on this creature — in part because he knows that the ring has inflicted great suffering upon Gollum. Frodo knows firsthand the burden of carrying the ring, and sees that he could become what Gollum is, if the ring has its way. Examples can be drawn from real life, as well. One reason that some people who are well-off give aid to those in need is that the well-off realize that if they were in need they would want the aid of others. There is an intuitive plausibility to the claim that I must believe that the same sort of suffering could happen to me in order to have compassion on others.

However, in her discussion of these issues, Nussbaum rejects this condition, and I think that she is right to do so. There are some things that almost certainly will not happen to me (such as forced conscription), but it need not follow that I cannot have compassion on child soldiers who are forced to fight. In place of this condition, Nussbaum argues that we must make a particular judgment, namely, that the suffering of other people impacts our own flourishing. I must take the flourishing of others to be one of the important aims of my own life. When I encounter someone who suffers, relieving that suffering should be important to me. To do this, I must widen my circle of concern beyond family and friends to others in my community, country, and world. To be compassionate, I must ask, "What would I want others to do for me, if I were in their shoes?" When we do this, our attention turns to those who are the worst-off in society — the poor, the ill, and the exploited — and compassion then directs us to raise the floor of society. I would argue that compassion directs us to at least seek to ensure that the basic needs of every human being are met, including food, shelter, and basic medical care. True compassion, it seems, allows for nothing less than this, given the dignity and frailty of human beings.

As followers of Christ, we have additional motivation and rationale for taking the welfare of others as one of our own important commitments: Jesus modeled this in the way that he lived and died. In his letter to the Philippians, the apostle Paul urges the church at Philippi to "Do nothing from selfishness or empty conceit, but with humility of mind regard one another as more important than yourselves; do not merely look out for your own personal interests, but also for the interests of others" (Phil. 2:3-4). A Christian view of a life well lived includes an unselfish concern for the welfare of other people. The Christian prescription for a good life includes a heavy dose of self-denial, losing our lives for the sake of Christ, with the result being that we actually find our lives (see Matt. 16:24-25). So the type of self-denial and concern for others that can be expressed through compassion impacts our own flourishing as human beings, according to Scripture. Our concern for others ultimately reflects the love that exists among the members of the Trinity, and as such should certainly be one of the primary aims of our lives. It is also a way in which we can be a part of the answer to the Lord's Prayer: we can be instrumental in providing daily bread for those who are in need. So, we should add to Nussbaum's discussion of Aristotle that those of us who are followers of Christ show compassion in part because we believe that this is God's clear will for our lives. It is a way we can reflect God's character and advance his kingdom on earth.

There is one final cognitive component of the virtue of compassion that I would like to add to this discussion. In a certain sense, people sometimes *deserve* to be shown compassion. Compassion is not an issue of *charity,* but rather it is an issue of *justice.* This claim is related to the belief that Jesus possessed when he felt compassion on the people in the aforementioned passage from Matthew, namely, that the people were worthy of being shown compassion. In order to fully understand the claim that we should believe that compassion is an issue of justice, some distinctions that moral philosophers often use will be helpful.

There is a threefold way to classify actions, from the moral point of view. Some actions are *morally forbidden,* such as murder. Such actions should never be performed, they are prohibited by morality. Other actions are *morally required.* A morally required action is one that we are obligated to do, morally speaking. For example, spouses are morally required to remain faithful to one another. Finally, some actions are *supererogatory.* Literally, this term means "beyond duty." A supererogatory act is not morally required — we are not obligated to perform it — but it is still a very good thing to do. Such actions are morally heroic, in the sense that it would be permissible to refrain from doing them but we praise those who do perform them. For example, donating a kidney to a stranger in order to save her life is a supererogatory action. It is a morally heroic act, but not one that we are morally required to perform. If I refrain from doing this, it does not follow that I have done something immoral.

These distinctions are relevant to compassion in the following way. In many contexts, we tend to think of compassionate actions as good things to do, but not in the sense that we are morally required to do them. We often think of compassionate acts, especially as they relate to the poor, as supererogatory acts of charity.[5] My claim is that exemplifying the virtue of compassion in our everyday lives is a matter of justice, rather than an optional matter of charity. The basic reason that compassion is an obligatory matter of justice, apart from the biblical injunctions, is that

5. I am using "charity" here in its contemporary sense, rather than in the sense used in some older translations of the Bible in which charity is the translation given for agape.

human beings have great value as image-bearers of God. Genesis 1:27 states that humans are created "in the image of God," but what does this mean? A variety of answers have been given to this question, but for our purposes, it is enough to point out that being made in God's image means that we are God's representatives, and that we are representational of who God is.[6] We are free, relational, morally responsible, self-conscious beings. We reflect and represent who God is as human persons made in his image. God is the locus of ultimate value, and we, as human beings created in his image and to reflect his character, share in that value. This has important implications for ethics generally, and the virtue of compassion specifically. Given that all human beings are made in the image of God, all human beings possess a basic dignity, a fundamental value such that they have a conditional right to have their basic needs met.[7] Hence, in some contexts, especially when a person's basic needs are at stake, showing compassion is an obligatory matter of justice rather than an optional matter of charity.

The Emotional Aspect of Compassion

There is a strong tradition in ethics that is wary of the emotions. Some strands of thought include the view that emotions don't matter, but rather what matters is doing one's duty, regardless of how one feels about it. There is a kernel of truth here, as we should do what's right even if we don't "feel like it." This is an important point in a culture where feelings, in practice, serve to justify much of what we do or fail to do. However, to disregard emotions because they are sometimes unreliable or irrational is a mistake. If we are concerned not only about *doing* what is right, but *being* a good person, then emotions are quite important. The ideally good person not only does what is right, but feels the right way about doing what is right. For example, Karina might decide to give a sum of money to

6. Robert L. Saucy, "Theology of Human Nature," in *Christian Perspectives on Being Human: A Multidisciplinary Approach,* ed. J. P. Moreland and David M. Ciocchi (Grand Rapids: Baker, 1993), pp. 17-52.

7. The right is conditional because we may forfeit it. For example, if I am able to work and work is available, but I choose not to do so out of sloth or for some other bad reason, it does not follow that others are obligated to help meet my basic needs.

Compassion International in order to provide for a child in another country, because she believes that this is her duty. However, if she feels cold and indifferent towards the child, and gives her monetary gift grudgingly, there is something lacking, from the moral point of view. It is good that she has done the morally right action, but it is also desirable that she possess a morally praiseworthy character. With respect to emotions, this would entail that Karina feel neither cold nor indifferent, and that she cheerfully offers her monetary gift for the benefit of the child. It is true that it is better for Karina to give the money without the proper emotions than not to give the money at all. It is not *necessary* to feel compassion in order to engage in compassionate acts, and the lack of feeling does not justify a lack of action. It is better to do the compassionate thing without the relevant emotions than, having no such emotions, to fail to act compassionately. But if we aspire to genuine moral excellence, we will aspire to have the relevant emotions, because this says something about our character. To be an intellectually and morally virtuous person involves the right sort of connections between reality, our beliefs, our feelings, and our actions. Ideally, then, the compassionate person sees the reality of suffering, the worth of human beings, has the appropriate emotional response, and acts to alleviate the suffering.

With regard to feeling and emotion, it is important to point out that compassion involves pain for the one possessing this virtue. To feel compassion for someone is to feel pained by that person's suffering. As stated above, Jesus felt compassion for the people. Paul tells us in Romans 12:15 to "weep with those who weep." Consider the fact that this is antithetical to the contemporary understanding of happiness as an intense feeling of pleasant satisfaction. We don't "feel good" when we feel compassion for others, we feel pained. Ultimately, we will likely feel good as a by-product of being compassionate. However, the primary point of compassion, and of the other moral and intellectual virtues, is not having pleasant emotional experiences, but rather being a good, wise, and Christlike person.

A practical problem with all of this is that it often seems that emotions lie outside of our control. We cannot control how we feel. This is true, insofar as we cannot directly control how we feel. If somebody offered me one million dollars to feel compassionate towards the poor, there is no guarantee that I could do it. However, over time, I could indirectly control whether or not I have such a feeling. I might read about the virtue of compassion, read biographies of those who lived out this virtue, engage in some of the relevant spiritual disciplines, meditate on appropriate biblical texts, pray for the acquisition of this virtue, and simply attend to the plight of the poor in our world. Then, over time, I would likely come to have certain beliefs and possess the right kind of emotions.

Even if, after some honest self-assessment, we come to the realization that we are missing the emotional aspect of compassion, we need not despair. We can, as followers of the Way of Christ, learn from him and from wise teachers in his Way how to become compassionate. There is the opportunity for genuine and deep moral and spiritual growth if we live as apprentices of Jesus. In the long run we should seek to have the proper emotions as well as the proper beliefs and actions if we are seeking to be like Christ in all aspects of our being. And in the long run we can expect fruit in this area of our lives if we take the proper steps in partnership with the Spirit of Christ.

The Active Aspect of Compassion

Of course, belief and emotion are not all that is required to be a compassionate person. We must, ultimately, do compassionate acts. Jesus' compassion moved him to *act.* In Matthew 14 Jesus felt compassion which moved him to feed and to heal. In Matthew 9, after feeling compassion for the people, Jesus implores his disciples to pray for laborers to go out into the harvest, and then sends the Twelve on a mission to cast out unclean spirits, heal, and proclaim the kingdom of heaven. So Jesus himself acts in compassionate ways, and implores his followers to go and do likewise. The very purpose of the incarnation, life, death, and resurrection of Jesus is bound up with his compassion for lost human beings.

South African Archbishop Desmond Tutu once said that "Compassion is not just feeling with someone, but seeking to change the situation. Frequently people think compassion and love are merely sentimental. No! They are very demanding. If you are going to be compassionate, be prepared for action!"[8]

Interestingly, the term "compassionate" has a verb form. Bishop Joseph Butler (1692-1752), an influential British pastor, theologian, and phi-

8. *Psychology Today* (March/April 2005). Accessed online, July 5, 2007 (http://psychologytoday.com/articles/pto-20050429-000005.html).

losopher whose writings still receive the attention of philosophers today, observes in a sermon on compassion that when we

> rejoice in the prosperity of others, and *compassionate* their distresses, we, as it were, substitute them for ourselves, their interest for our own; and have the same kind of pleasure in their prosperity and sorrow in their distress, as we have . . . upon our own.[9]

This passage from Butler is pregnant with meaning and insight, but note how he speaks of compassion. We are to *compassionate* the distresses of others. True compassion includes assisting others who are in distress.[10] For Butler, as for Christ, compassion necessarily involves action.

As an action that we engage in, compassion often involves sacrifice. Perhaps it requires that we give up some of our comfort, our time, or our talent. As Butler pointed out, it involves taking the distress of others to be as significant as our own distress. As such, it involves a turning away from what philosopher Immanuel Kant (1724-1804) called "the dear self."[11] We often find self-love at the bottom of actions that otherwise appear to be morally right, including acts of compassion. However, even if this assessment is descriptively accurate, this does not count against the claim that we ought to act out of a genuine and unselfish concern for others. Nor does it entail that we shouldn't seek to take the flourishing of others to be as or more important than our own. This is demanding, to be sure, but it remains within our reach, as we seek to alleviate the distresses of not only the poor and the sick, but also those closest to us.

Compassionate Spouses, Friends, and Parents

When we think of compassion, we often see it as a virtue to be expressed toward the sick, the suffering, and the poor. These individuals are surely

9. Joseph Butler, *Fifteen Sermons* (London: G. Bell and Sons, 1914), p. 83 (emphasis added).

10. See also Butler, *Fifteen Sermons,* p. 87.

11. Immanuel Kant, *Grounding for the Metaphysics of Morals,* 3rd edn. (Indianapolis: Hackett, 1993), pp. 19-20. For more on Kant's views here and their connection to faith in God, see Kelly James Clark and Anne Poortenga, *The Story of Ethics* (Upper Saddle River, NJ: Prentice-Hall, 2003), pp. 66-71.

important subjects of compassion. However, the scope of compassion goes beyond such individuals, and includes all of the people that we encounter in our everyday lives. Here I will focus on opportunities for compassion in the context of marriage, parenthood, and friendship. Strangely, it is often in these contexts that compassion is most difficult to express. People often treat family members, for example, in ways that they would never dream of treating complete strangers.

Marriage and friendship provide numerous opportunities for showing compassion, and numerous temptations to display a variety of vices, such as callousness and selfishness. Compassion may take a variety of forms within marriage. Certainly when our spouse is in physical or emotional pain, we should exercise compassion by seeking to bear the burden that he or she carries. One less obvious way to show compassion to our spouse relates to patience, grace, and forgiveness. We know our spouses better than anyone, and we see their weaknesses and strengths day after day. This is one of the blessings of marriage, inasmuch as a deep level of intimacy is good and fulfilling. However, this up close and personal view of our spouse can hinder compassion. For example, a husband will ideally ask for forgiveness for his impatience and self-centeredness when he has displayed it with his wife, but if this is an ongoing pattern it will be difficult for her to continue to extend forgiveness to him. If he is making a good-faith effort, and not simply asking for forgiveness while doing nothing to foster change in his character, compassion can come into play as follows. The wife can see that this is an especially difficult area of struggle for her husband, and have compassion on him as he seeks to overcome this particular area of sin. It can be helpful here for her to consider her own particularly difficult struggles, which can enable her to empathize with those of her husband, even if they are different from her own. There are numerous other ways that compassion should occur within a marriage or a close friendship. Simply seeing the relevance of this virtue for marriage and friendship is an important step in improving the quality of these vital human relationships.

Turning to our role as parents, we recall that Jesus taught us by his words and actions that children are valuable, and that their needs and well-being are important. In Mark 10:13-16 the disciples rebuked those who were bringing the little children to Jesus. Christ, however, was indignant at this and took the children in his arms and blessed them.

This has significance for the centrality of compassion for the parent-child relationship. As parents, we can tend to fail to see our kids as our "neighbors" — whom we should love and offer compassion towards.[12] Jesus commands us to love our neighbors as ourselves, and showing compassion towards our neighbors is one way to show love. We make the same mistake that some of the people in Jesus' day made, which he addressed with the parable of the good Samaritan. Part of the point of the parable is that everyone is our neighbor. Even Samaritans fall within the scope of neighborly love. We often overlook the fact that our children fall within the scope of this command as well.

We can have compassion on our children as they face the challenges and struggles of growing up, both physically and emotionally. One reason that we may fail to show compassion is that we expect more of our children than is reasonable. For example, it is not reasonable to expect a six-year-old to be at the same level of moral development as a sixteen-year-old, but in my experience Christian parents often have such (or greater) expectations. Some Christian parenting literature advocates expecting "first-time obedience" with children, and there is perhaps nothing wrong with this as an ideal. However, as an iron-clad standard this is not only unrealistic but also misguided, and is perhaps motivated more by pride than concern for the child's well-being and flourishing. Sometimes circumstances will call for grace, rather than a rigid application of some principle of parenting. Part of showing love and compassion to our children is realizing what stage of development they are in, the strengths and weaknesses of their particular personalities, and how the challenges of life feel to them. We too easily dismiss their struggles or challenges as "insignificant," which in the grand scheme of things may be true. However, we must recall that failure to score a basket or to receive an invitation to a party that everyone else is attending can be very difficult emotionally for children. To fail to empathize with our kids in such situations is to show callousness, not compassion.

It is clear that the demands of compassion are high, and that we must rely on God to help us develop this trait. The aim of the final section is to help us overcome the barriers that get in the way of compassion, and begin to develop this important virtue.

12. I owe this point to Curt Gardner.

Some Practical Advice for Developing Compassion

Compassion is something that many of us find easy to praise, but hard to practice. As already noted, Bishop Butler was a strong advocate of the virtue of compassion. His words are as timely today as when he first spoke them, given our propensity to direct our attention away from the suffering that exists in our world:

> In many cases, it is very much in our power to alleviate the miseries of each other. . . . [But] men, for the most part, are so engaged in the business and pleasures of the world, as to overlook and turn away from objects of misery; which are plainly considered as interruptions to them in their way, as intruders upon their business, their gaiety and mirth; compassion is an advocate within us in their behalf; to gain the unhappy admittance and access, to make their case attended to.[13]

Butler notes that we see those who are suffering as barriers to our own happiness, recreation, and liberty. They interfere with our plans and projects. But compassion should move us to shift our attention to their suffering, and to ways we can alleviate it. In our contemporary culture, distractions seem omnipresent. Cell phones, iPods, the internet, and all of the rest of our electronic gadgetry, as well as our general focus on and thirst for entertainment, often stand between us and those who need our aid. These gadgets are not intrinsically bad and can be very beneficial. My point is that they have the potential to feed our tendency towards self-absorption. In so many ways, this vice is encouraged by the world around us, whether directly by advertising or in more subtle ways through our general, culturally-induced understanding of the good life — which focuses on the individual rather than the community, and perhaps especially on the lives of celebrities. When we do face the reality of suffering around us, we might feel bad and perhaps even write a check. Then we move on and forget about it, as our attention is directed elsewhere. A good part of the battle is to merely attend to the cases of those who are in misery, as so much in our lives tends to turn our focus away from such individuals. So one way to develop the virtue of compassion is to simply turn our focus towards those who suffer.

13. *Fifteen Sermons,* p. 100.

Another barrier to developing compassion is self-deception. We may try to get ourselves off the hook, so to speak, by lying to ourselves. We might tell ourselves that "There's not that much suffering in the world," "There's nothing that I can do," or "The poor are just lazy." If these things were true, then we might be relieved of our obligations to help those in need. But they aren't, and so we're not. Another way we deceive ourselves is by magnifying the concerns and troubles in our own lives, which then prevents us from attending to the deeper and more serious suffering of others. When we contemplate the relative significance of our suffering compared to that of the AIDS orphan in Africa, the child soldier in Uganda, or any family in a war zone, we can undergo a reality check that is useful as we seek to cultivate compassion.

An important aspect of the life of Jesus is that he was *with* those who suffered. He spent time with the sick, the poor, and the social outcasts. We must follow his example. This is difficult, given the socioeconomic segregation that exists in much of society. Many churches reflect this segregation, which adds to the difficulty. We must be intentional about crossing the socioeconomic barriers that exist, and in my own limited experience it is worth the trip. I've learned important lessons from time spent in conversation with those in poverty and those suffering from drug addiction, for example. There are other ways to be with those who are in need. For example, Compassion International allows one to direct a monthly gift toward a particular child, and one then has the opportunity to correspond with that child and encourage him or her via letters and gifts.[14] The support enables the child to receive education, health care, spiritual input, and a safe place to play. This is a different but still valuable way to be with those who are in need.

A very useful strategy for growing in compassion is to develop and employ our God-given faculty of the imagination. In Hebrews 13:3 (NIV), we are commanded to employ the imagination as a means to love others: "Remember those in prison *as if* you were their fellow prisoners, and those who are mistreated *as if* you yourselves were suffering" (italics added). The italicized words highlight the need for using our imaginations to love and care for those who are in prison and mistreated. To do so, we must imagine what it is like for them to undergo imprisonment and mistreatment, respectively. If we do this, we will have a sense of soli-

14. See http://www.compassion.com.

darity with such people, and this can foster compassion. And this specific incarnation of compassion is an important part of authentic Christian spirituality (see Matt. 25:34-40). Regarding the imagination, the contemplation of works of art can help us care about and seek to help those who suffer. And we need not take a trip to the museum; simply watching a movie can accomplish this. For example, a viewing of recent films such as *Hotel Rwanda* or *Blood Diamond* can engage us in powerful ways and help motivate us to do our part in protecting innocent lives, even those on the other side of the planet. We must put ourselves in the shoes of others and try to imagine what life is like for those who suffer from poverty, illness, war, homelessness, and the like. As we seek to understand others, we may begin to feel part of what they feel, and this may fuel compassion in us.

Finally, an excellent way to develop compassion is to participate in (or create) communities of compassion. By banding together with others who share our concerns, we can help create momentum and integrate a commitment to compassion in our lives as we work together to make real changes. Existing organizations such as Habitat for Humanity provide a fairly easy entry point into doing something. Many churches provide help to the poor in the form of food banks, job training, and financial support. If your church doesn't do this, why not take the lead? There are also opportunities to band together via movements such as the ONE campaign, Save Darfur, International Justice Mission, and Right to Play.[15] These organizations not only provide concrete assistance on the ground, but they also work at removing some of the social and political causes of poverty and suffering through their grassroots lobbying efforts.

Conclusion: Kingdom Priority

Consider the scathing words of Jesus to the Pharisees in Matthew 23:23-24:

> Woe to you, scribes and Pharisees, hypocrites! For you tithe mint and dill and cummin, and have neglected the weightier provisions of the

15. Each of these groups has a presence on the internet. See, respectively, http://www.one.org; http://savedarfur.org; http://www.ijm.org; and http://www.righttoplay.com.

> law: justice and mercy and faithfulness; but these are the things you should have done without neglecting the others. You blind guides, who strain out a gnat and swallow a camel!

All too often we follow the path of the Pharisees, focusing on the less important at the expense of the more important. The more important and significant matters of God's kingdom are justice, mercy, and faithfulness. As we've seen, compassion is a matter of justice for all humans who are created in God's image. It is also a concrete way to extend mercy to those in distress. And it is clear that if we want to be apprentices of Jesus, we ought to follow him in his commitment to the virtue of compassion.

Questions for Further Reflection

1. How can I show compassion to those who are suffering from poverty, disease, and war? What resources do I have that could benefit others?
2. What aspect of compassion is most difficult for me — the cognitive, emotional, or active aspect? How can I develop this aspect of compassion?
3. Are there particular people in my everyday life that I have an especially difficult time being compassionate towards? Why is this? How, practically speaking, can I change?
4. How can I encourage compassion in my home, church, and community? What are some specific things that I can do?

Forgiveness

R. Douglas Geivett

PETER: Lord, how often will my brother sin against me and I forgive him? As many as seven times?
JESUS: I do not say to you seven times, but seventy times seven.

Introduction

"Watch out for that guy. He's a snake in the grass." I was given this advice by a friend about a mutual acquaintance. In due course, it would turn out that the real snake in the grass was my supposed "friend," who had a habit of dealing treacherously with people who threatened his fragile ego.

The word "treachery" is potent, to be sure, and it must be used judiciously. The *act* of treachery is potent, as well, and it must be managed with wisdom. Treachery occurs when one person in a position of apparent intimacy with another person exploits that relationship to achieve some personal goal at the expense of real injury to the other person. The treacherous person acts with highhanded perfidy against another person, thereby violating the faith and trust of that person. Often, one act of treachery leads to a series of others as the faithless individual nervously seeks to cover his tracks and control exposure of whatever damage he has caused.

I've had many helpful conversations with others about the nature of forgiveness and wish to thank them for their contribution to my understanding of this vital issue: Peter Everett, Howard Geivett, Greg Jesson, Holly Pivec, Ronald Tacelli, and Doug Wubbena.

Treachery bespeaks unilateral injury within a relationship. It's a one-way street. One party harms another who does not "have it coming." And frequently, the injured party doesn't *see* it coming. The injured person's character may or may not be unimpeachable. If it's not completely unimpeachable, there is, nevertheless, a significant disproportionality, a real undeservedness, of the harm inflicted by the treacherous party. The harm done is *asymmetrical.*

This chapter is not about treachery, but about the call to forgive in contexts of asymmetrical wrongdoing. There clearly are cases of asymmetrical wrongdoing, or unilateral harm. We know this from experience and we should know it from our study of Scripture. Unfortunately, some are in denial about this. They believe that in every instance of interpersonal conflict, every party to the conflict is blameworthy. This attitude is confused. It is also confusing. A victim of personal injury is twice injured if members of his community blame him no less than his assailant. This double injury is further compounded if the victim loses his grip on the reality of injustice done to himself. There are other confusions, to be addressed in this chapter.

Cases of asymmetrical wrongdoing are plentiful. Our most poignant experiences of asymmetrical harm provoke fresh consideration of the call to forgive. Our common vexation about how "difficult it is to forgive" already presupposes a certain understanding of what it means to forgive, an understanding that I believe to be a *mis*understanding of the nature of forgiveness.[1]

1. The virtue of forgiveness is vital to healthy relationships. But successful relationships and joyful community depend also on social and emotional intelligence and a rich stock of interpersonal skills. In the 1980s, Howard Gardner developed the idea of multiple intelligences. See his *Frames of Mind: The Theory of Multiple Intelligences,* 10th edn. (New York: Basic Books, 1993). Following his lead, many have seized upon the idea of "emotional intelligence." For a practical manual on this, see Daniel Goleman, *Emotional Intelligence* (New York: Bantam, 1997). Also, much valuable work has been done on the challenge of coping with especially difficult people, such as psychopaths, sociopaths, and unhealthy narcissists. I especially recommend Robert D. Hare, *Snakes in Suits: When Psychopaths Go to Work* (New York: Harper, 2007), and Nina Brown, *Working with the Self-Absorbed: How to Handle Narcissistic Personalities on the Job* (Oakland, CA: New Harbinger Publications, 2002).

Is Forgiveness a Virtue?

It is usual to think of forgiveness as an act or process. For this reason, it will seem, initially, that forgiveness is not any kind of virtue. But because forgiveness is a *moral* act (or process), performed (or engaged in) by a person toward another person — at least in contexts of asymmetrical wrongdoing, it is natural to think that there is some virtue or cluster of virtues that a person might have that would qualify her as "a forgiving person." Such a person forgives "habitually," you might say, because when she forgives she does so *from virtue.* She does not simply perform an act that — intentionally or not — results in forgiveness. She has a *disposition* to act (consciously or unconsciously) "forgivingly," as a person of character who has the relevant virtue or virtues. It is *characteristic* for her to forgive. She is apt to be known by others as that kind of person. And so, she, and not merely her act, is praiseworthy.

This is what it means to regard forgiveness as a virtue, and why a discussion of forgiveness belongs in a book on the virtues.

We could say that there are two senses of the phrase "a forgiving person." There is a weak or limited sense where the attribution is restricted. You call me a forgiving person because you observe me performing an act of forgiveness. Maybe it's you that I've forgiven. Out of gratitude, you regard me as forgiving. And so I am, in this instance. But am I characteristically forgiving? I may be, but I need not be for you to regard me the way you do. Your calling me a forgiving person in this context really is only an indirect way of evaluating my action, which may not issue from any special virtue of forgiveness. My response to future offenses is unpredictable if I don't have the virtue that goes with forgiving habitually.

In the stronger, unrestricted sense, the *explanation* for my action in forgiving you is rooted in the fact that I have the virtue of forgiveness. This is the sense of being "a forgiving person" intended throughout this chapter. In the strong sense, a forgiving person is one who exhibits expertise in forgiveness. This is important, for we learn virtue best from those who exhibit virtue. And so, we learn forgiveness — that is, we learn how to *be* forgiving — by attending closely to what forgiveness looks like when practiced by a person with the virtue of forgiveness.[2]

2. Robert C. Roberts has introduced the term "forgivingness" to refer to the vir-

Forgiveness in the Teaching of Jesus

Another aid to learning virtue is direct instruction. Instruction about virtue is important, for it enables us to recognize a virtuous person should we ever encounter one. There's a critical dialectic between these two modes of learning, however. The most trustworthy instruction in the art of forgiving, for example, comes from one with the virtue of forgiveness.

Jesus of Nazareth is greatly admired for his many virtues and the character of his moral instruction. For Christians, this admiration is unqualified. A true disciple of Jesus recognizes, with others, the exceptional insight of the man, and marvels at his moral constitution. But the true disciple of Jesus also stands in relationship with Jesus. Thus, he knows himself to be loved by Jesus, morally inspired by Jesus, and, yes, forgiven by Jesus. The words and actions of Jesus resonate with greater moral authority for anyone who has experienced Jesus' forgiveness.

And so we turn to consider explicit instruction by Jesus about the call to forgive and the nature of its corresponding virtue.

The Lord's Prayer

Jesus instructed his disciples in the art of prayer. Probably he did this on more than one occasion, for the circumstances surrounding the two gospel accounts we have differ in some respects.

Reflecting on "the Lord's prayer," we notice a natural connection between the problem of interpersonal reconciliation — where forgiveness of wrongdoers is a critical component — and the in-breaking of the kingdom of God.

The Lord's Prayer in the Gospel of Matthew In the Gospel of Matthew, Jesus' counsel on prayer is embedded in a lengthy discourse known as the Sermon on the Mount. Depending on how you count units of material in this discourse of 107 verses, the portion on prayer in chapter 6 comes to nine or eleven verses (6:5-13 or 6:5-15). The connection between 6:14-15 and 6:5-13 argues for the larger delimitation. This matters because 6:14-15

---

tue of forgiveness and developed a compelling account of this virtue. See Roberts, "Forgivingness," *American Philosophical Quarterly* 32.4 (1995): 289-306.

focus narrowly on the call to forgive, and in direct connection with what is included in the prayer of 6:9-13.

The complete unit, then, has three parts. In the first part, verses 5-8, Jesus gives general instructions about praying with proper humility and sincerity. This is followed, in the second part, by a sample prayer that reflects the attitude of a properly prayerful person (verses 9-13). This sample prayer has been called "the Lord's prayer." It is the "Our Father," or *Pater noster,* recited in churches worldwide on Sunday mornings. (The prayer in Matthew resembles the prayer attributed to Jesus in the Gospel of Luke, to be considered next.) Finally, in the third part of the passage, Jesus stresses an issue raised by the kind of prayer he commends — what it is that motivates the bit in the prayer about forgiving others.

Jesus begins with a few sobering remarks about how we are to pray. The first thing he says is this: "And when you pray, you must not be like the hypocrites" (Matt. 6:5). That's an interesting start in light of our discussion of forgiveness and the kingdom of God. You may surmise that the hypocrites are outside the kingdom, though they probably think both that they are in the kingdom and that they have a special place in the kingdom.

Observe next that Jesus commends concision in our prayers. God is not impressed with long-winded invocations and bluster (6:7-8). God isn't fooled by the ornate oratory of our public prayers or the mantra-like repetitiveness of so much praying that we do.

Following these brief introductory remarks, Jesus says, in the second part of this passage, "Pray like this." The prayer is truly a model of brevity. You would expect this compact prayer to contain what is most important. It does. Here is the prayer itself (vv. 9-13):

> Our Father who is in heaven, may your name be sacred. May your kingdom come; may your will be done on earth as it is in heaven. Give us today our daily needs. And forgive us our sins as we also forgive those who sin against us. And do not let us yield to temptation, but deliver us from the evil one.[3]

3. Here I've adopted the translation given by Grant R. Osborne in his *Exegetical Commentary on the New Testament: Matthew* (Grand Rapids: Zondervan, 2010), p. 223. Notice that "daily bread," more familiar to us from the *Pater Noster,* is rendered "daily needs." This is because the word "bread," in its cultural context, generally "stands for food and then for all a person's needs" (Osborne, *Matthew,* p. 229). While there is some disagreement among interpreters, "the majority . . . take it as a metaphor

A dominant feature of this prayer is a confident expectation of the imminent in-breaking of the kingdom of God. God the Father rules the heavens, and his very name is holy. "May your kingdom come" sounds like a request. But the mood is more complex than that. It's reasonable to interpret this sentence as both imperative (i.e., a request) and indicative (i.e., a statement of fact). The one who prays this way aligns himself with God's own purposes on the earth.

This is reinforced by what follows: "may your will be done on earth as it is in heaven." Of course, the Father's will is done when his children obey his commands. So this is a prayer of submission to the commands of God and of intention to do what the Father wills. For this is the *how* of God's breaking into the world with his kingdom.

It follows naturally, then, that our Father, who knows what we need before we ask him (see 6:8), supplies our physical needs on a day-to-day basis (6:11), much as he did with the children of Israel as they wandered in the wilderness. Since the in-breaking of God's kingdom is both imminent and already present, it is enough if our daily needs are met as they arise. Meanwhile, we acknowledge our sins and entrust ourselves to the Father's promised forgiveness; and we practice the same kind of forgiveness toward others who sin against us (6:12). That God's kingdom comes, that the Father's will is done, that our physical needs are supplied daily, and that we are forgiven by our heavenly Father, are all facts. And our forgiveness of others is to be a matter of fact, as well.

The forgiveness part of this representative prayer is especially important to Jesus. We know this from what he says following the prayer (vv. 14-15):

> For if you forgive others who sin against you, your heavenly Father will forgive you. But if you refuse to forgive others, your Father will not forgive your sins either.[4]

---

for a person's daily needs" (p. 229). Also, the word "sins" is used in place of "debts" or "transgressions," though it should be understood that the word "debt" for sin in the prayer signifies the effect of sinning: it constitutes a debt owed to the person we have sinned against. Finally, following Osborne and the best contemporary translations, I've omitted the familiar ending to the *Pater noster,* "For Thine is the kingdom, and the power, and the glory, forever. Amen." It's almost certain that these words did not appear in the original manuscript of this gospel.

4. This, again, is Grant Osborne's translation (*Matthew,* p. 223).

God doesn't forgive the unforgiving. What else can these words of our Lord mean? No hermeneutical gyrations designed to resolve the meaning of Jesus' words into something he didn't intend will subvert the sobering knowledge we have that God requires us to forgive others as a condition for being forgiven by him. These are words to make the hair on the back of your neck stand up. If you understand the significance of sin that God does not forgive, you can connect the dots.[5]

If you understand the significance of Jesus' words, *then* you can connect the dots. But extreme care must be taken in connecting the dots. While this isn't the place for a full-scale development of the point, it needs to be noticed that Jesus is concerned with kingdom living and the eruption of the kingdom in our lives and in the world through kingdom

5. Chris Brauns takes this as a warning about the possibility that the unforgiving person is not actually saved. He says, "people who are unwilling to forgive should be warned in the most serious way possible. Indeed, Jesus taught that if we are either unable or unwilling to offer forgiveness, we should question the reality of our salvation." (See Brauns, *Unpacking Forgiveness: Biblical Answers for Complex Questions and Deep Wounds* [Wheaton: Crossway Books, 2008], p. 120.) He repeats, in no uncertain terms, *"Those unwilling or unable to forgive should fear for their salvation"* (p. 123; italics in the original). Thus he's compelled to answer, in several pages of the first Appendix, the direct question, "How can I be sure that God has forgiven me?" (pp. 195-98). There are two reasons why I'm not convinced that this is Jesus' meaning. First, Jesus' Sermon on the Mount is about participation in Christ's kingdom. Moving in and out of the kingdom during the present time is largely a matter of participation through fellowship with God and each other on God's terms. This should not be confused with gaining or losing salvation, or finding that you never were saved to begin with. Having said that, it is possible, as we'll see when we examine Matthew 18, to be turned out of fellowship by unrepentance, yet with the hope of eventual restoration. Second, it is a key principle in 1 John that true *experience of God* — signified by the biblical term "fellowship" — depends essentially on brotherly love. See 1 John 2:9-11; 3:10-17; 4:7–5:2. Anyone who does not love his Christian brother lives in darkness, and he lies if he claims to love his brother. A wrongdoer who will not repent of his sins against a brother is one who "hates his brother," and so is an injured person who will not forgive a repentant brother. (1 John 5:2 points out that general disobedience to the commands of God is a clue that the one who disobeys does not love the children of God. When one sins, it is an offense against the whole community. See also 1 Pet. 1:22.) Our salvation does not hang in the balance. But the intimate experience of God that we crave (and seldom find, for all of the spiritual technologies we apply) is on the line. And that is a lot to forfeit for the sake of pride. Thankfully, rupture in fellowship need not be permanent (see 1 John 1:9).

living. Sin and unforgiveness disrupt the equilibrium of the kingdom. They manifest a breach in fellowship. God's kingdom consists in fellowship between God and ourselves and amongst ourselves (see all of 1 John). Confession of sin and forgiveness of sin are vital to that fellowship. And if one does not forgive as he has been forgiven by the Father, then he stands apart from fellowship with God.

This should matter to a generation of Christians who long for special experiences of God. True experience of God's presence depends on activities of moral repair: confession of sin, repentance, and forgiveness.

The Lord's Prayer in the Gospel of Luke The Gospel of Luke recounts an event inaugurated by Jesus' own praying. On this occasion, seeing that Jesus had finished praying, one of his disciples was inspired to ask, "Lord, teach us to pray" (Luke 11:1). Apparently, this disciple, who must have had some experience with prayer, felt a need to understand prayer better. Something about the example of Jesus led him to seek the Lord's counsel. Surely Jesus was delighted with the request, for he answers with a sample prayer, much like the one included in his discourse on the mount:

> Father, hallowed be your name. Your kingdom come. Give us each day our daily bread. And forgive us our sins, for we ourselves forgive everyone who is indebted to us. And lead us not into temptation. (Luke 11:2-4, NASB)

This prayer model does not include the petition for God's will *to be done on earth as it is in heaven.* But it's there by implication in the words, "Your kingdom come."

God's kingdom is realized on earth through the obedience of his people to his will. Old Testament theologian Bruce Waltke distinguishes between "God's universal kingdom and the particular kingdom that is in view in the Lord's Prayer."[6] He says, "By the former, theologians mean God's activity in exercising his sovereignty over all things, even giving the nations their pagan deities (cf. Deut. 4:19). By the latter, they mean God's activity in establishing a realm in which his subjects obey *ex animo* his law."[7] On the one

6. Bruce K. Waltke, *An Old Testament Theology* (Grand Rapids: Zondervan, 2007), p. 146.

7. Waltke, *Theology,* p. 146.

hand, there is God's sovereign, all-inclusive kingdom; on the other hand, there is God's "mediatory kingdom," which is progressively realized on the earth. Quoting George Ladd, Waltke adds, "While God *is* King, he must also *become* King."[8]

Waltke's choice of the Latin phrase is especially apt: obedience is to be *ex animo.* The phrase literally means "from the heart or spirit." It is, I believe, another way to speak of acting *from virtue.* Central to the in-breaking of God's kingdom on earth, during the interval between the two advents of Jesus Christ, is for those who have the mind of Christ to exhibit the character of Christ in all that they do. Their actions spring from an internal state equivalent to a unified set of well-developed virtues.

Jesus' prayer alludes to several virtues that lie at the heart of this emerging kingdom process:

- Reverence — exhibited by our regard for God as sovereign over all, who rules from heaven;
- Affection — indicated by our familiarity with God as our heavenly Father;
- Faithfulness — shown in our heartfelt desire for God's moral will to be fulfilled throughout the earth, including our own lives;
- Humility — reflected in our acknowledgment of complete dependence on God for our daily sustenance;
- Gratitude — implied in the thanks we give for the forgiveness we enjoy and demonstrate through the forgiveness we offer to others.

Is there anything else? Yes. *Forgiveness.* For right at the center of the prayer is Jesus' tacit exhortation to appeal to God for forgiveness of our sins, *for we ourselves forgive everyone who is indebted to us.*

In Matthew 6 we saw that God's forgiveness of us provides a model and incentive for our forgiveness of others. Here in the Gospel of Luke we see that our confidence in God's forgiveness when we confess our sins is linked to our habit of forgiving those who sin against us. This is a complement to the principle revealed in Matthew 6, not an inversion of that principle.

We could not pray with integrity what Jesus teaches here if we were not in the habit of forgiving the sins of others against us. I say habit be-

8. Waltke, *Theology,* p. 146.

cause habit is implied in Luke's account of the prayer Jesus commended. This habit is rooted in the forgiveness virtue.

Jesus is saying quite a lot here about how our management of relational conflict pertains to the coming of God's kingdom here on earth and in the present moment. We only pretend to be agents of God's kingdom if we are indifferent about the sins we commit against one another, strung out on bitterness that prevents us from forgiving one another, and resolute in our hardness of heart that forestalls repentance and precludes reconciliation.

The real work of the kingdom is reconciliation. Reconciliation between God and ourselves, and also between you and me. We have the ministry of reconciliation, says the apostle Paul (see 2 Cor. 5:18-21). If we cannot reconcile with each other, then how can we appeal to others to be reconciled to God? There is no place in God's kingdom for ambassadors who bicker.[9]

The most potent force on behalf of God's kingdom, and in winning others to his realm, is the love of believers for one another — without qualification, and without exception.[10] If we must bicker, let us at least not become bitter. Let us resolve our disputes for the sake of God's kingdom. The stakes are too high for squabbling. As Paul warned, "But if you bite and devour one another, take care lest you be consumed by one another" (Gal. 5:15, NASB).

In the Lord's sample prayers, Jesus teaches his disciples how to pray. In doing so, he also teaches them about forgiveness of one another. While the importance of forgiveness is clearly linked to the in-breaking of God's kingdom, and the failure to forgive has fearful consequences, the method of forgiveness remains a mystery.

Not to worry. In Matthew 18, Jesus answers our questions about *the what* and *the how* of forgiveness.

9. This is not to say that Christians cannot or should not ever disagree. Certainly, there is room for disagreement. But Christians should not fall into petty altercations. More important, they should act with moral dignity whenever they disagree. They compromise that dignity when they bicker. But I mean something quite strong by "bicker," namely sins of one kind or another against each other. I thank Michael Austin for suggesting that I clarify the difference between this and general disagreement.

10. See Tertullian, *The Apology* 39; see also Francis A. Schaeffer, *The Mark of the Christian* (Downers Grove: Inter-Varsity Press, 1972).

Matthew 18 — Protocol and Parable

The forgiving person, I've argued, is forgiving even when he is not performing some special act of forgiveness or engaged in some current process of forgiveness. This, it turns out, has much broader application than has generally been noticed.

First, if you have wronged me and you have not yet repented, but I have the virtue of forgiveness, then I will exercise that virtue in anticipation of forgiving you when you repent. Further, recall that there is no true forgiveness without an unjust act to forgive. So, as a forgiving person, I will continue to take seriously the nature of your offense, and deem you responsible for doing something morally wrong. Correctly regarding your action as morally objectionable will have different implications for different circumstances. What is proper for me to think or do or desire, as a person with this virtue, is context-relative.

Second, because you and I share much of the same social space as members of the same community (as in any relationship we will), those other members of our community *who also have the virtue of forgiveness* will *act from this virtue* in relationship to your action, its implications,[11] and its effects (e.g., the suffering you have caused me). Though they are not the direct targets of your wrongdoing, their having the virtue of forgiveness is important. This is not because they are free to forgive you for an injury you've caused me to suffer. Rather, they have duties to perform in helping to bring a wrongdoer to repentance. This is a moral fact, ripe for further exploration.

Jesus on the Protocol of Forgiveness Consider Jesus. He is the paradigm of the forgiving person, our ideal model. Like his heavenly Father, Jesus was fully imbued with the virtue of forgiveness. This means, at the very least, that he knew how to forgive and did forgive as it was fitting. At every authentic opportunity to forgive, Jesus came through with forgiveness. But that is only the very least of the significance that Jesus maximally possessed this virtue. There's more.

It is also clear that Jesus was an ideal teacher in the way of forgiveness. And we are blessed with his essential instruction about forgiveness.

11. See Pamela Hieronymi, "Articulating an Uncompromising Forgiveness," *Philosophy and Phenomenological Review* 62.3 (2001): 529-55.

We can be sure that we have the heart of what he wanted us to understand about forgiveness, through the messages and actions that have been recounted for us in the New Testament gospels.

Did Jesus ever counsel others to forgive? He did, of course. But why should anyone act on his advice? Because Jesus had the virtue of forgiveness. His having the virtue would itself be exemplified in his wise counsel regarding forgiveness. For example, he would not counsel premature forgiveness. Nor would he recommend forgiveness in the absence of repentance, unless it was right to do so.

Jesus' most explicit teaching about forgiveness is recorded in Matthew 18:15-19:

> If your brother sins against you, go privately and reprove him. If he listens, you have won your brother. But if he does not listen, take one or two others with you, so that, with the word of two witnesses, or even three, the whole matter may be resolved. But if he refuses to listen to them, tell it to the church. And if again he refuses to listen, even to the church, then regard him as if he was a Gentile or a tax collector. I tell you truly, whatever you bind on earth shall be bound in heaven, and whatever you loose on earth shall be loosed in heaven.[12]

How often, when someone has injured us, have we been advised, counseled, commanded to forgive, by members of our community? This is one of the most familiar rituals of contemporary Protestant Christianity. But this counsel is muddled, at best, and spiritually injurious at worst.

When you have been *seriously* wronged,[13] should you not follow the wise counsel of Jesus? If, in following his counsel as recorded in Matthew 18, you are dealing with a recalcitrant wrongdoer who has injured you, by all means, search out one or two members of your community to join you in confronting him with his sin. But choose wisely. It is a near certainty that even the most likely candidates for this critical responsibility will tell

12. This is my translation. Unless otherwise noted, all subsequent Scripture translations are my own.

13. When Jesus says, in Matthew 18:17, "If your brother sins against you," he speaks of hostile action. See Osborne, *Matthew,* p. 693 n.1. It is clear from the whole context of Jesus' instruction in Matt. 18:17-20 that "these are substantial and not just trivial sins" (*Matthew,* p. 685).

you to "get on with forgiving the person already." This casual reflex betrays a shortage of the virtue of forgiveness among such "counselors."

The tragedy is, when you've been wronged, there may be no one to whom you can go. Or the pain of injustice you've already experienced may be compounded by absurd counsel that presumes to be the wisdom of God.[14]

This is yet another arresting indicator of the sad state of the Western church. We have allowed ourselves to slip into patterns of behavior that we think have the authority of Scripture, but are simply means of skirting responsibility.

Oddly, injured members of our community are likely to be rebuffed when they ask for assistance in dealing with a sinning member. When that happens, further injury is done to offended parties. For all intents and purposes, leaders, who should "man up" and take a firm stance regarding sin against a brother or sister, often conspire with the wrongdoer through inaction or, worse, a leveling of the playing field.

Conveniently, many leaders today presume that when there has been a rupture in relationship between two members of their community, both are blameworthy. Of course, this frequently is the case. But it is not always the case. And leaders are ill-prepared for the reality of asymmetric wrongdoing.

We know it to be a reality because of Jesus' own teaching. His counsel in Matthew 18 presupposes a context of asymmetrical harm done by one person to another person. The corrupt action and its disastrous effects are unilateral. Faithful exegesis requires this interpretation.

What then? A great portion of Jesus' teaching in this passage focuses on the responsibilities of others to intervene on behalf of injured persons. This is an important protection for the injured person. If he is rebuffed when he approaches the wrongdoer about his sin, he should be able to have confidence that others will validate the wrongness of what has been done, and step up with aid in holding the wrongdoer accountable.

In every such instance of significant wrongdoing, there is always the possibility that others will need to take action. Initially, one or two of them

14. So often, when a believer has been wronged and caused real grief, his advisors are like Job's friends, who came to comfort him in his distress, and to advise him about the right course of action. Their counsel only made matters worse by adding to Job's distress and misrepresenting God's view of the matter. See Job 42:7-19.

may need to accompany the offended person — with the purpose of confronting the wrongdoer with his sin and challenging him to repent. If that fails, because there has been no repentance, then the case of wrongdoing is to be made known to the rest of the fellowship. And if that doesn't do the trick, the guilty person is to be removed from active participation in the community. "Regard him as if he were a Gentile or a tax collector," Jesus says (verse 17). In other words, treat him as if he were an unbeliever, someone who is not a member of the community.[15]

Jesus entrusts his disciples with awesome responsibility here (see verses 18-19). But God stands behind the responsible action of an obedient community.[16]

I emphasize the role of other believers in the forgiveness process for two reasons. First, the church needs to hear and apply this message. Much suffering has occurred and been compounded because leaders with the virtue of forgiveness were not available to intervene on behalf of an injured person and validate that person's experience of injustice. Second, the point comes into clearer focus when we consider forgiveness as a *virtue,* rather than simply as an act or process. Considered as an act or process, it looks like the burden of forgiveness settles wholly on the shoulders of the injured person. That is not the way things are meant to be.

Within every community of believers in Jesus, there must be some who have the virtue of forgiveness, if only because their good example and wise counsel would go far to repair damaged relationships, and, failing that, wounded souls. But persons of virtue are needed to act on behalf of

15. See Osborne, *Matthew,* p. 687.

16. The best pastoral treatment of forgiveness today is the book *Unpacking Forgiveness: Biblical Answers for Complex Questions and Deep Wounds,* by Chris Brauns (Wheaton: Crossway Books, 2008). Brauns ably develops and defends the view that a wrongdoer must repent before he can be forgiven. He defines forgiveness on the human level, in parallel with how divine forgiveness works, this way: "Forgiveness is *a commitment by the offended to pardon graciously the repentant from moral liability and to be reconciled to that person, although not all consequences are necessarily eliminated*" (p. 56). Everett L. Worthington, Jr., resists this conception of forgiveness and joins others in mistaking forgiveness for a displacement of negative emotions (see Worthington, Jr., *Forgiving and Reconciling: Bridges to Wholeness and Hope* [Downers Grove: InterVarsity Press, 2003], pp. 41-42). He explicitly denies that repentance is a needed condition for forgiveness to occur (see pp. 51-52). His exegesis of relevant Scripture passages is breezy and is held hostage by his enthusiasm for clinical results that he has documented in dealing with people who have been wronged.

the wounded and to call wrongdoers to account. Our leaders must themselves have the virtue of forgiveness. Unless we can turn to members in our community who understand the requirements of forgiveness and have the virtue themselves, moral repair within the community will falter. Going it our way rather than Jesus' way is a disaster for God's kingdom.[17]

Jesus' Parable on Forgiveness Peter, the most frequently visible disciple of Jesus, precipitates further instruction about forgiveness with a candid question: "Lord, how often should I forgive my brother who sins against me?" Peter may have paused briefly before he ventured what probably seemed to him a generous estimate: "How about seven times seven?" (Matt. 18:21).[18]

Jesus replied, "No Peter, more like seventy times seven." He then told his crestfallen disciples another of his parables (vv. 23-35).

The parable of the "unforgiving servant" is unusually long.[19] Here we have thirteen verses to illustrate a basic point. The central figure is the servant of a king. This servant is mandated to pay a significant debt that he owes the king but cannot pay. He pleads for leniency and the king, showing great compassion, forgives the debt. Wouldn't you know, the next thing that happens is a repeat of the same dire situation. Only this time, the king's servant is owed a smaller amount by a fellow servant. Now *he* demands repayment. But this other servant is no more able to repay his debt on demand than the first servant had been when confronted by the king.

Already we know what the first servant should do. But if we've heard enough of Jesus' parables, we also suspect that the servant does the wrong thing, and this will be a lesson for us.

Sure enough, the first servant blows it. The second servant cannot come up with what he owes; he pleads for more time to produce the money. This sounds familiar. But the first servant insists on repayment,

17. Margaret Urban Walker makes a valuable contribution on this point in chapter 5 of her book *Moral Repair: Reconstructing Moral Relations after Wrongdoing* (Cambridge: Cambridge University Press, 2006). L. Gregory Jones develops an exceptionally rich account of "the craft of forgiveness" in the communal life of the church. See his *Embodying Forgiveness: A Theological Analysis* (Grand Rapids: Eerdmans, 1995).

18. I'm paraphrasing.

19. See Matthew 13 for a comparison with several other parables.

on pain of going to jail. He sticks to his guns and throws the unfortunate fellow-servant into prison.

If the parable ended here, we would already recognize the incongruity of the first servant's action. The recipient of mercy shows no mercy toward others. But Jesus makes a further point.

Fellow servants of the imprisoned man are grieved by what has happened. They report to the king. The king is furious. He summons the unforgiving servant and hands him over to be punished until he is able to repay the debt that had at first been forgiven him.

What's the point of the parable? Jesus says: "In the same way my Father will also do this to you unless each of you forgives his brother or sister from your heart" (18:35).[20]

This parable changes nothing that I've said so far in this chapter. Sin is here likened to a debt. Forgiveness wipes the slate clean. But forgiveness isn't automatic. If forgiveness was to be automatic, there would be no "debt." So the first servant pleads for mercy. The king's response outstrips the servant's request. The servant asks for more time; the king decides to release the man from his debt.

And so it is with forgiveness. When one sins against another, the sinner incurs a kind of debt. This debt is owed to the one he has wronged. And this debt is owed unless and until it is repaid or forgiven. The one who has been wronged has a claim on the wrongdoer.

In the parable, repayment is initially required. But in response to an entreaty for mercy, and the promise to repay in due course, the debt is cancelled. The servant may seem completely sincere in his intention to repay the debt. He was clearly distressed by the demand to repay, and feared what would happen since he could not. If the king felt compassion, it was because of the servant's attitude. Consider the relief the servant must have felt when the king cancelled the debt.[21]

Yes, the servant was relieved. But was he also grateful? Certainly not. If he had been grateful, he would have forgiven the second servant who was equally desperate. In his refusal to grant the second man's request,

20. See Osborne, *Matthew,* p. 697, for this translation.

21. We must understand the extent of the debt he was forgiven. As the story goes, he owes ten thousand talents. Jesus deliberately exaggerates the amount. Incurring such a large debt was hardly possible. A single talent would be somewhere between 75 and 100 pounds of gold or silver. The servant owes ten thousand times that!

this servant demonstrated that he did not respect the king. He did not admire the king for his character. He simply felt lucky to be off the hook for what he had owed. Admiration for the king would have issued in the same compassion the king had shown and a merciful act toward the second servant pleading for more time.

So the servant's refusal to be merciful toward another in debt to him revealed an attitude that already existed when the servant was himself forgiven. He was, very simply, a fraud.

People often read the parable backwards or upside down, as if the second half came first. One servant demands that another servant repay a debt. The debtor is unable. So the first servant imprisons the poor bloke. This merciless servant is summoned to pay his own debt to the king. Now, what will the king do when the servant pleads for more time? That depends on the king's character and what the king knows about the servant. The king is a man of compassion, so he's inclined to forgive the man his debt. But what does he know about the servant? If he knows of the servant's recent action toward another servant, will he forgive the debt? Almost certainly not. What else might happen is a matter of speculation.

But in the actual order of events, it's presumed that the forgiven servant will be a forgiving servant, not because of any guess about his own character, but because he has been the blessed recipient of forgiveness. His own experience should positively dispose him to be equally merciful.[22]

The first servant's unpleasant actions have unpleasant consequences. But notice, the consequences are, in principle, temporary and conditional. If he is ever able to repay his debt, the king will restore the servant in some way. (Considering the amount he owes, to be sure, it's unlikely that he'll ever be released.)

Remember that this parable is presented to reinforce Jesus' answer to Peter's question. Peter was concerned with the statute of limitations on the number of times to forgive an errant brother or sister. Jesus' answer revealed that Peter was asking the wrong question. There is no statute of limitations. ("Seventy times seven" is a figure of speech.) Keeping track

22. There is great irony in this parable, as there is in many of Jesus' parables. The amount owed by the second servant is said to be a hundred denarii. While this is a significant amount, it doesn't begin to compare with the first servant's debt of ten thousand talents. The ratio is about 6,000 to 1. See the discussion in Osborne, *Matthew,* pp. 694-97.

violates the very idea of forgiveness. As Jesus says at the end of his parable, we are to forgive "from the heart" (18:35). This is the fundamental point of the parable. And forgiving from the heart is an act of virtue.

What about the Forgiveness Prayer of Luke 23:34a?

So far, I have said nothing about the "forgiveness prayer" of Luke 23:34a, where Jesus, speaking from the cross, says,

> Father, forgive them, for they know not what they do.

Many take these words of Jesus to be the chief interpretive key to understanding interpersonal forgiveness. Jesus, as our example in the life of faith, here demonstrates the grace that we should exercise towards all those who cause us harm. And we are to note, especially, that repentance is not required of the wrongdoers in this passage.

This, I believe, is a mistake. Luke 23:34a does not provide clear guidance about whether and how we are to forgive those who sin against us.

As I've suggested, the Jesus protocol of Matthew 18 provides the fundamental interpretive key for understanding forgiveness in circumstances of asymmetrical wrongdoing within the believing community. Interpreting Scripture in light of Scripture, much else that the Bible teaches about forgiveness must be understood in reference to Jesus' express teaching about what to do in Matthew 18.

What, then, are we to make of Luke 23:34a?

First, we must acknowledge that the words of Matthew 18 bear the full authority of Jesus. They are no less poignant than what he says on the cross. And they are sandwiched among a number of things Jesus had to say about forgiveness (in the Lord's Prayer in the Sermon on the Mount, and in the parable of Matthew 18, for example). More to the point, these words of Jesus are written expressly for instruction in the way of forgiveness. A correct understanding of Luke 23:34a must reckon with this significant difference.

Second, neither Jesus, when speaking from the cross, nor Stephen, when he says something very similar while being stoned by enemies of the gospel (Acts 7), expresses his own forgiveness of the people persecuting them. Each appeals to God to forgive, presumably because the offense committed in their cases is a special offense against God, and it would be presumptuous for them to arrogate to themselves what only God (the Father, in Jesus' case, as obedient Son) can do. So their prayers of forgiveness are appeals to God on behalf of others.[23]

Third, with both Jesus and Stephen, the sins are committed by pagan enemies. Jesus does explicitly instruct his disciples to love their enemies, and his prayer no doubt issues from this love he has for his own enemies. But Jesus' persecutors do not pretend to be his friends, members of the same community, committed to the same kingdom values, seeking to live together in obedience to God's commands, and so forth. Brothers and sisters in the kingdom of heaven, like those referred to by Jesus in his Matthew protocol, stand in a different relation to those against whom they sin. And this disrupts kingdom life for all. Responsibilities toward them differ in significant ways. And one is that of holding an errant brother or sister accountable for wrongdoing. This is not merely for the good of the one wronged. It is for the good of the in-breaking kingdom and kingdom community. This includes all members, others who are vulnerable to the wrongdoer's further actions, the wrongdoer himself or herself, leaders, and so forth. (See Matt. 5:44-45, where treatment of enemies and fellow disciples is contrasted.)

Fourth, there is a consistent thread in Scripture to take different steps with errant believers than with enemies of the kingdom. The goal in the case of believers, of course, is reconciliation. And this certainly cannot happen without repentance. At least, nearly all would agree about that. The person wronged can make all the right overtures that many people (mistakenly, I think) associate with forgiveness, to encourage repentance and, ultimately, reconciliation. The list of virtues in 1 Corinthians 13 provides guidance in this.

Fifth, believers are no less remiss if they disobey Jesus' Matthew 18 teaching about this aspect of life in the kingdom than they would if they did not learn the proper lesson from Jesus' example on the cross.

Sixth, it is especially clear that God's forgiveness of us does depend on our repentance, both at regeneration and throughout our lives as believers (1 John 1:9 is addressed to believers). Repentance for regeneration

23. There are a few passages in which Paul defends his apostleship and expresses his thanks to God for showing him mercy when he persecuted the church, out of ignorance. (See 1 Tim. 1:12-14.)

brings one into initial fellowship with God. But continued fellowship (not salvation of the "going-to-heaven" sort) is dependent on obedience. And this is why confession is so important. It restores fellowship with God. And so it is among believers who sin against each other.

Jesus' words in Matthew 18 shouldn't leave us in much doubt about how forgiveness should proceed. Surely, if Jesus meant something radically different than what I've outlined about Jesus' protocol, then Jesus might have left us with instructions that would not so easily misdirect us. As it is, believers have trouble practicing what is there commanded.

Jesus must have had a pretty good reason for instructing us the way he does. If his counsel was followed more consistently, I believe, there would be a great deal more healing than there usually is. And what more fitting means to goad a sinner back into proper fellowship than to ordain a means of this sort?

Finally, it has to be noted that the textual evidence for the authenticity of Luke 23:34a is mixed. As I. Howard Marshall has pointed out, "the textual status of v. 34a is very uncertain." He reviews the arguments for and against authenticity, then concludes, "The balance of evidence thus favors acceptance of the saying as Lucan, although the weight of the textual evidence against the saying precludes any assurance in opting for this verdict."[24] This leaves the interpreter less than firm grounds for regarding the passage as the interpretive key to forgiveness.

Forgiveness in the Epistles

Several other passages of the New Testament confirm and amplify what Jesus taught about forgiveness. Here we consider four key passages from the epistles of Paul.

24. See I. Howard Marshall, *The Gospel of Luke: A Commentary on the Greek Text* (Grand Rapids: Eerdmans, 1978), pp. 867-68. I want to thank Greg Jesson and Doug Wubbena for vigorous discussion about the significance of Luke 23:34a for understanding the call to forgive.

Ephesians 4:32

Be kind and compassionate toward each other, practicing forgiveness among yourselves, since God also forgave you in Christ.

How does this compare with what Jesus taught about forgiveness?

The participial phrase "practicing forgiveness among yourselves" modifies the main verb in the passage. The main verb in the verse is the verb "to be." Believers are to be kind and they are to be compassionate or tender-hearted. The phrase "practicing forgiveness among yourselves" is included in order to clarify. The phrase indicates an underlying means of being kind and compassionate. So forgiving or not forgiving is an effective test of genuine kindness and tender-heartedness.

This is illuminating. We should wonder how anyone can tell whether we are kind or tender-hearted. We do sometimes confidently say that some person has these attributes. But what is our evidence? It's possible for an apparently kind act to come from some other place in the agent's heart and not really be kindness incarnated. The same goes for compassion.

Compare forgiveness. Can it be faked? Not so easily. This is because forgiveness releases another person from retribution for his actions. That either happens, or it doesn't. The person you claim to forgive will surely know whether you have forgiven, if he understands what forgiveness is.[25]

So a particularly compelling way to demonstrate kindness and compassion is to forgive those in your circle, the believers who share the social world that you must navigate.

The apostle also draws the now familiar parallel between the reasonable expectation that we would forgive each other and the forgiveness we

25. It may be easier to fake repentance than it is to fake forgiveness. The first thing to say about this is that it is no reason to withhold forgiveness. If you suspect counterfeit repentance, there must be some basis for this. A truly repentant person will wish to convince you that his repentance is genuine. This should make it easier to tell. And if you are a forgiving person — that is, if you have the virtue of forgiveness — then you will accept appropriate criteria for determining the sincerity of repentance. If you are mistaken, you have done nothing wrong in seeming to forgive one who has not really repented. Your forgiveness won't "take," you might say. But your conduct will look the same either way. In search of appropriate criteria for determining the sincerity of repentance, you could turn to 1 Cor. 13, briefly discussed below.

enjoy because of what Christ did to reconcile us to God. We are to forgive each other, since, after all, God has forgiven us. Jesus drew attention to the same basic rationale for forgiveness: we have been forgiven by God.

Recall what this means. God has forgiven us. But we had, first, to repent. The apostle has not stripped this out of the equation. In fact, he tacitly affirms it when he draws the parallel between God's forgiveness of us and our forgiveness of one another. The comparison with God's forgiveness is basic. We simply would not know what forgiveness is if we didn't know God's forgiveness, both conceptually and experientially. *Conceptually* because we have to consider that God was just (and no less compassionate than he would be otherwise) in requiring us to repent as a condition for forgiveness. God's compassion is revealed precisely in God's willingness to forgive the repentant. *Experientially* because we know ourselves to be forgiven in light of what Christ has done for us.

One more point about this passage. The challenge of forgiveness is raised within the context of believers in relation to believers. Practicing forgiveness is supposed to be natural to the one who seeks to imitate God, "as beloved children" (Eph. 5:1, which directly follows the exhortation of 4:32). This, too, parallels the overt teaching of Jesus.

Paul does not neglect the sobering possibility that some within earshot of his admonitions are not really in Christ. Earlier in the surrounding passage he describes the life pattern of the Gentiles (a term used in context to designate the unregenerate). This pattern is marked by all sorts of sordid things. Callousness, sensuality, and greediness are given special mention. Paul knows that a person could affiliate with the church and yet be just like the Gentiles in these respects. He says in Ephesians 4:20-24:

> But you did not learn Christ in this way, if you heard him and were taught in him — as you certainly have been. The truth is in Jesus. You were taught to take off the old self — corresponding to your former life orientation, which is corrupt in its correspondence with deceitful desires — to be renewed in your mind by the Spirit, and to put on the new self, that was created in God's likeness, in righteousness and holiness stemming from the truth.[26]

26. This is my translation of a difficult instance of Greek syntax. Following Clinton E. Arnold, I think it best to preserve the sense of three infinitives arranged in

If a believer suffers because of the callousness, or sensuality, or greed of another who claims to be a Christ-follower, then the one who causes this suffering had better demonstrate his genuine repentance, lest he be considered indistinguishable from the Gentiles. Moving out toward the larger context of this epistle to the Ephesians, we should notice the reinforcement of Paul's 4:32 admonition in 4:1-3 and 5:21.

Colossians 3:13

Paul echoes the sentiment of Ephesians 4:32 in his epistle to the Colossians, where he commends "bearing with one another, and forgiving each other if anyone has a complaint against another. Because the Lord has forgiven you, you should also" (Col. 3:13).

Again we find the participial phrase "forgiving each other," paired this time with "bearing with one another." The preceding verse says that, as people "chosen of God, holy and beloved," we are "to put on a heart of compassion, kindness, humility, gentleness and patience." The practice of forgiveness, as we saw before, gives evidence of these character traits in our souls.

Notice the language Paul uses in verse 12: "put on a heart of. . . ." Compare Colossians 3:15, which says, "Let the peace of Christ rule in your hearts." This language further attests to the idea that these are all virtues that are being described.

Romans 12:14-21

Paul's counsel in his epistle to the Romans is instructive. He writes:

> Bless those who persecute you; bless and do not curse. . . . Repay no one evil for evil. Give careful thought to what is right in the sight of all. If possible, insofar as it depends on you, be at peace with all people. Dear ones, do not take revenge, but allow for God's anger. For it is

---

an orderly sequence: "to take off," "to be renewed in," and "to put on." See Arnold, *Exegetical Commentary on the New Testament: Ephesians* (Grand Rapids: Zondervan, 2010), pp. 285-90.

> written, "Vengeance is mine, I will repay, says the Lord." "But if your enemy is hungry, feed him; if he is thirsty, give him something to drink. For in doing this, you will heap burning coals upon his head." Do not be overcome by evil, but overcome evil with good. (Rom. 12:14, 17-21)

There is no mention here of *forgiveness,* but the sentiment expressed relates directly to our topic. The apostle is talking about relationships between believers and their *enemies.* Jesus exhorted his disciples to love their enemies.[27] When he spoke of forgiveness, it was in connection with filial relationships, that is, relationships among those who have become children of God and are, in effect, siblings.

But love is clearly a common denominator in the Christian's behavior toward his enemies and toward fellow-Christians. To the church at Galatia, Paul wrote,

> So then, as we have opportunity, let us do good to all people, and especially to those who belong to the household of faith. (Gal. 6:10)

The Romans passage recites texts from the Hebrew Bible. Deuteronomy is Paul's source for the attribution of vengeance to God, a truth that is supposed to induce patience when we are mistreated.[28] Paul appeals to Proverbs 25:21-22 for the psychological insight that doing good to your enemies will be a major nuisance to them. This is presumably because they will know themselves to be unworthy, which will spoil their enjoyment of the good things you do for them. They may come to feel ridiculous.

Some who read Romans 12 will be puzzled by a seeming tone of vindictiveness in Paul's words. How can it count as love for your enemies when the good you render them leaves them at the mercy of a vengeful God, or is motivated by a desire to make them squirm?

The question, I think, misunderstands the passage. First, there are the simple facts of the matter. On the one hand, God's people are to treat their enemies with kindness. Doing so will have certain consequences, whether or not God's people act in order to produce those consequences. The consequences will include the psychological angst that is generated

27. See Matt. 5:38-47; Luke 6:35-37.

28. See Deut. 32:35; for the same theme, see Prov. 20:22; Ps. 94; 1 Thess. 4:6; Heb. 10:30.

when a disciple of Jesus loves his enemies. And God's people will be vindicated by a completely just God, who waits patiently for sinners to repent.[29] The believer can do nothing about any of these things. They are simply true.

Second, if the believer is motivated by Paul's words, we must understand how this is to work. The believer can leave the business of exacting justice to God, who is perfectly just. We may think we have the capacity to judge correctly what our enemies deserve for the harm they have done to us. But this is mistaken. We may be too harsh. Alternatively, we may be too lenient. Better that we should leave room for the wrath of God than to take matters into our own hands. God wants us to leave these concerns to him. And though we may tremble at how terrible it is for sinners to fall into the hands of the living God (Heb. 10:30-31), God will one day balance the scales of justice. Meanwhile, we are to love our enemies. And, if our enemies are anything like the enemies of that bleached-out prophet Jonah, our kindness will lead some, at least, to a knowledge of the truth and to repentance. Thus will they escape divine judgment.[30]

Do we serve our enemies with food and water *so that* they will feel as if burning coals have been heaped upon their head? Well, we may. But if we do, that is only our instrumental goal. Our ultimate goal is to *overcome* evil with good (Rom. 12:21). Perhaps the discomfort induced by kindness toward our enemies will bring them to their senses. If that should happen, then they won't be enemies any longer.[31]

The apostle Peter was convinced that when we suffer because of our enemies, some of them will wonder at our allegiance to Jesus Christ and inquire about our reasons.

> But even if you should suffer for righteousness, you are blessed. Do not fear what they fear, and or be troubled. But in your heart regard Christ as Lord, always being prepared to give a defense to anyone who asks for a reason for the hope that is in you. But do this gently and respectfully,

29. See 2 Pet. 3:9, 15; 1 Tim. 2:1, 4; Rom. 11:32; Ezek. 18:23; 1 Pet. 3:20.

30. See 2 Tim. 2:24-26.

31. Notice how the New Testament speaks of our membership in a "household": Eph. 2:19; Gal. 6:10; Heb. 3:6; 4:17. That we should be prepared to see our enemies repent is stressed by C. S. Lewis in "The Weight of Glory," *The Weight of Glory, and Other Addresses,* revised and expanded edn. (New York: Macmillan, 1980), pp. 3-19, esp. 18-19.

> having a good conscience, so that, when you are slandered, those who revile your Christ-like behavior may be put to shame. (1 Pet. 3:14-16)

Shame is a good thing if it leads to repentance!

1 Corinthians 13

For all of its legendary appeal, the message of 1 Corinthians 13 has yet to sink in. Why are we so inclined to trade brotherly love for personal influence — for "having a ministry with impact"? Why do we value miraculous powers — or, in popular contemporary lingo, "signs and wonders" — over love for one another?[32] Let's face the harsh reality. We often do really believe and behave as if everything else we do for God's kingdom is more important than dealing God's way with interpersonal conflict. But we are on solid ground in rejecting this moral disease within the church today.

1 Corinthians 13 is Paul's answer to narrow-minded obsessions with power and influence that afflicted the first-century church at Corinth and that afflict the church today. In the absence of love, nothing else we do "for the cause of Christ" counts for much. In fact, our actions may be counterproductive. That, I suppose, is the point in saying that speaking with the tongues of men and of angels — that is, super-duper public speaking — without also having the virtue of love, is tantamount to noisy gonging and cymbal clanging (v. 1).

Verses 4-7 lie at the heart of this chapter:

> Love is patient. Love is kind, and is not jealous. It does not boast, nor is it arrogant. Nor is it fractious.[33] Nor is it ego-centered. Nor is it resentful. Nor does it keep track of wrongs that have been suffered. Nor does it rejoice at wrongdoing, but rejoices with the truth. It bears all things, it believes all things, it hopes all things, it endures all things.

Here we have the anatomy of love: what it is and what it isn't. It's a remarkable list. There's counsel here for the person who would grow in the

32. See 1 Cor. 1:22; cf. Matt. 12:38.

33. That is, love doesn't cause a bunch of trouble with others, or create tension within the community.

virtue of forgiveness. On the receiving end of unilateral injury, *patience* is evidence of love. Perhaps the wrongdoer will repent. Perhaps his actions will be revealed for what they are. In any case, God will, in his own time, avenge and bring the wrongdoer to justice. Meanwhile, while there is still time there is still *hope.*

The one who has been wronged does not *keep* these wrongs before his mind in his further dealings with the wrongdoer. This is not to say that he forgets the injustice. But he does not retaliate. He does not say, resorting to Latin, *"Osculare pultem meam!"*[34] On the contrary, he is *kind.* The wrongdoer benefits from this loving disposition, whether he knows it or not. If he knows it, he may seek to exploit it. But love *endures all things.*

The loving person is not easily *provoked* or *resentful,* looking for some fault to hold against another. Nor is he, even when he judges rightly that he has been severely and unjustly treated, *aroused* to shameful action. He is calm in response to provocation. His response is measured and befitting a person of virtue.

The loving person also *rejoices with truth.* In contexts that call for forgiveness, this means that he will bring the truth to light. He will not shrink from bold action where accountability for injustice is needed. The complement to this is that he *does not rejoice at wrongdoing.* When someone is wronged, he notices it and does something about it.

There is healing truth here for wrongdoers, as well. By seeking to grow in these same virtues through specific, observable acts, a repentant wrongdoer can demonstrate his sincerity and thus facilitate reconciliation.

No wonder it's said that "love covers a multitude of sins."[35]

The Virtue of Forgiveness in Community Life

As we consider the fuller implications of forgiveness construed as a *virtue,* we should come to see that the virtue of forgiveness may be "operational" even apart from exercising forgiveness in the usual sense of the term — where a wrongdoer is forgiven by the person who has been

34. Translated, this means "Kiss my grits." See Henry Beard, *Latin for Even More Occasions* (London: HarperCollins, 1992), p. 71.

35. 1 Pet. 4:8.

wronged. I use the term "operational" in its literal sense. Any person who has the virtue of forgiveness *will act like it.* Ideally, she will display this virtue in her conduct whenever the occasion for doing so arises. Unfortunately, we tend to think that the only occasion calling for a person to display this virtue is when that person has been wronged by another person. Coming to grips with forgiveness as a virtue will help us see why this is inadequate.

We start with the point that possessing a virtue means behaving in ways consistent with having that virtue, in circumstances that call for exhibiting that virtue. If forgiveness is a virtue, then being a forgiving person means behaving as a forgiving person would in any circumstance that calls for exhibiting that virtue. And having that virtue does not depend on being wronged by another person. The virtue of forgiveness does not come and go through cycles of wrongdoing. The virtue of forgiveness is a stable feature of the forgiving person's character; it is always present and ready to condition all that the forgiving person does.

To be sure, to be a forgiving person is to have the disposition to forgive a wrongdoer whenever preconditions for forgiveness, such as repentance, have been satisfied. But having that disposition depends upon having the capacity for sober awareness of the injustice of a wrongdoer's act. Otherwise, there would be no point in forgiving, since there would be nothing to forgive. This capacity for perceiving injustice is a constituent of the virtue of forgiveness. The forgiving person knows what kinds of circumstances call for forgiveness. The forgiving person recognizes these circumstances for what they are when they arise.

Now this capacity to recognize circumstances that call for forgiveness is not limited to those who have been wronged in particular cases. "Outside observers" endowed with the virtue of forgiveness will also, under the right conditions, recognize the need for the forgiveness process in particular circumstances. Recognizing the aptness of forgiveness, or of pursuing the steps toward forgiveness, requires also seeing that an injustice has been done.

In addition to having the capacity for sober awareness of the injustice of a wrongdoer's act, the person who is wronged, if she has the virtue of forgiveness, will also know how to regard the wrongdoer. And how the injured person, now supposed to have the virtue of forgiveness, regards the wrongdoer depends on aspects of the wrongdoer's demeanor. When confronted with his wrongdoing, he may listen and repent. If he does not repent, then the forgiving person does not forgive. If he repents, then the forgiving person forgives. Forgiveness isn't even a possibility without repentance.[36]

What, now, about outside observers who have this virtue of forgiveness? They, too, will be sensitive to the wrongdoer's aspect, and regard the wrongdoer from the virtue of forgiveness. This does not mean that they will forgive the wrongdoer. For one thing, it is not their place to forgive, for they have not been wronged.[37] Nor will they urge the person who

36. If you think you've forgiven an unrepentant person, think again. You may not harbor resentment toward the person. But that is not forgiveness, at least not on Jesus' terms. This is why, for all the excellent points he makes about resentment and forgiveness, Joseph Butler (1692-1752) is not altogether right about what it means to forgive. (See Butler's two sermons "On Resentment and Forgiveness of Injuries," in *Fifteen Sermons Preached at the Rolls Chapel,* 2nd edn. (London, 1729). According to Jesus, the opportunity to forgive arises with repentance. The call to repent really is not optional, in the protocol that Jesus provides. So the opportunity to repent should arise, and it does arise when members of the fellowship do their part. If the wrongdoer does not repent, then he is to be excluded from fellowship.

What if the Jesus protocol is ignored? Unfortunately, especially when the offense committed significantly injures another person — physically, emotionally, or otherwise — it is common for the wrongdoer to persist in his ways. Having injured another person, he may continue with sins against the person, possibly to insulate himself from any suspicion of wrongdoing within the community. He may threaten the person he's wronged. Or he may take preemptive action to undermine the credibility of the person, should he seek the aid of others in confronting him with his sin. And if his wrongdoing becomes known to others within the community, but nothing is done about it, then he is, in effect, enabled in his sinful acts, and he may take courage in this to cause further injury if it is to his advantage. It's time we reckon with these dynamics, which are played out with disastrous effect more often than we would like to admit.

We are not to give wrongdoers "the benefit of the doubt," especially if there is no doubt about wrongdoing. In his letters, Paul warned pastors and churches that there was skullduggery in the church and that it had to be weeded out. He even named names (see 2 Tim. 4:14-15, with 1 Tim. 1:18-20). From the clues we have about these people, we might suppose that some of them were unhealthy narcissists, with dangerous ego-projects and little capacity for admission of wrongdoing (see Phil. 1:15-17; cf. 2 Cor. 11:12-15; Acts 20:29-30; Gal. 1:7; 2:4; Titus 1:10-11; 2 Pet. 2:1-3). In 1 John, the author links bad doctrine with bad behavior, and warns his readers to be on guard against both. This letter emphasizes the need for Christians to love one another. Evidence that they do not is a bad sign.

37. They have not been wronged directly. But as members of the same community, whose spiritual health depends on interpersonal harmony, they are indirectly

has been wronged to forgive the wrongdoer. For having the virtue of forgiveness includes insight into the conditions under which forgiving someone is the proper thing to do. At the very least they will know that there can be no forgiveness without repentance. So those who have this virtue who have not been wronged will not counsel the suffering party to forgive, unless there is satisfactory evidence of repentance.

We must now consider more deeply the significance of having the virtue of forgiveness. A proper act of forgiveness is carried out with a reasonable sense of having been wronged.[38] This includes self-regard. The forgiving person knows that he has been wronged. He is right, then, to feel wronged. Having the virtue of forgiveness will tend to produce in the injured person the right balance of sentiment about having been wronged. He may grieve. He may even be angry. He may mourn the loss of what has been taken from him — some concrete possession, possibly, or perhaps his reputation, maybe his confidence in himself and his ability to move forward in his vocation. Having been wronged, he has a legitimate claim on the wrongdoer, who has attempted an illicit claim on or against him.

So the forgiving person's emotional state, after being wronged, will be ordered by his having this forgiveness virtue.

Those who have not been wronged will not be induced to feel the way the injured person feels. However, if they have the virtue of forgiveness, they will *sympathize* with the person who has been injured. This sympathy is a positive force in the forgiveness dynamic. Forgiving persons aware of the circumstances where wrongdoing has occurred — "on their watch," as it were — will not begrudge the injured person his perfectly proper emotional state or his attitude toward the unrepentant wrongdoer.

What, then? Others in the community, and especially the leaders, will affirm the injured person's proper evaluation of the act. They will validate the injured person's sense of injustice.

This is a crucial feature of healthy community life. We can understand this better if we contrast it with standard operating procedure. It is standard practice for community members to engage in different behaviors, depending on their position in the community. If they have a rela-

---

harmed, along with the rest of the community. Also, the moral authority and trustworthiness of leaders within the community is at stake when significant wrongdoing occurs.

38. This, again, assumes asymmetric wrongdoing of a significant kind.

tionship with the wrongdoer, and they are reluctant to risk losing that relationship, they probably will, at best, sideline themselves, hoping to "stay out of it." At worst, they will accommodate the wrongdoer in more proactive (and sometimes even provocative) ways. If they are community leaders, with an interest in peacemaking, they will be tempted to "level the playing field" and assume — often against the evidence — that "both parties are to blame." They may advise reconciliation, and seek to facilitate this. But their methods are bound to be ham-handed, at best.[39] Unless, I want to emphasize, they have the virtue of forgiveness.

The task of collecting and assessing evidence of wrongdoing is delicate, to say the least. How this is handled will itself depend on whether those responsible have and exercise the virtue of forgiveness. It is certainly easy to fumble the evidence of wrongdoing. The potential for further injury is great. But if the protocol that Jesus recommended is followed by people who have the virtue of forgiveness, then wisdom will prevail. The wrongdoer will be confronted with his wrongdoing, rebuked, and invited to repent. If all goes well, he will.

How members of the community respond when there are "tensions in the air" depends on their stable of virtues. In a bona fide case of wrongdoing that cannot justly be called bilateral (i.e., where both parties are equally responsible), community members have a responsibility both to the wrongdoer and to the person wronged.

This is rarely played out the way Jesus desired.

Why Forgive?

I've spoken of emotional states and how they are ordered by the forgiveness virtue. Having the virtue of forgiveness leaves plenty of room to experience a wide and fluctuating range of emotions when we've been wronged. This topic deserves fuller development at another time.

Here, though, we have to confront one popular answer to the question, Why forgive?

You can tell a lot about someone's conception of forgiveness by his answer to the question. Many psychiatrists and psychotherapists have

39. They may even fuel the difficulties that have arisen because of the wrongdoer's actions.

noted that forgiveness is good for the wounded soul. Three authors will serve as illustrations of this trend.

Edward M. Hallowell is a practicing psychiatrist, a Harvard University faculty member, and the director of the Hallowell-Ratey Center for Cognitive and Emotional Health. He is also the author of the book *Dare to Forgive: The Power of Letting Go and Moving On.*[40] The eighteen chapters of this self-help book are divided into two parts. Part one answers the question, What is forgiveness? Part two explains how to forgive. Between the two sections is a self-assessment quiz for determining how forgiving you are.

Already this should sound a little dubious.

Hallowell's take on the question in the first part of his book is neatly indicated by five chapter titles:

1. "Forgiveness Is a Gift You Give Yourself."
2. "Forgiveness Detoxifies Hurt and Hatred."
3. "Forgiveness Sets You Free."
4. "Forgiveness Improves Your Health."
5. "Forgiveness Is Brave."

Forgiveness is a process that (1) begins with feeling wronged and wondering what to do, (2) moves next to "reliving what happened and reflecting on it" in order to answer the question, "What do I want this pain to turn into?" (3) proceeds with the work of getting past anger and resentment, and (4) ends by "taking stock and moving forward."[41]There are actually twenty individual steps involved in this fourfold process.[42] (I'm not making this up.) The entire process is designed for recovery from the pain of injury.

Another book, enthusiastically endorsed by Rabbi Harold Kushner, is *Forgiving for Good: A Proven Prescription for Health and Happiness,* by Dr. Fred Luskin, director of the Stanford University Forgiveness Project.[43] Several chapters are devoted to exploring "the reasons you are better off

40. Edward M. Hallowell, *Dare to Forgive: The Power of Letting Go and Moving On* (Deerfield Beach, FL: Health Communications, Inc., 2004).

41. Hallowell, *Dare to Forgive,* p. 72.

42. Hallowell, *Dare to Forgive,* pp. 87-88.

43. Fred Luskin, *Forgive for Good: A Proven Prescription for Health and Happiness* (San Francisco: HarperCollins, 2002).

when you choose to forgive."[44] The good doctor offers this virtual guarantee: "I have conducted research studies that conclusively prove that what I am teaching you works, and I describe these studies in detail."[45] So it's no surprise to find a chapter on "The Science of Forgiveness." Among other things, forgiveness is:

- "the peace you learn to feel";
- "for you and not the offender";
- "taking back your power";
- "about your healing";
- "a trainable skill";
- "becoming a hero instead of a victim."[46]

It's difficult to recognize the teaching of Jesus in these pleasant postulates. But of course, Jesus didn't live in the modern scientific age.

The truth is, there is psychic value in forgiveness. Often, the person who forgives is rewarded with feelings of peace and victory over resentment and anger that eat away at the wounded soul. And there is much to commend in these books. The trouble is, they don't reflect the true nature of forgiveness and its first-order benefits. And the reason is that the real thing has been sanitized for consumption by a society of self-obsessed "victims" who want to get back into the happiness groove as quickly as possible. Pressed into service for this purpose, forgiveness becomes something else — what I call "therapeutic forgiveness."[47]

A reductive account of forgiveness is to be expected from secular theorists. But some Christian thinkers have joined this chorus. The classic example is Lewis B. Smedes, whose book *Forgive and Forget: Healing the Hurts We Don't Deserve* has sold in the hundreds of thousands.[48]

44. Luskin, *Forgive for Good,* p. 64.

45. Luskin, *Forgive for Good,* pp. 64-65.

46. For these items, see Luskin, *Forgive for Good,* p. vii.

47. Others have also adopted this terminology. See especially L. Gregory Jones's chapter on "Therapeutic Forgiveness," in his carefully researched and theologically sophisticated book *Embodying Forgiveness: A Theological Analysis* (Grand Rapids: Eerdmans, 1995), pp. 35-69.

48. Lewis B. Smedes, *Forgive and Forget: Healing the Hurts We Don't Deserve* (New York: HarperCollins, 1984). My copy brandishes yet another endorsement from Rabbi Harold Kushner.

There is much wisdom in this compassionate volume. Smedes says, for example, that "you will know that forgiveness has begun when you recall those who hurt you and feel the power to wish them well."[49] This doesn't say what forgiveness is, of course, and it's not true without exception. There are cases, I believe, where someone wronged gets over the personal pain of an injury and even re-acclimates to relationship with the wrongdoer, without actually forgiving the wrongdoer.

It is disquieting, however, to see the same preoccupation with feeling good after being wounded. When woundedness results in anger and resentment, the wounded person must find release in forgiving the person with whom she is angry. Because the anger and resentment that naturally emerges from woundedness is often directed at God, Smedes even speaks of "forgiving God" — a concept that is foreign to Scripture.[50]

I believe in therapy. I accept that woundedness can be relieved through therapy. And I concur with many of the principles described in these books.[51] But their distortion of forgiveness itself is disturbing. A telltale sign discernible in each of them is confusion about the place of repentance in the forgiveness dynamic. What Jesus considered essential, these authors consider optional, or even irrelevant. For them, repentance has to be optional; otherwise, forgiveness in the sense of emotional recovery lies beyond the power of the wounded person.[52]

49. Smedes, *Forgive and Forget,* p. 29.

50. Smedes is not alone in commending a therapeutic approach to forgiveness to Christians. See also Grace Ketterman and David Hazard, *When You Can't Say "I Forgive You": Breaking the Bonds of Anger and Hurt* (Colorado Springs: NavPress, 2000), and Worthington, Jr., *Forgiving and Reconciling,* mentioned in note 16 above.

51. A seminal work on the role of forgiveness in the counseling context is Ronald D. Enright's essay, "Counseling within the Forgiveness Triad: On Forgiving, Receiving Forgiveness, and Self-Forgiveness," *Counseling and Values* 40.2 (January 1996). Philosopher Jeffrie Murphy examines Enright's contribution to "forgiveness boosterism" in his own book on forgiveness. See Jeffrie G. Murphy, *Getting Even: Forgiveness and Its Limits* (Oxford: Oxford University Press, 2003), chapter 7, "Forgiveness in Psychotherapy" (pp. 73-86).

52. Advocates of therapeutic forgiveness are rightly concerned about the anger and hatred that arise in contexts of asymmetric wrongdoing. What is needed, however, is wisdom in dealing with anger, even when forgiveness is not possible, and often as a precursor to forgiving a person who does repent. David W. Augsberger understands this. He, too, objects to the clinical model of forgiveness that is so popular today. According to the "common cultural misunderstanding" of forgiveness, forgive-

Is Forgiveness a Christian Virtue?

The Christian conception of forgiveness is distinctive. (1) The obligation to forgive is backed by the singular authority of Jesus. (2) Human forgiveness is modeled on God's forgiveness of us. (3) Forgiveness follows repentance, which makes it an unlikely secular value. Sure enough, there is virtually no emphasis on the need for repentance in secular accounts of forgiveness.[53] (4) Jesus is our only reliable model of uncompromised forgiveness in action. He gently but purposefully says to us, "Take my yoke upon you and learn of me" (Matt. 11:29). And he notes, in reference to himself and his disciples, that "a student, after he has been fully taught, will be like his teacher" (Luke 6:40). (5) The ultimate incentive to forgive is to preserve the unity of the church in the bond of peace (Eph. 4:3; cf. Col. 3:14). (6) The practice of forgiveness is essential for kingdom-like living during the interval between Christ's first and second advents, in preparation for the splendor of his kingdom fully realized. (7) For the church to woo the world to Christ, its people must demonstrate uncommon harmony with each other, and this requires faithful practice of forgiveness. If seven weren't the perfect number, we might add an eighth point, that the inculcation of this virtue is due to the Holy Spirit working in us (see Gal. 5:22-23). But this, you could say, is in the background of each individual point.

The point of enumerating these several truths is to indicate the worldview context in which the virtue of forgiveness is rightly understood and properly motivated. *Forgiveness is a Christian virtue.*[54]

---

ness is confused with "a therapeutic release of hatred" (*Hate-Work: Working through the Pain and Pleasures of Hate* [Louisville: Westminster John Knox Press, 2004], p. 220). He agrees that we must "critique . . . those cheap and easy varieties of pardon that require no repentance or consideration of repentance" (p. 86). For the therapeutic value of Augsberger's treatment of "hate-work," I commend his book. For valuable secular advice on dealing with anger, I recommend the cognitive-behavioral approach developed, in much practical detail, by Matthew McKay, Peter D. Rogers, and Judith McKay, in their book *When Anger Hurts: Quieting the Storm Within,* 2nd edn. (Oakland, CA: New Harbinger Publications, 2003).

53. We witness the secular reduction of this dimension virtually every time we hear of a politician's apology in response to a demand for an apology by another politician or the press.

54. For more along these lines, see Marius Reiser, "Love of Enemies in the Context of Antiquity," *New Testament Studies* 47 (2001): 411-27.

Jesus once said to his disciples,

> Temptations to sin are sure to come, but woe to one through whom they come! It would be better for him if a millstone were hung around his neck and he were cast into the sea than that he should cause one of these little ones to sin. Pay attention to yourselves! If your brother sins, rebuke him, and if he repents, forgive him, and if he sins against you seven times in the day, and turns to you seven times, saying, "I repent," you must forgive him. (Luke 17:1-4, ESV)

Jesus remains on point. The order is always the same:

1. Person A sins against Person B.
2. Person B rebukes Person A.
3. Person A repents of his sin against Person B.
4. Person B forgives Person A.

The fourfold sequence is a progression, where each step depends on the previous step. Person A is fully responsible for having started the cycle in the first place. The first responsibility of Person B is to *rebuke* Person A. Think of it. Have you ever been counseled to follow the advice of Jesus? I haven't. But I have been told, usually immediately, "Forgive your brother." Usually there is a third person, Person C, who tells Person B, "You must forgive your brother." This exonerates person C of all further responsibility, and it is very convenient for person A.

What must Person B do once he has rebuked Person A for his sin? Jesus does not say he is to forgive. Again, responsibility falls to Person A. He is to repent. *If* Person A repents, *then* Person B is to forgive.

One of the most egregious failures of the Christian church has been its disregard for Jesus' teaching regarding sin, repentance, and forgiveness. It is egregious, first, because it is disobedience, pure and simple. Second, untold injury has been compounded for all those who have been shamed into premature forgiveness, while their original injury festers interminably. And third, the people of God are injured as a community.

This last point is true on several levels. Offenders are protected and empowered. Having dodged appropriate confrontation — and the proper consequences for their sin and for stubborn refusal to repent — offenders are loosed upon other members of the community, who may suffer similar indignities and the whole sorry debacle begins anew. Leaders display their timidity and compromise God's ordained authority pattern for addressing sin in the community of faith. How many leaders who deplore the moral lassitude of the church have a track record of confronting sin the Jesus way?

If there is a forgiveness virtue, as I have argued, then evidence of its presence as a character trait should be visible in various ways:

- The forgiving person will forgive the repentant person who has injured him.
- The forgiving person will not forgive unless there has been repentance.
- The forgiving person will support those who have been injured by the sins of others, rightly validating the injured person's feeling of injustice.
- The forgiving person will respond to rebuke with repentance when he has sinned against another.

Accountability for sin among believers makes good sense. Whereas Jesus commanded love of our enemies without injecting confusion with commands to forgive them, he judiciously established a different plan for addressing, or even forestalling, the rancor that sometimes occurs among believers. The only influence the church has with its enemies is the influence of unrestrained love. But the church must exercise its influence much differently when its unity and its values are threatened by members who sin against other members. It must display the virtue of forgiveness.

When we contemplate the challenge of Jesus' teaching about forgiveness, and wonder where we will find the strength to do things Jesus' way, we might respond as his disciples did when they were presented with this same challenge, and said to the Lord:[55]

Increase our faith!

55. Luke 17:5.

Questions for Further Reflection

1. If you believe that Christians should forgive even if the wrongdoer does not repent of his wrongdoing, how do you respond to the chapter's exposition of Matthew 18?

2. Why have believers generally failed to follow the protocol Jesus commands in Matthew 18? Where does the process usually break down? Why is this? What can be done to restore this practice among believers? What difficulties will have to be overcome?

3. In footnote 14, Geivett likens the advice believers typically receive when they have been wronged to the counsel Job received from his dubious and unreliable friends. What counsel did his friends give and how did they justify their advice to Job? What, in God's own eyes, was wrong with how they counseled Job? What did God command them to do to set things right? How does this parallel the situation today, where Christian leaders often ignore the forgiveness protocol Jesus commanded?

4. It will often be challenging to determine whether an instance of wrongdoing is asymmetrical, as this is defined in the chapter. And it will frequently be difficult to collect and evaluate the evidence of wrongdoing. What criteria would you recommend for leaders to use in fulfilling their responsibilities in the forgiveness process outlined in this chapter?

5. What should you do if a believer has wronged you and you have attempted to follow Jesus' protocol, but you have been stonewalled by other Christians in your community?

Humility

Andrew Pinsent

The Puzzle of Humility

> Let a certain saving ambition invade our souls so that, impatient of mediocrity, we pant after the highest things and (since, if we will, we can) bend all our efforts to their attainment. Let us disdain things of earth, hold as little worth even the astral orders and, putting behind us all the things of this world, hasten to that court beyond the world, closest to the most exalted Godhead. There, as the sacred mysteries tell us, the Seraphim, Cherubim and Thrones occupy the first places; but, unable to yield to them, and impatient of any second place, let us emulate their dignity and glory. And, if we will it, we shall be inferior to them in nothing.
>
> Pico della Mirandola (1486)[1]

Most people would not regard this passage from the *Oration on the Dignity of Man* as a humble statement, at least if they think of humility as being low, deferential, and submissive. In a style that marks a watershed

1. Giovanni Pico della Mirandola, *Oration on the Dignity of Man* [1486], trans. A. Robert Caponigri (Washington, DC: Regnery, 1956).

I am most grateful to Eleonore Stump for reviewing earlier drafts of this chapter. I also thank Joseph Carola and Marcus Holden for their helpful comments and Theodore Vitali for encouraging me to pursue research in this field.

from that of the great Christian thinkers of antiquity or the Middle Ages, Pico praises the brilliance of humanity, our mastery of the world and, above all, our ability to fashion ourselves into whatever we wish. He even claims we have the power, should we choose to exercise it, to imitate the highest of the angels and ascend to the very throne of God.

Although such hubris can be regarded as playful rhetoric, historians have often interpreted the *Oration* as a spiritual manifesto of the Renaissance, a period of growing self-confidence in which many of the prevalent cultural attitudes of contemporary society were first formed. The writer urges us to shape our own destiny rather than defer and submit to anything. Contemporary society has imbibed this spirit, expressed in myriad slogans that proclaim one or other variant on the theme, *"You can be whatever you want to be!"* Given its association with being deferential and submissive, what place does humility have in our present world? And indeed, in the light of the many achievements of humanity, why *should* we be humble? What can humility do for us except inhibit our efforts to excel? Is it not better to strive for greatness, to reach for the stars rather than crawl in the dust?

Even if such questions are rarely consciously articulated, the attitudes behind them are widespread and persuasively account for the neglect and even rejection of the virtue of humility.[2] Yet any attempt to respond to these questions from a philosophical perspective faces a number of peculiar challenges. First and most important, classical non-Christian philosophers of virtue ethics have little or nothing to say about humility. In Aristotle's *Nicomachean Ethics,* which presents a grand survey of all the principal moral and intellectual virtues that pertain to human nature and flourishing, humility is only conspicuous by its absence. Similarly, in Plato's dialogues, humility is scarcely mentioned.[3] By contrast, Scripture greatly

2. For a recent analysis of the contemporary neglect of humility as a virtue see, for example, Kari Konkola, "Have We Lost Humility?" *Humanitas* 18.1-2 (2005): 182-207. Konkola cites evidence for a loss of attention to humility within Christian as well as in secular accounts of the virtues. He notes that post-Reformation England maintained a basic continuity with the medieval Catholic emphasis on the importance of humility. By contrast, many contemporary Christian reference works are often silent on the subject.

3. It is sometimes argued that the virtue of humility is wholly absent in the works of Aristotle and Plato, a claim made, for example, in Jay Newman, "Humility and Self-Realization," *Journal of Value Inquiry* 16 (1982): 277. I argue that the classical tradition does not entirely neglect humility, as Plato, *Laws* 4.716a shows. Nevertheless, it is in-

extols humility. Jesus in the Gospel of Matthew says, "Take my yoke upon you, and learn from me; for I am gentle and humble in heart, and you will find rest for your souls" (Matt. 11:29, NRSV).[4] The First Letter of Peter says, "Humble yourselves therefore under the mighty hand of God, that in due time he may exalt you" (1 Pet. 5:6), and the Letter of James reminds us that "God opposes the proud, but gives grace to the humble" (James 4:6). A similar emphasis runs through the whole Christian tradition, where literally thousands of references to humility and its importance can be found in the writings of the church fathers, scholastic theologians, and doctors of the church. Cassian, for example, refers to humility as the "the mother of all virtues and the surest foundation of the whole spiritual superstructure,"[5] and Augustine calls it the "safe and true way to heaven . . . which lifts up the heart to the Lord."[6] For Aquinas humility is in the first place of importance in removing obstacles to the virtues, given that it opposes pride.[7] Therefore, though humility is negligible in the classical pantheon, Christianity has evidently given a greatly increased emphasis to this virtue. This emphasis in turn raises further questions about how to examine humility from a philosophical perspective. Does humility belong in the list of natural virtues? Alternatively, is humility a uniquely Christian virtue? If so, what can be said about humility to those who do not accept the truth of Christian revelation? Furthermore, how should those who do accept revelation understand humility? Is humility something that can be reasoned about, or should the need for this virtue merely be accepted as God's will for us?

---

disputable that such exceptions are rare and that the emphasis given to humility in the Jewish and Christian traditions is different in kind from what is found in classical sources of virtue ethics.

4. Citations from Scripture are taken from the Revised Standard Version (RSV) unless marked NRSV, indicating the New Revised Standard Version. For this passage, the NRSV has been used since it translates *tapeinos* explicitly and correctly as "humble."

5. John Cassian, *Conferences* 2.19.2, trans. Edgar C. S. Gibson, in Nicene and Post-Nicene Fathers, Second Series, ed. Philip Schaff and Henry Wace (Peabody, MA: Hendrickson, 1994), vol. 11.

6. Augustine, *City of God* 16.4, trans. M. Dods, in Nicene and Post-Nicene Fathers, ed. Philip Schaff (Peabody, MA: Hendrickson, 1989), vol. 2.

7. Aquinas, *Summa Theologica* (hereafter ST) 2a2ae, q.161, a.5, ad 2. A good translation of the *Summa* is the 1911 edition by the Fathers of the English Dominican Province and originally published by Benziger Brothers, Inc. This translation has been reprinted under license by Christian Classics (Notre Dame: Ave Maria Press, 1981).

A second and associated problem is that when any attempt is made to examine humility within classical philosophical accounts of the virtues it does not quite fit into *any* of the available categories. Aquinas places humility within modesty or temperance in what appears, at first, to be an Aristotelian approach, arguing that it restrains us from an immoderate and disordered desire for greatness.[8] A similar approach can be seen in some contemporary philosophical work, in which humility is treated as a kind of temperance that restores one's self-estimation to a mean founded on right reason from a bias towards exaggeration.[9] To say, however, that temperance is the *most appropriate* of the Aristotelian categories does not mean that this is the *best* way of describing humility. As an illustration, among

8. ST 2a2ae, q.161, a.4. Aquinas does make use of Aristotelian categories to demarcate the matter of the principal virtues, including temperance, but in fact his treatment of the virtues diverges from that of Aristotle in many details, including that of humility. I explore this issue in "The Gifts and Fruits of the Holy Spirit," a chapter of the *Oxford Handbook of Aquinas,* ed. Brian Davies and Eleonore Stump, forthcoming from Oxford University Press in 2011.

9. Norvin Richards, *Humility* (Philadelphia: Temple University Press, 1992), adopts this approach in one of the relatively few contemporary philosophical studies of humility. Richards claims that "humility consists . . . in *understanding oneself so well* that one is disinclined to over-estimation" (p. 86). Such a definition does indeed describe two important characteristics of humility, namely self-understanding and disinclination to over-estimation. This definition also parallels Aquinas's categorization of humility as a species of temperance, insofar as temperance restores a proper mean from a tendency (in most cases) towards excess. Nevertheless, the objection has been raised as to whether mere accuracy in an assessment of one's own merits is sufficient to define humility. See, for example, Ewin's review of Richards's work: R. Ewin, "Review of 'Humility' by Norvin Richards," *Australasian Journal of Philosophy* 72.1 (1994): 125-26. Working within a Kantian framework, Jeanine Grenberg, *Kant and the Ethics of Humility: A Story of Dependence, Corruption and Virtue* (Cambridge: Cambridge University Press, 2005), also associates humility with proper self-esteem. Grenberg describes humility as the achievement of the inner condition of the proper valuation of the self in relation to duty. Similarly, David Horner has suggested that the virtues of magnanimity and humility "keep one within a rational balance with regard to great, difficult honors." In other words, the combination of these two virtues gives one a truthful awareness of one's gifts and abilities; see David A. Horner, "What It Takes to Be Great: Aristotle and Aquinas on Magnanimity," *Faith and Philosophy* 15.4 (1998): 434-35. Nevertheless, while such approaches seem to describe certain aspects of humility well, the notion of humility as proper self-valuation lacks the extravagance in self-giving or self-emptying that seems to characterize humility in the Christian and Jewish traditions.

the set of all possible two dimensional objects, a circle may be the most appropriate way of categorizing a sphere. This does not mean, however, that a circle is the best way of describing what a sphere is *in itself*; in fact, to describe a sphere as a circle is geometrically misleading. Similarly, to say that humility is a part of temperance may be true insofar as it is the most appropriate way of categorizing humility within an Aristotelian framework. Nevertheless, to regard this as a sufficient description of humility in itself is highly misleading. While it is true that humility restrains us from a disordered desire for greatness, to think of humility merely in terms of temperance does not seem to capture the essence of humility. In the Christian tradition, humility is associated with a kind of *extravagance* of self-giving or self-emptying, an extravagance which seems quite alien to treating humility as a minor category of temperance, relegated to the level of sensible eating.[10] But where else does humility fit if not within temperance, and if humility cannot be placed within a classical theory of virtue ethics at all, what alternative framework can we provide?

A third major problem with humility arises from this difficulty of finding an appropriate philosophical framework. Virtues in a classical approach are usually seen as good principally because they are conducive to an end, namely human flourishing or happiness. For example, denying oneself some immediate pleasures is helpful training in temperance, which will in turn help promote one's flourishing. But how is it possible to justify humility in this way? Humility, to use a description of Aquinas, conveys the notion of "a praiseworthy self-abasement to the lowest place."[11] If, however, an account of humility cannot be given within a broader framework of human nature and flourishing it is hard to see what conceivable good can arise from such self-abasement. Indeed, is such abasement even just? Unfortunately, far from answering the questions raised at the beginning of this chapter, such a description of humility seems only to confirm rather than answer the objections. Surely volun-

10. The treatment of humility as an Aristotelian mean between two extremes of excess and deficiency has also been criticized within the Jewish tradition. James Diamond has noted how Moses Maimonides, who otherwise extols the Aristotelian mean, specifically excludes humility from the moderation of other virtues. For Maimonides, humility is an *extreme* self-abnegation or self-effacement that is a necessary protection against hubris. See James Arthur Diamond, "Maimonides on Kingship: The Ethics of Imperial Humility," *Journal of Religious Ethics* 34.1 (2006): 89-114.

11. ST 2a2ae, q.161, a.1, ad 2.

tary abasement hinders our efforts to excel? Furthermore, insofar as the promotion of humility is strongly associated with the Christian tradition, one might argue that Christianity is a pernicious influence that restrains us from excellence. This line of argument leads, of course, to the well-known objection of Nietzsche, who denigrated Christian ethics as the morality of resentful slaves.

So humility is, to say the least, philosophically challenging. Aristotle does not identify it as a virtue and it does not fit properly within his categories. Even worse, what is generally connoted by humility, namely self-abasement, seems low, mean, miserable, and lacking in any obvious consequent good. Therefore, for many people, humility might actually be seen as a vice rather than a virtue, and Christianity, which has so strongly advocated humility, as a hindrance to human progress and fulfillment. The rhetorical challenge of Pico della Mirandola cited at the beginning of this chapter remains unanswered: why *should* we be humble rather than striving for the greatness of the gods?

Despite the difficulties set out above, there are grounds for answering this challenge in the rather paradoxical nature of humility in those to whom it is attributed. A dramatic example in Scripture is that of Moses. Scripture describes him confronting an evil king, working miracles, leading over six hundred thousand people out of slavery, giving God's law to these people, and leading them for forty years through a wilderness to their Promised Land. These are not the typical actions of a low or servile individual. Yet Scripture also describes Moses as being more meek or humble than anyone else on earth (Num. 12:3). This implies that humility is not incompatible with greatness of leadership, action, and achievement; many additional examples of this paradoxical mix of humility and greatness can be found in Christian history. One example who comes to mind is Dante. In a famous scene from the *Divine Comedy,* Dante encounters in Limbo the souls of the five greatest poets who had ever lived prior to his own time. These souls welcome him as follows:

> And they honored me far beyond courtesy,
> for they included me in their own number
> making me sixth in that high company.[12]

12. Dante Alighieri, *The Divine Comedy,* trans. John Ciardi (New York: North American Library, 2003), *Inferno* 4.100-102.

Here in his own poem Dante explicitly describes himself as the sixth greatest poet of all history. Is such a description compatible with humility? Although we might be slightly uncomfortable with his bold self-assessment, the truth is that Dante probably *is* one of the greatest poets of all time, perhaps even the greatest. Dante simply acknowledges this fact and, if anything, makes a rather conservative assessment of his abilities by placing himself sixth. If, instead, he had disparaged his abilities this would have been a falsehood, and thus surely incompatible with the notion of virtue. So it seems that humility is not a matter, as is sometimes wryly remarked, of intelligent people pretending to be stupid. On the contrary, humility can be compatible with greatness, as in the case of Moses, and even with the acknowledgment of one's own greatness, as in the case of Dante.

In what, then, does humility consist, and why has Christianity placed such an emphasis on it? Why does Scripture proclaim the humble ones to be exalted and the proud cast down (Luke 1:51-52), and what is it about humility that makes it possible to be humble and yet great at the same time? In particular, is there a philosophical way to explain the paradoxical nature of humility and its worth, the reasoning of which is acceptable even to those who do not accept the truth of Christian revelation?

Although there is no mention of humility in Aristotle's *Nicomachean Ethics,* a passing reference in one of Plato's dialogues indicates a line of inquiry that human reason might make to answer these questions. The ancient Christian writers Clement of Rome and Origen both cite this passage in arguments for the compatibility of elements of Plato's philosophy with Christianity,[13] but the key point for the present study is the implication that something of the importance of humility can be known by the power of human reason:

> ATHENIAN. Now, then, our address should go like this: "Men, according to the ancient story, there is a god who holds in his hands the beginning and end and middle of all things, and straight he marches in the cycle of nature. Justice, who takes vengeance on those who abandon the divine law, never leaves his side. The man who means to live in happiness latches on to her and follows her with meekness and humility *(tapeinos).* But he who bursts with

13. Clement of Rome, *Stromata* 2.22; Origen, *Against Celsus* 6.15.

> pride *(megalauchia),* elated by wealth or honors or by physical beauty when young and foolish, whose soul is afire with the arrogant belief that so far from needing someone to control and lead him, he can play the leader to others — there's a man whom God has deserted. And in his desolation he collects others like himself, and in his soaring frenzy he causes universal chaos. Many people think he cuts a fine figure, but before long he pays to Justice no trifling penalty and brings himself, his home and state to rack and ruin. Thus it is ordained. What action, then, should a sensible man take, and what should his outlook be? What must he *avoid* doing or thinking?"
>
> CLINIAS. This much is obvious: every man must resolve to belong to those who follow in the company of God.[14]

In this version of the text of *Laws* 4.716a-b, the Greek word *tapeinos,* which also means low, lowly or obsequious, has been translated as "with humility." The contrast with *megalauchia* (meaning pride, arrogance, or great boasting) in subsequent lines implies that the word "humility" faithfully translates the disposition that Plato commends. Indeed, the same Greek word appears in New Testament passages extolling humility, for example, "learn from me; for I am gentle and humble (*tapeinos)* in heart" (Matt. 11:29). The text from *Laws* 4 is, therefore, an unusual but valid instance of the disposition of humility being commended in classical non-Christian philosophy. It is also notable that there are further parallels with Christian thought, especially given that Plato associates humility with following God and the eventual goal of becoming dear to God and God's *friend.*[15]

Furthermore, what is also significant about this passage from *Laws* 4 is that it lays out in considerable detail what happens to anyone who *abandons* humility, namely the person who "bursts with pride" and thinks that he has no need of someone to control and lead him. Plato

14. Plato, *Laws* 4.716a-b, trans. Trevor J. Saunders, in *Plato: Complete Works,* ed. John M. Cooper and D. S. Hutchinson [1970] (Indianapolis: Hackett Publishing Company, 1997), p. 1402.

15. The connection between Plato's conception of humility and being a friend of God is made clear in the subsequent paragraph, *Laws* 4.716c-d: "On this principle the moderate man is God's friend, being like him, whereas the immoderate and unjust man is not like him and is his enemy." Trans. Trevor J. Saunders.

lists the dire consequences as follows: being deserted by God, trying to play leader to others of like mind, throwing things into chaos, and, in a short time, ruining oneself, one's family, and one's city. Since humility is, as Plato points out in the passage above, related to divine matters such as following God, we should not, perhaps, be surprised if humility is difficult to define. Nevertheless, the destructive consequences of *not* being humble, of bursting with pride, are serious, concrete, and recognizable to everyone.

Plato's *Laws* therefore suggests a way in which the rhetorical challenge of Pico della Mirandola may be answered. Rather than starting by examining the nature and importance of humility in itself, a more fruitful approach may be to consider its opposite, namely pride. By understanding pride and its destructive consequences, it will be possible to begin to understand humility and its benefits. From this foundation, it will then be possible to address the deeper issue in some detail, namely why Christianity has given a particular emphasis to humility and to the way that it can be achieved in daily life.

The Problem with Pride

What is pride and why is it a problem? The word "pride" is sometimes used in a positive sense as, for example, when someone says to parents who are watching their child excel, "You must be so proud!" Nevertheless, the word usually denotes a serious moral failing, traditionally regarded not only as a sin but as the root of all sins. Aquinas explains the meaning of pride as follows:

> Pride denotes immoderate desire of one's own excellence, a desire that is not in accord with right reason.[16]

What does it mean, however, to have a delight in or desire for one's own excellence that is not in accord with right reason? Some clarification may be found by considering how pride is manifested in practice. Aquinas defines four kinds of pride.[17] The following paragraphs make use of these

16. ST 2a2ae, q.162, a.4.
17. ST 2a2ae, q.162, a.4.

definitions, but modify and augment them slightly to highlight the connections of pride, relatedness, and gift.

The first kind of pride is as follows:

> P1 Ascribing an excellence to oneself that one does not possess.

Clearly P1 is against right reason because it is simply wrong. To ascribe an excellence to oneself that one does not have is to fail to match reason to reality. Under this category comes empty boasting, which is one of the most obvious and unpleasant manifestations of pride, and which tends to alienate rather than impress people when they perceive the mismatch of words and reality. P1 is also detrimental to the proud person in that choices made on the basis of an exaggerated and unwarranted estimate of personal excellence risk going awry. In extreme cases this may even prove destructive to one's person, family, or society. The skier who overestimates her ability on a dangerous ski slope risks disaster, as does the military general whose self-belief is exaggerated to the point of ignoring all views contrary to his own.

Yet the more subtle problem with P1 pride is not only that a person thinks she has what she does not have, but given that she thinks she *already* has some particular excellence, she will not strive for it or ask for it from another. The person who believes erroneously he is already a great pianist or conversationalist or philosopher will not be ready to receive instruction from others and to strive for improvement. P1 pride is therefore also detrimental to a person since it is closed to potential excellence, so that she is worse off by missing out on some good that she might otherwise have had.

The second kind of pride is less obvious, recognizing genuine excellence but failing to recognize the correct cause:

> P2 Thinking that one has acquired for oneself some excellence that one has received as a gift.

P2 is against right reason because the person with P2 pride wrongly attributes the cause of his own excellence. He may actually consider himself the cause of a particular excellence, as when a person delights in a scientific breakthrough he has made when the seminal idea really came from someone else. More subtly, even when he does not actively think he has caused his own excellence, he may simply delight in the excellence but be forgetful of the person who has brought this about.

P2 pride also has serious consequences for relationships. While P1 pride prevents a person from receiving a gift (because she thinks she already has it), P2 pride prevents a person from acknowledging that a gift *is* a gift. Since a gift necessarily relates to a giver, P2 pride implies a failure to acknowledge the relationship between giver and recipient. An example might be that of children who fail to honor the parents who have given them their very lives and provided them with so many gifts. This means that like P1 pride, which has the characteristic of self-imposed closure, P2 pride is also 'cold' in the sense that it is deleterious to relationships or fails to establish or acknowledge a relationship that should exist. Furthermore, P2 pride specifically concerns a failure to recognize *causes.* Now to know the causes of a thing is the true meaning of knowledge, according to Aristotle,[18] and such knowledge, particularly of the more universal causes of things, tends to be difficult to acquire. There is therefore a hint here that, far from being associated with greatness, pride can be considered a kind of intellectual laziness or blindness. Conversely, the humility that opposes pride involves not passivity, but an active engagement of a mind that recognizes the true causes of the excellences of things. This suggests a connection between humility and knowledge, especially the knowledge of first causes and principles which is *wisdom.*[19]

The third kind of pride acknowledges a personal excellence and its cause correctly, but fails to recognize the true "cause of the cause":

> P3 Thinking that some excellence that one has received as a gift is due to one's own merits.

P3 is against right reason because the person with P3 pride assumes that she is the "cause of the cause" of her own excellence. This is one of the most subtle forms of pride and it is worth examining what it means with

18. Aristotle, *Metaphysics* 1.1.981a24-30.

19. This description of wisdom comes from Aristotle, *Metaphysics* 1.1.981b26-29. With regard to the possible connection of humility and wisdom, based on the acknowledgment of the true causes of things, it is notable that Christianity regards Mary the mother of Jesus as an exemplar of humility and also gives her the traditional title "seat of wisdom."

some care. Take, for example, the case of a great basketball player. He knows, correctly, that he is a great basketball player. He also knows, correctly, that this greatness has been achieved as a result of his own hard work over many years together with many natural gifts such as health, coordination, height, and so on. If, however, he believes that God gave him these gifts because God knew that he *would* use them well, in other words, that he *deserved* those gifts in the light of what he would do with them, this is an example of P3 pride.

P3 pride also damages relationships in that, from the perspective of the person with P3 pride, the relationship with the giver has a contractual quality and follows the logic of commutative justice, *"You are doing something for me because I can do something for you."* Gifts are received in the manner of a business transaction rather than as genuine *gifts* and, as a consequence, there is again a kind of 'coldness' about P3 pride. Although a relationship exists it lacks the characteristics of genuine love, in which the will for the good of the other and for union with the other are not conditional upon receiving some good *from* the other. P3 pride therefore acknowledges a relationship but only an *inadequate* relationship.

The fourth kind of pride can be present even in the absence of all the others. This kind of pride may acknowledge a personal excellence and its causes correctly, but does not rejoice at the presence of this excellence in others:

> P4 Thinking that some excellence that one possesses is greater insofar as others do not have it.

In other words, part of the delight of the person with P4 pride is that she possesses this excellence and others do not. Many examples of this kind of pride could be cited from daily life, such as the brilliant academic who unfortunately also enjoys being more brilliant than others, or the leader in business or government who surrounds herself with weak subordinates in order to be more conspicuously successful in the sight of the world. Perhaps the clearest illustration of this kind of pride, however, can be found in one of the parables of Jesus:

> Two men went up into the temple to pray, one a Pharisee and the other a tax collector. The Pharisee stood and prayed thus with himself, "God, I thank thee that I am not like other men, extortioners, unjust, adulter-

> ers, or even like this tax collector. I fast twice a week, I give tithes of all that I get." But the tax collector, standing far off, would not even lift up his eyes to heaven, but beat his breast, saying, "God, be merciful to me a sinner!" I tell you, this man went down to his house justified rather than the other; for every one who exalts himself will be humbled, but he who humbles himself will be exalted (Luke 18:10-14).

In this parable, the Pharisee acknowledges God as the cause of what he has and thanks God for his gifts, but part of his delight is not just that he has these gifts but that others lack them. Consequently, even if he avoids the first three kinds of pride, he is still guilty of P4 pride. Indeed, Jesus warns that it is not the Pharisee but the tax collector, who simply asks for God's mercy, who goes home justified.[20]

P4 pride damages the relationship between giver and recipient, principally because the recipient fails to understand the *nature* of the gift and the giver. A lesser good, such as chocolate cake, is a finite thing. A smaller slice for one person implies a larger slice for another, and in this instance one's own good fortune might be enhanced if the fortune of another is diminished. For greater goods, however, this kind of arithmetic breaks down. It is the mark of great goods that they are not diminished by being given away, and this is especially true of the love of God. The saints rejoice in other saints as well as in God, but the person with P4 pride fails to understand this, treating love as a lesser good in which her own spiritual good fortune is augmented by the failures of others. That is why the Pharisee *thanks* God that he is not like other people, but in doing so only shows that he does not know the nature of love and, by implication, that he does not really know God.

This analysis reveals that the four kinds of pride are opposed to justice, in that they frequently fail to attribute to each what is his due, and they are opposed to truthfulness, in that they fail to recognize the proper

20. Rebecca Konyndyk DeYoung has argued that humility is a disposition to consider oneself small in relation to God and magnanimity is a virtue of "acknowledged dependence" on God. See Rebecca Konyndyk DeYoung, "Aquinas's Virtues of Acknowledged Dependence: A New Measure of Greatness," *Faith and Philosophy* 21.2 (2004): 219. This solution is consistent with the rejection of P1 and P2 pride, but does not, I believe, fully explain the rejection of P3 and P4 pride, since, for example, the Pharisee in the parable acknowledges dependence on God but still suffers from P4 pride.

causes of things. Therefore, as Plato affirms in the *Laws,* pride will tend to be contrary to the good order of society. Given that pride always involves an error with regard to the presence, true cause, or desirability of an excellence, actions made on the basis of pride will not be properly informed. They will tend, sooner or later, to the disadvantage or even destruction of the proud person and her society. Furthermore, this analysis shows that all forms of pride are detrimental to any relationships in which a person is the recipient of genuine love. There is a 'coldness' and loneliness about pride: it either prevents a person receiving love because he believes he already has what is being offered (P1 pride), or he receives without acknowledging the giver (P2 pride), or he receives believing he deserves what is given (P3 pride), or he misunderstands the nature of the gift (P4 pride). Since love and friendship are held to be good things, and since humility is the virtue opposed to the pride that inhibits such relationships, this is already a partial answer to the question of why we should be humble.

Nevertheless, this analysis has not yet given a clear answer to the question of why Christianity has given such a remarkable emphasis to humility. Having outlined humility with reference to pride, it is now necessary to examine what is specifically new in the case of Christianity.

What Is Specifically Christian about Humility?

To ask why Christianity has so strongly emphasized the importance of humility is to ask about the relative importance of humility with respect to the other virtues. As noted previously, humility is almost never mentioned in classical non-Christian philosophy. By contrast, humility suddenly gains a very prominent role with respect to the other virtues in the transition to Christian moral theology. Such a re-ordering implies that the transition to Christianity involves a fundamental change in the principles upon which the ordering of the virtues is based. Since the most important principle in the ordering of virtues is the end that is sought, in other words human perfection, it is necessary to examine how the understanding of human perfection changes in the transition from a classical to a Christian perspective.

What is the understanding of human perfection in classical non-Christian philosophy? According to the most influential classical treatment of virtue, Aristotle's *Nicomachean Ethics,* the perfection that we seek is flourishing or happiness.[21] From an examination of the nature of human beings, Aristotle concludes that what specifies human flourishing is to be active in philosophical contemplation (that is, to act in conformity with the highest faculties of the mind) in a "complete life," that is, with bodily sustenance, the company of friends, and the personal property to live well and perform deeds in conformity with moral excellence.[22] Aristotelian human perfection is, in effect, a well-ordered personal life and earthly city in which the highest activities of the mind can flourish. Having determined this goal in outline, Aristotle's account of the moral and intellectual virtues is then ordered in such a way as to promote this goal.

By contrast, Christians understand human perfection to be *personal* and *relational.* What specifies the happiness of heaven is a *relationship* with the three persons of God, the Father, the Son, and the Holy Spirit. Christian teaching about heaven also implies that its flourishing encompasses all that human beings naturally desire. The heavenly city and the communion of saints, for example, are clearly analogous to the Aristotelian notion of flourishing in the well-ordered earthly city and the company of friends. Nevertheless, all aspects of heaven are ordered towards a relationship with the persons of the Godhead. Indeed, the First Letter of John even claims that this flourishing will be something like a face-to-face relationship with God when he says, "We shall be like him, for we shall see him as he is" (1 John 3:2).

Now there are many ways in which one thing can be related to another, and so it is worth examining with some care what such a "personal relationship" means. Merely having a relationship with God does not, in itself, seem enough to specify what is different in the transition to Christianity. After all, one could argue that Aristotle's understanding of happiness also involves a relationship with God. Aristotle claims we have a natural desire to know, and to know is to know the causes of things. Since his reasoning also leads him to conclude that there is a

21. Aristotle, *Nicomachean Ethics* 1.4.1095a14-1095a19. Although the traditional translation of the word *eudaimonia* in Aristotle's text is "happiness," it is usual to use the word "flourishing" in contemporary philosophy.

22. Aristotle's treatment of the nature of happiness can be found in books 1 and 10 of the *Nicomachean Ethics.* The key definition is in 1.7.1098a16-18.

first cause of all things,[23] the most complete satisfaction of what we seek by nature involves our knowing this first cause, in other words knowing God. One could even argue that a relationship with God is *the* good towards which natural perfection is ordered, if all aspects of happiness support philosophical contemplation, and knowing the first cause is the most perfect activity of such contemplation. What, then, is different about Christianity?

The answer seems to lie in the first part of the quotation from 1 John cited above, "We shall be like him." Knowing God in the Aristotelian sense of knowing a first cause of what exists is not the same as knowing God by being *like* God. The former is proper to human nature, but to be *like* God, enjoying a face-to-face relationship with God, is certainly not.[24] God is disproportionately greater than the whole of creation, so to say that we shall be *like* God implies participating in the divine nature, establishing a personal relationship between two kinds of beings that are naturally so *dis*proportionate that the difference between them cannot be bridged even in thought.[25] The example of a journey may help to convey a sense of the contrast. Take the case of Paul deciding to go to Corinth. Even if God prompts and aids the journey, it seems that Paul can conceive of Corinth as his destination and reach there by means of his natural powers, that is, without any obvious recourse to a special intervention by God. If Paul decides to set out for the moon the challenge is far greater, although just about within reach of the resources of an entire modern nation. If, however, Paul wants to go to the Andromeda Nebula, all human efforts are in vain. At two million light years distance, the Andromeda Nebula, like nearly the whole universe, is utterly beyond the reach of any human traveler. Yet it is at least possible to *imagine* such remote places. By contrast, Paul, the writer of the First Letter to the Corinthians, asserts:

> What no eye has seen, nor ear heard, nor the human heart conceived, what God has prepared for those who love him. (1 Cor. 2:9, NRSV)

23. Aristotle, *Physics* 8.1-6.

24. "He [the Lord] said, 'You cannot see my face; for no one shall see me and live'" (Exod. 33:20, NRSV).

25. Aristotle, in fact, states explicitly that we cannot be friends with any gods, since they surpass us most decisively in all things. Cf. *Nicomachean Ethics* 9.8.1159a3-9.

When Paul says that the human heart has not even *conceived* what God has prepared, he is emphasizing that the goal of Christian flourishing is something incomparable to even the most remote imaginable aspirations within the natural order of creation. To see God face to face in the heavenly city is something unknown and even unknowable by the power of unaided human reason.

Here the radical distinction between the Aristotelian and Christian understanding of human perfection becomes clearer. Perfection in the Aristotelian sense is something that human reason can know by extrapolating the characteristics of human nature to their proper fulfillment. Furthermore, the self-knowledge of our natural perfection and our means for achieving it is something about which there could be a correct mean between two erroneous extremes.[26] We might, for example, overestimate or underestimate the extent of our justice or temperance, or our capacity to become just or temperate. By contrast, perfection in the Christian sense is unknowable by unaided reason, since it is specified by knowing the divine persons, knowledge even of the *existence* of whom is beyond unaided reason.[27] This relationship with the divine persons is only made possible by participating in the very nature of God. In this context, the self-knowledge of our perfection and the means for achieving it are *not* things about which there could be a moderate view between two erroneous extremes. We cannot have too excessive an aspiration for a

26. This possibility of erring towards excess or deficiency in terms of *natural* human perfection would explain why, when attempts are made to place humility within an Aristotelian scheme of the virtues, it tends to be placed under temperance. Additional support for this plausible view comes from the fact that we tend to err towards overestimating rather than underestimating our natural excellences, just as most people err by eating and drinking to excess rather than deficiency when they have the opportunity. Therefore, just as temperance has acquired the connotation of a reduction rather than an increase in consumption, humility in such a scheme would plausibly acquire the connotation of making oneself "smaller" in one's own estimation. Nevertheless, the problem with this approach is that humility in the Christian tradition does *not* have the connotation of mere temperance but of an *extravagant* self-giving or self-emptying.

27. There are no proofs for the existence of the Trinity in classical philosophy in the way that there are proofs for the existence of God. Indeed, Aquinas makes it a principle that although we can know that God exists by the power of natural reason (ST 1, q.2, a.2), we cannot know the Trinity by natural reason but only by revelation (ST 1, q.32, a.1).

personal, face-to-face relationship with God because this goal exceeds all aspirations. On the other hand we cannot have too deficient a view of our innate capacity for attaining this relationship because we have *no* power to attain it by ourselves.

This contrast of the poverty of means with respect to the awesomeness of the end begins to show why humility is so central to a Christian understanding of the virtues. History and Christian tradition show that beings with intellect and will have a tendency, or rather a temptation, to seek to become like God by means of their natural powers. What is wrong with Pico della Mirandola's rhetoric cited at the beginning of this chapter is not that he urges us to "fly to the court beyond the world and next to God," but the implication that we can *raise ourselves* to this goal, in other words that we can *make ourselves* like God. This is the pattern of the temptation of Adam and Eve in the Garden of Eden when the serpent says, "You will be like God" (Gen. 3:5). It is also the pattern of the fall of the king of Babylon in Isaiah, which Christian tradition has interpreted as a spiritual reference to the fall of Lucifer:

> You said in your heart, "I will ascend to heaven; above the stars of God I will set my throne on high; I will sit on the mount of assembly in the far north; I will ascend above the heights of the clouds, *I will make myself like the Most High.*" But you are brought down to Sheol, to the depths of the Pit. (Isa. 14:13-15, emphasis added)

When any created being aims to *make himself like the Most High,* this is a kind of pride. This is not pride in an everyday sense, however, such as, for example, an excessive admiration for one's own appearance or an empty boast about one's ability on the sports field or in the academy. In these cases, cultivating the virtues of justice and truthfulness may be sufficient as remedies for such exaggerations. Indeed, the existence of such remedies may help to explain why classical non-Christian philosophers do not usually emphasize the special virtue of humility in the good ordering of the earthly city. By contrast, it is an *insane* pride to attempt to bridge the gulf between human nature and God by means of natural powers, to *seize* participation in the divine nature. Such language may seem rather abstract and esoteric. Nevertheless, any choice in which God offers divine life if we follow one course of action and warns of death if we follow another is a choice with practical implications. Indeed, simply to choose to act in serious defiance of God is to break our personal relationship with God and to usurp God's place by seeking our own way to perfection. Therefore, in the Book of Genesis, the simple action of eating the wrong piece of fruit leads to the fall of the entire human race.

Because of this offer of a personal relationship with God, and the concomitant temptation to seize divine participation by natural powers, humility has a special and unique place in Christian moral theology. The need for this virtue is still further highlighted by the fact that it is naturally powerful beings, even those that are *perfect* by the standard of nature, who are particularly vulnerable to this kind of temptation. The problem is that their powers in the natural order may encourage them to transpose these powers erroneously to the supernatural order. Christianity therefore emphasizes the special virtue of humility in order to cast out the four kinds of pride with respect to the goal of Christian perfection, that is, the personal relationship with God in the kingdom of heaven. A person cannot believe and act as if she *already* has the relationship that God offers (P1 pride); nor receive this as a gift without acknowledging God as the giver (P2 pride); nor believe she *deserves* what God is giving (P3 pride); nor misunderstand the nature of the gift by wishing to exclude others from this union (P4 pride). Whatever our powers in the order of nature, we cannot raise ourselves to heaven. The divine union offered us can only be received *as* a gift, a gift given solely out of love and a gift which is itself Love.

So in terms of attaining heaven, humility appears to be essential. Furthermore, it is also possible that humility is intrinsic to *enjoying* heaven. Knowing anyone in a personal relationship involves not only knowing the other, but also knowing how the other person knows oneself. What specifies heaven is a relationship with the persons of the Godhead. Assuming that personal relationships of this kind bear some analogy to those of the natural order, this suggests that to know God personally is also to know, in some way, how one is *known* by God. In other words, in knowing God one also, in a sense, sees oneself from God's perspective.[28] Although the saints participate in the divine nature, this is a likeness in kind rather than in scale. Any enjoyment of God *as* God implies that the saints "look

28. This participation in God's stance toward things is one of the consequences of the gifts of the Holy Spirit, in Aquinas's interpretation of the gifts. See my "The Gifts and Fruits of the Holy Spirit" in the *Oxford Handbook of Aquinas.*

up" at God (it is, of course, necessary to resort to metaphorical language here), and they, in turn, see themselves as "small" (though wholly beloved) in comparison with God. Nevertheless, their smallness or humility is a cause for joy rather than regret. G. K. Chesterton explains this kind of joy in the following passage:

> If a man would make his world large, he must always be making himself small. Even the haughty visions, the tall cities, and the toppling pinnacles are the creations of humility. . . . For towers are not towers unless we look up at them, and giants are not giants unless they are larger than we are. . . . It is impossible without humility to enjoy anything.[29]

Therefore humility is linked, paradoxically, to greatness rather than smallness. Making oneself small *before God* is not smallness absolutely. On the contrary, it is the proud person who is in fact mean and low, since he is preoccupied (to borrow the words of de Tocqueville) with the contemplation of a very small object, namely himself.[30] The humble person, by contrast, can enjoy the greatest gift of all.

The Nature and Acquisition of Humility

Humility is most easily defined as the virtue that opposes pride, that is, the virtue which opposes ascribing to oneself an excellence one does not possess, or wrongly thinking of oneself as the cause of one's own excellence, or wishing to be the exclusive possessor of that excellence. Such a definition is perfectly compatible with persons being great — as in the cases of Moses and Dante — provided they also acknowledge the true causes of these qualities and rejoice in the qualities of others. Nevertheless, what makes Moses and Dante humble in the proper sense is not so much that they acknowledge the true causes of their natural greatness, such as their leadership or poetical abilities, but their profound sense that their natural qualities, no matter how formidable, do not suffice for the gift of a personal relationship with God. Therefore Moses refuses to

29. G. K. Chesterton, *Orthodoxy* (London: Bodley Head, 1908), chapter 3.
30. Cf. Alexis de Tocqueville, *Democracy in America,* chap. 18.

move on from Mount Sinai until God promises to go with him (Exod. 33:3-16), and Dante cannot take a single step up Mount Purgatory toward God unless the light of grace is shining on him.[31]

Therefore, what makes humility so central to the Christian understanding of the virtues is not so much the problem of everyday pride about natural excellences, a pride which can be countered by justice and truthfulness, but the offer of a personal relationship with God that is central to the Christian gospel. This offer carries the concomitant risk of an insane pride with which a person seeks to become *like God* by her own powers. Consequently, Christianity gives a special emphasis to opposing pride, not by promoting moderation in our self-understanding, but humility characterized by two *extreme* dispositions: first, a sense of the majesty of God and of the gift offered to us; second, a sense of the poverty of any natural means we possess for securing this goal for ourselves. By opposing a self-regarding pride in these matters, humility gives us the correct disposition to *receive* the gift of a personal relationship with God, and also to *rejoice* in God who gives us this gift and who is so much greater than ourselves.

All of these conclusions are illustrated by the *Magnificat* (Luke 1:46-55), the New Testament song of Mary when she has conceived Jesus Christ by the power of the Holy Spirit. Mary says, "My soul magnifies the Lord," which shows how humility makes us want to "enlarge" God rather than ourselves in our own souls. She says, "He has regarded the low estate of his handmaiden," which shows how humility makes us see ourselves as small in God's sight. Nevertheless, this smallness is not a cause of her regret but of her joy, because from this perspective she can rejoice in God who is so much greater than herself; therefore, Mary also says, "My spirit rejoices." Then she says, "Henceforth all generations will call me blessed," which is not an empty boast, because it is true; therefore, she excludes P1 pride. She adds, however, "For he who is mighty has done great things for me," in which she acknowledges the true cause of this greatness, namely God, and so she excludes P2 pride. Since there is no sense in which she considers this greatness deserved, she excludes P3 pride. Finally, she expands her hymn of thanks to include her whole nation, "He has helped his servant Israel, in remembrance of his mercy." In other words, she does not rejoice in the exclusiveness of her gift, which would be P4 pride,

31. Dante, *Purgatorio,* Canto 17.

but rejoices that through this gift the whole people of God and all generations will be blessed.

Given that humility is so important, how, then, can we achieve this casting out of pride? The philosophical analysis presented in this chapter suggests an important conclusion. Since human reason more clearly understands pride rather than humility, it is to some extent within our own power to discern our own pride. Hence the definitions of the four kinds of pride listed in this chapter can be of some practical help in diagnosing pride, especially in some of its more subtle forms. Nevertheless, given the very nature of humility in disposing us to receive God's gifts as gifts, it is not, in fact, within our power to acquire humility for ourselves, as if humility itself were not a gift. A self-help book entitled *How to Be Humble* or *Teach Yourself Humility* would miss the entire point — though, of course, within the history of Christianity there have been many attempts to systematize the stages in the acquisition of humility.[32] All such attempts should be read with a degree of caution. At best they show some of the marks of humility in a certain mode of life. The problem is that someone could have all the external characteristics listed in such accounts of humility while, in truth, being insanely proud. Furthermore, there is no one pattern of humility that can be encoded in a single set of rules. Humility is much more of an internal disposition, one that produces humble kings as well as humble beggars.

How, then, does God give us this gift? The whole history of the church suggests that God forms humility in his people in a most unusual way, constantly disrupting the apparent but false association that reason tends to make between natural powers and supernatural fruitfulness. Indeed, he often entirely inverts the natural order of strength and weakness in such things: "He has put down the mighty from their thrones, and exalted those of low degree" (Luke 1:52). So while it is true that God sometimes makes use of a person's exceptional natural gifts, such as intelligence or political ability, God can just as easily make use of someone's

32. An example is the *Rule of St. Benedict,* which proposes a series of steps to acquire humility. Examples are: submitting to one's superior in all obedience for the love of God (third step) and not speaking unless asked a question (ninth step). Although these may well be genuine marks of humility in a certain mode of life, they are not easily applicable to more generic contexts. Indeed, some of the steps would be incompatible with many kinds of Christian vocations.

simplicity, weakness, or foolishness. Indeed, he frequently seems to *make* someone weak, or allow a person to fall, precisely to bring about the disposition of trusting in him alone. It is only when Peter has betrayed Christ and been forgiven that he is humble enough to be the leader of the church; it is only when Paul has persecuted Christ to the point of murdering his followers that he is conscious enough of his own failures to be the greatest of all missionaries. Humility properly disposes us to receive God's gifts *as* gifts — and even that disposition is itself the fruit of God's grace.

Questions for Further Reflection

1. As an internal disposition, humility can be found in kings as well as in beggars. What is the evidence in the Old Testament that King David has humility?

2. In the New Testament, Jesus Christ invites us to "learn from me; for I am gentle and humble in heart" (Matt. 11:29). In what ways does the life of Jesus Christ show the nature of humility?

3. Much of the practice of humility involves an acknowledgment of the true causes of good gifts. Taking 2 Corinthians 9:1-15, or another suitable text, mark off some of the many references to gifts and givers. Discuss what kinds of pride such acknowledgments help to cast out.

4. Discuss the ways in which Christians can exercise virtues of leadership in the contemporary world and yet still achieve humility.

Index of Names and Subjects

Note that **boldface** page numbers in this index indicate chapter-length treatments of virtues.

Index of Scripture References